Osler's
Bedside Library

Osler's Bedside Library

Great Writers Who Inspired a Great Physician

Michael A. LaCombe, MD
David J. Elpern, MD
Editors

Co-editors and Contributors:

Charles M. Anderson, PhD
Pamela Brett-MacLean, PhD
Albert Howard Carter, III, PhD
Jeremiah Conway, PhD
John K. Crellin, MD, PhD
Lynn C. Epstein, MD
Marin Gillis, LPh, PhD
Bernadette Höfer, PhD
Claire Hooker, PhD
Brian Hurwitz, MD
Lyuba Konopasek, MD
Paul S. Mueller, MD, MPH
Allan D. Peterkin, MD
M. Sara Rosenthal, PhD
Audrey Shafer, MD
Jerry Vannatta, MD
Arnold Weinstein, PhD

Louise Aronson, MD, MFA
Arthur L. Caplan, PhD
Rita Charon, MD, PhD
Jack Coulehan, MD, MPH
Thomas P. Duffy, MD
Toby Gelfand, PhD
Saba Hoda, MD
Martha Stoddard Holmes, PhD
Joel D. Howell, MD, PhD
Liva H. Jacoby, PhD, MPH
Stephen S. Lefrak, MD
T. Jock Murray, MD
Maureen Rappaport, MD
Lawrence J. Schneiderman, MD
Ronald D. Stewart, MD, DSc
Seth Vannatta
Omid Zargari, MD

AMERICAN COLLEGE OF PHYSICIANS   PHILADELPHIA

Director: Linda Drumheller
Editorial Coordinator: Angela M. Gabella
Cover and Design: Lisa Torrieri
Interior Designer: Michael Ripca
Compositor: SPi Technologies, Inc.

Manufactured in the United States of America

Printing and binding by Sheridan Books, Inc.

Library of Congress Cataloging-in-Publication Data

Osler's bedside library : great writers who inspired a great physician / Michael A. LaCombe, David J. Elpern, editors.
    p. cm.
  Includes bibliographical references
  ISBN 978-1-934465-49-3 (hardcover: alk. paper)
  ISBN 978-1-934465-47-9 (paperback: alk. paper)
  1. Medicine–Literary collections. 2. Authors–Literary collections. 3. Osler, William, Sir, 1849-1919. 4. Medical writing. 5. Medicine in literature. 6. Literature and morals. I. LaCombe, Michael A., 1942- II. Elpern, David J.
  PN6071.M38O75 2010
  808.8'03561–dc22
                                        2009030465

Dedication

For:

Stanley M. Aronson, Murray Bronet, Margaret Caplan, Nancy Corson Carter, Jane Case, Nazaré Conway, Anne Coulehan, Janet Crellin, Susan Duffy, Martha E. Elpern, Mel H. Epstein, Abraham Fuks, Hadi Hoda, Bruno Höfer, Nora Howell, Bill Jacoby, Margaret Mary LaCombe, Jacob Lander, Jane Langridge, Mel MacLean, Nancy Mueller, Jock Murray, Shannon Murray, Kirsten Niles, Solomon Papper, William A. Peck, Edith Peterkin, Barbara Schneiderman, Elizabeth Sewell, Ben Shykind, Ruth Dougherty Stoddard, Robert Townsend, Gordon Wright and Sara Zargari.

Introduction

Presented here are those classics you have always intended to read. I know, you haven't had the time.

Osler had the time.

You have that stack of journals.

Osler read every scientific journal published in Canada while at McGill.

There are students and residents to be taught.

Osler taught them at the bedside, and, what is more, gave them keys to his home, calling them his latchkey children.

Perhaps you are writing a textbook, or rather editing one, as it is done today.

Osler single-handedly wrote the standard medical textbook of his day, *The Principles and Practice of Medicine*.

Osler was a genius, you say. Yes, he was, but so are you. Perhaps you can't teach or write as well as he did, but you can read, can't you?

Well then, your argument will run, the books presented in this compendium are out of date, arcane, and irrelevant today. There are a few who have argued this with lists of their own. I don't believe that, and if you will scan the biographical sketches of the contributors at the back of the book, you will have to agree that I am in good company.

The book you are holding is intended to get you to read, meant to pull you away from television, set aside that modern novel, and return to the classics as you have to admit you have always intended to do. There are 30 books and/or authors listed here in the table of contents. They include Osler's own personal list of those 10 books of which he said in *Aequanimitas*:

> A Liberal education may be had at a very slight cost of time and money. Well filled though the day be with appointed tasks, to make the best possible use of your one or of your ten talents, rest not satisfied with this professional training, but try to get the education, if not of a scholar, at least of a gentleman. Before going to sleep read for half an hour, and in the morning have a book open on your dressing table. You will be surprised to find how much can be accomplished in the course of a year. I have put down a list of ten books which you may make close friends. There are many others; studied carefully in your student days these will help in the inner education of which I speak.

Osler called this list of 10 books his *bedside library for medical students*. They are presented here, slightly out of order for editorial reasons to be explained below, each introduced by a scholar who will present excerpts of the work to whet, we hope, your appetite for this inner education. After these 10 are 20 other works selected for their accessibility, their variety, and for their adjunctive supplement to this education.

This is the first such book of its nature in that it contains excerpts from pre-1913 texts that Osler had in his library, now called the Bibliotheca Osleriana at McGill, with a catalog of his collection by the same name. But there does exist an earlier wonderful book by Wallis and Miller, *75 Books from the Osler Library*, containing essays of works Osler owned, treasured, and read. I refer you to that fine text as well.

We start with Plutarch, one of Osler's 10 books, and I admit this is a personal choice. A print of the cover illustration of this book, a painting by Alexandre-Charles Guillemot entitled *Erasistratus Discovers the Cause of Antiochus' Disease*, captures a moment in medical history from about 275 BC and told centuries later in *Plutarch's Lives*. Next comes Browne's *Religio Medici*, Osler's favorite book. At the Osler Library, there are over 30 editions of this work, and they are shelved next to his ashes. After the remaining eight of Osler's 10 books come two poets, seven consummate storytellers, six philosophers, three dramatists, one compelling journal, and finally, a legendary physician perhaps unknown to you.

Were I to ask you who might have been the greatest physician of all time, whom would you name? Who was it who memorized his bible by the age of 14, who by 18 had read all the existing medical textbooks and began practicing medicine, who cured a king and in payment was given use of the royal library, who wrote 450 books, one of which, his textbook of medicine, was used by European medical schools as the standard text for seven centuries, who first described the transit of Venus seen with the naked eye, whose book on tonic intervals and rhythmic patterns was a standard text on musicology, and who sought to integrate all aspects of science and religion in a grand metaphysical vision?

Unless you are Persian, you will not know the answer to this question, and yet George Sarton, arguably the greatest historian of science who ever lived, said of Avicenna:

> Were you to ask historians of medicine to name the three greatest physicians who ever lived, they would all name Avicenna and argue over the other two.

A word or two about the contributors to this book:

There are at least three card-carrying Oslerians here, one member of the *Baker Street Irregulars*, one Aussie whose essay on *Middlemarch* is simply perfect for our purpose here, one Brit, several Canadians, one bona fide philosopher (Conway), and a favorite teacher of mine, Arnold Weinstein of Brown, all of whose lectures I have attended by means of *The Teaching Company*. One contributor, Rita Charon, earned her PhD in English *after* her MD and *after* beginning a job in academic medicine. Try doing that after rounds. The great majority of these contributors teach and/or direct programs in medical humanities at their universities. I am humbled by their work for this book.

Years ago I wrote a short piece about an elderly patient who goads her physician into reading Thackeray's *Vanity Fair*. A cardiologist from Colorado wrote me a letter, stating that he had shown my story to his daughter, who abruptly turned to him and said, "Well, how about it, Dad?"

And so, I ask you, how about it?

Michael A. LaCombe, MD
Augusta, Maine

Acknowledgments

Fortunate is the author who gains a publisher with just the shred of an idea. For that great fortune, I am indebted to Steve Weinberger of the American College of Physicians. Thank you for your immediate acceptance of the idea, and for your support.

Deepest gratitude to Bob Spanier for his unqualified support of this important text.

To Diane McCabe, wise, quiet intellect, huge asset to the College, and long-time valued friend, thank you.

For their support of this project, I am grateful to Marla Sussman, to Angela Gabella, who could find a typo in a Chinese dictionary, and to Linda Drumheller of the publications division of the College and of ACP Press, who has made this a better book. Great thanks as well to Tom Hartman for his editorial advice.

Thanks to Basho, my coeditor David Elpern, the most well-read physician I know, invaluable in researching excerpts in the public domain and in critiquing submitted manuscripts.

Thanks to Zoe Alanna Elpern who labored over this manuscript, substituting for every excerpt not in the public domain, equally compelling quotations from pre-1913 works of the authors included and who, where necessary, found quotes for the book. Thanks to Aaron Rothschild who found suitable illustrations from old texts, adding much richness to this one.

To my contributing editors—I remain humbled by your scholarship. A special thanks to Bernadette Höfer, who came to my rescue in the 11th hour with her fine essay on Molière.

Thank you to Christopher Lyons, curator of the Osler Library at McGill University, for his advice in compiling this book.

And finally, deepest gratitude to my wife, Margaret Mary, who in another life would have been the quintessential reference librarian, as she is the perfect partner.

Contents

Contents

Osler's Ten

Plutarch's Lives

Osler, Plutarch, and the Intimate Observation of Human Behavior

Louise Aronson

In an address entitled "The Hospital as College," delivered to the New York Academy of Medicine in 1903, Sir William Osler detailed his "conception of how the art of medicine and surgery can be taught":

> ...teaching the student begins with the patient, continues with the patient, and ends his studies with the patient, using books and lectures as tools, as means to an end.... Teach him how to observe, give him plenty of facts to observe, and the lessons will come out of the facts themselves.... The whole art of medicine is in observation...to educate the eye to see, the ear to hear and the finger to feel... (1).

Note that Osler refers to the art of medicine, not the science, though clearly he believes both essential to clinical competence. Indeed, earlier in the lecture, he lauds the then recent move of much preclinical teaching from the lecture hall to the laboratory where "the student learns to use the instruments of precision, gets a mental training of incalculable value, and perhaps catches some measure of the scientific spirit" (2). Thus, he viewed practical scientific education as the necessary first step in physician training but considered its application to the care of patients an art. Second, for Osler, proficiency in the art of medicine required extensive practice of skilled observation using the five senses by a scientifically "fairly well-trained man" (3). Third, although Osler here describes the patient as the fundamental text and books as tools to be used by physicians in the pursuit of clinical excellence, elsewhere in *Aequanimitas* he describes the significant value of books for a physician: to keep him on the proper moral course (4), to give him the knowledge to understand his practice (5), to acquire the "wisdom in life which only comes to those who earnestly seek it" (6), and in making him into a "truly good man" (7).

Osler's vision of medical training and practice provides critical insight into the prominent position of Plutarch in his "top 10" list of bedside reading for physicians. For not only does the classic author's greatest work, *Plutarch's Lives*, appear on the list, but so do three other authors who drew heavily on Plutarch's oeuvre in creation of their own: Shakespeare, Montaigne, and Emerson. Although few specific references to why Osler held Plutarch in such high regard exist, both men placed heavy emphasis on the importance of learning from the best and worst of human lives and on the cultivation of good personal character. Both also made their marks in history as a result of their skills in close observation and their sensitive, erudite approaches to the interpretation of human experience.

Lucius Mestrius Plutarchus, believed to have lived from AD 45 to 120, is considered among the earliest moralists and, after Augustine and Aristotle, one of the most influential classic philosophers (8). He left two works, the *Moralia*, a collection of advice, criticism, essays, and speeches designed to provide readers with a moral education, and the *Lives* (also known as *Parallel Lives*), a series of biographies of the most influential soldiers and statesmen of the ancient world, most arranged in pairs of a Greek then a Roman and followed by comparisons of the pairs' moral vices and virtues. In many ways, *Plutarch's Lives* were the first modern biographies (9). Written in an intimate, accessible style, they were clearly intended to entertain and to instruct. Equally significant, rather than simply recounting events and actions as had his predecessors, Plutarch originated the now-common emphasis on the interior life of his characters. His writings, hugely popular in his own time, were rediscovered in the High Renaissance and, until recently, were considered essential reading for educated Westerners. It is easy to understand how the exceedingly well-read Dr. Osler came to Plutarch. But why might a modern physician read at least part of this 1452-page classic text?

Let me begin to answer that question by describing the passage from Plutarch's biography of Demetrius, which provides the narrative background for the painting by Guillemot featured on the cover of this volume (10). This episode provides one of the first literary examples of psychosomatic illness and depicts a physician using physical diagnosis and what we refer to today as "cognitive skills" in service of his patient (11). It also demonstrates Plutarch's characteristic emphasis on values in human affairs and his tendency to digress to recount entertaining and often significant smaller stories within the larger story of the chapter.

The account begins with the announcement that Demetrius' daughter, Stratonice, had remarried the son of her first husband and been proclaimed

Queen of Upper Asia. Plutarch then elaborates. Stratonice was not yet 20 years old when she married Seleucus I, a Syrian king past middle age with a grown son. The son, Antiochus, fell "passionately in love" with his step-mother and, recognizing his desire as inappropriate, "determined on death, and thought to bring his life slowly to extinction by neglecting his person and refusing nourishment, under the pretence of being ill" (12). King Seleucus, fearing for his son's life, asked for help from the physician Erasistratus who quickly made the diagnosis of love but knew that he must discover the root cause of the problem in order to find a cure. His approach—which in appropriately Oslerian fashion begins and ends with the patient—and the moment of diagnosis are relayed as follows by Plutarch:

> He therefore waited continually in [Antiochus'] chamber, and when any of the beauties of the court made their visits to the sick prince, he observed the emotions and alterations in the countenance of Antiochus...passions and inclinations of the soul...the presence of other women produced no effect upon him; but when Stratonice came, as she often did...he observed in him all Sappho's famous symptoms, his voice faltered, his face flushed up, his eyes glanced stealthily, a sudden sweat broke out on his skin, the beatings of his heart were irregular and violent...(13).

Guillemot's painting depicts this moment: the demure Stratonice walking by, the prostrate Antiochus, and the surprised physician, one hand on his patient's pulse and the other on his heart.

But the story doesn't end there, for now Erasistratus must use the art of medicine to save his patient's life. He tells Seleucus that his son has an incurable love and then tricks the king into providing the cure himself. Erasistratus claims Antiochus is in love with his—Erasistratus'—wife. When Seleucus asks the physician to give up his wife to save Antiochus' life, Erasistratus counters that he won't since Seleucus would not do so himself if their positions were reversed. The king replies "with the greatest passion, shedding tears as he spoke," that he would part not just with Stratonice but also with his empire to help his son. At this point, Erasistratus reveals the truth and declares the king "the proper physician for your own family." The scene concludes with Seleucus promising Stratonice to Antiochus in marriage, making them king and queen, and noting that if Stratonice "should manifest any reluctance to such a marriage, that she ought to esteem those things just and honorable which had been determined upon by the king as necessary to the general good" (14). Thus, we have a story which, in typical Plutarch fashion, tells volumes in a very short space and—though the modern clinician may question Erasistratus' ends justify the means approach—shows both a physician and a king making very human assessments of what is best for individuals and civilization.

While stories about physicians, illness, and medicine appear infrequently in the *Lives*, they are unfailingly apt and detailed in a way that reinforces Plutarch's message about the character of the affected individual. In the biography of Caesar, we get an account of a man who triumphs despite his epilepsy:

> For he was a spare man, had a soft and white skin, was distempered in the head, and subject to an epilepsy, which, it is said, first seized him at Corduba. But he did not make the weakness of his constitution a pretext for his ease, but rather used war as the best physic against his indispositions; whilst by indefatigable journeys, coarse diet, frequent lodging in the field, and continual laborious exercise, he struggled with his diseases, and fortified his body against all attacks (15).

Later in the same chapter, Plutarch describes a seizure aura long before that entity had been officially named by physicians:

> Others say, [Caesar] was not in the action, but that he was taken with his usual distemper just as he was setting his army in order. He perceived the approaches of it, and before it had too far disordered his senses, when he was already beginning to shake under its influence, withdrew into a neighboring fort, where he reposed himself (16).

Plutarch's insights into illness were not lost on Osler. In his 1898 revision of *The Principles and Practice of Medicine*, he quotes Strabo in Plutarch on "the lisping of the gout" (17).

Beyond its historic and literary merits, the *Lives* no doubt appealed to Osler for the same reasons that make the work meaningful to the reader of today. Throughout the book Plutarch tells stories rich in timeless, universal details about human traits and entanglements. Take, for example, this description of Antony that sounds (at least to this reader) very much like a description of a young, hip-hop stud:

> ...his beard was well grown...giving him altogether a bold, masculine look...he wore his tunic girt low about the hips, a broadsword on his side, and over all a large, coarse mantle...his vaunting, his raillery, his drinking in public...made him the delight and pleasure of the army (18).

Similarly, Plutarch's accounts of city–country life distinctions, romantic struggles, the brutality of wars, the maltreatment of certain peoples by others, and the effects of alcohol and "other debaucheries" on men, while not detailed in the manner of a modern writer, have an entirely contemporary feel. For the physician-reader, then, the *Lives* may be considered a master text in the empathetic study of human behavior. As Plutarch himself describes in his biography of Alexander:

> It must be borne in mind that my design is not to write histories, but lives. And the most glorious exploits do not always furnish us with the clearest discoveries of virtue or vice in men; sometimes a matter of less moment, an expression or a jest, informs us better of their characters and inclinations, than the most famous sieges, the greatest armaments, or the bloodiest battles whatsoever (19).

Plutarch's approach is essentially that of the expert clinician. While a merely competent physician might obtain an accurate medical history and perform a complete physical exam, an expert also observes and interprets a patient's gestures and expressions and listens for the telling silences and subtexts when taking a history (20).

These acute observations notwithstanding, there are three reasons why a modern physician might be put off by Plutarch: 1) his prioritization of morality over historical accuracy, 2) his writing style, and 3) the length of the work. Though reasonable, none of these objections should preclude the physician of today from reading the *Lives*. Unless one's primary purpose is historical study, the biographies provide a chronologic and sufficiently factual account of ancient events and people. And while his phrasing and sentence structure reflect the standards of his time and not ours, the writing is both charming and easily understood, making at least a sampling of this admittedly very long work well worthwhile.

Over a century ago, William Osler argued that physicians should practice close observation and broad reading to achieve excellence in the art of medicine. In recent years, universities and clinicians have tended to prioritize science and technology over other forms of knowledge and experience, often at the expense of patient care and physicians' personal and professional development. We modern clinicians would do well to follow Osler's lead in honing our observational skills, expanding our knowledge base, and contemplating the routes to a morally exemplary life by studying Plutarch, who notes that "acts of virtue...produce in the minds of mere readers about them an emulation and eagerness that may lead them on to imitation" (21).

Religio Medici

Osler's Beloved Mentor:
Sir Thomas Brown and *Religio Medici*

On 31 December 1919, the day before William Osler's funeral, the great physician's favorite copy of *Religio Medici*, the book he claimed had had the "most enduring influence" on his life, lay atop his coffin (1, 2). He had purchased the book as an 18-year-old university student, at the suggestion of his mentor, Father William Johnson, a naturalist and Anglican priest. *Religio Medici*, or the religion of a physician, had been written by Sir Thomas Browne, a 17th-century English physician, not long after he had completed his medical studies. For the young Osler, Browne's testament of faith became a source of inspiration as he struggled with the existential questions of the life and, later in his career, the book was an inseparable companion from which he often read passages to his students (3). Osler came to view *Religio Medici* "virtually as his surrogate Bible. Eventually he knew the *Religio* and Browne's other writings almost as well as his parents knew their Old and New Testaments" (4).

Given the strength of Osler's recommendation, I was surprised when I first read *Religio Medici* in search of the wisdom that had so enchanted the icon of North American medicine. On a cursory reading, Browne's ideas regarding religious tolerance, freedom of conscience, and natural science seemed commonplace, albeit embedded in flowery prose. Granted, these ideas would have been new, perhaps even radical, in the 17th century, but what endeared the book to Osler? When I slowed down a bit, I had to acknowledge that Browne's creatively discursive prose was itself a virtuoso performance that one could appreciate somewhat independently of the intellectual content. Was it style that attracted Osler? I also found it difficult to avoid fixating on Browne's several errors and misconceptions. Overall, I was tempted to agree with Perry Hookman who considered *Religio Medici* Osler's "one blind spot" and called it "a dark book filled with sanctimonious claptrap and prejudices" (5). Why on Earth, I asked myself, did the biblio-phile physician choose *Religio Medici* to include in his highly select bedside library for medical students? I figured there must be more to *Religio*—and to Osler's wisdom—than met my cursory 21st-century eye.

Okay, I decided, let's give it another try. So I embarked upon a more careful study of Osler's lifelong relationship with Sir Thomas Browne, "that most liberal of men and most distinguished of general practitioners" (6), and of his most famous book. I tried to triangulate Browne, Osler, and the questions of belief that concerned them both, albeit at a temporal distance of 250 years. A different, more complex picture began to emerge. It is this picture of Sir Thomas Browne as William Osler's beloved mentor that I'd like to share with you.

SIR THOMAS BROWNE

Thomas Browne was born to a middle-class family in London in 1605, early in the reign of James I and around the time Shakespeare wrote *Macbeth* and *King Lear*. Browne attended Oxford (1623–1626) and then studied medicine on the Continent at Montpellier, Padua, and Leiden, completing his MD degree at the University of Leiden in 1633. After returning to England, he practiced medicine for a short time in Yorkshire, where he probably wrote *Religio Medici* in 1635 or 1636 (7). Browne moved in 1637 to the provincial city of Norwich, where he lived until his death in 1682. He married in 1641 and began a family. The following year, *Religio Medici*, which had circulated for years among his friends in manuscript, appeared in print without his approval. Later, Browne published a corrected version of *Religio* and several other books, among them *Pseudodoxia Epidemica*, an inquiry into "false beliefs and vulgar errors"; *Hydriotaphia*, a meditation on funerary customs in different cultures; and *Christian Morals* (8, 9).

Many of Browne's case reports survive and illustrate his busy medi-cal practice, including patients with smallpox, gout, asthma, malaria, and rickets. During the Great Plague of 1665–1666, Dr. Browne remained in Norwich to care for his patients, rather than abandoning them and escaping to the countryside, as did most physicians in London, among them Thomas Sydenham (10). Browne seems to have kept up to date with medical devel-opments of his time, like William Harvey's demonstration of the circulatory system. He was elected a Fellow of the Royal College of Physicians in 1664 and, in recognition of his Royalist sympathies during the English Civil War, Charles II bestowed a knighthood on him in 1671.

Sir Thomas Browne seems to have been a stable, well-balanced man who manifested many attributes of a good physician. Samuel Johnson, one of Browne's early biographers, concluded, "He was never seen to be transported with mirth or dejected with sadness; always cheerful but rarely merry, at any sensible rate; seldom heard to break a jest, and when he did he would be apt to blush at the levity of it. His gravity was natural, without affectation" (11). Near the end of *Religio Medici*, Browne assessed his own life with these words, "Now for my life, it is a miracle of 30 years, which to relate, were not a history, but a piece of poetry, and would sound to common ears like a fable" (12). This is the voice of a young man secure in his powers, at peace with himself, and confident in the future, whose words remind me of the 19th-century Shaker hymn, "My life flows on in endless song above earth's lamentation." Perhaps the one virtue that Browne falsely—or at least, ingenuously—claimed was humility. He wrote, "I thank God, amongst those millions of Vices I do inherit and hold from Adam, I have escaped one, and that a mortal enemy to charity, the first and father-sin, not only of man but of the devil: pride" (13). Immediately after making this assertion, Browne "proceeded, with entertaining naivety, to list his six languages and his knowledge of the names of all the constellations and most of the plants of the country" (14).

RELIGIO MEDICI

When *Religio Medici* appeared in 1642, the book immediately generated controversy. Here was a young, unknown physician expressing religious convictions that could not easily be classified in any of the accepted categories of the day. Moreover, the author of this "religion of a doctor" expressed himself in imaginative prose with scope and mastery. The strong focus of the book on religious tolerance and freedom of conscience outraged Protestants and Roman Catholics alike. His disavowal of Catholic dogma and sacramentalism easily won *Religio* a place on the Vatican's Index of Forbidden Books. Critics initially varied in their reception of Browne's testament, but it quickly became a 17th-century bestseller. Subsequently, critics ranging from Samuel Johnson to James Russell Lowell praised Browne's elegant and imaginative prose (15). Writers like Charles Lamb, Samuel Taylor Coleridge, Thomas De Quincey, Herman Melville, and Edgar Allan Poe were passionate admirers of the book. In fact, as late as 1950, Sir Thomas Browne's biographer was able to assert that "*Religio Medici* appears on virtually every list of 'great books'" (16). As Jeremiah Finch wrote, "Behind the lively, bright exterior was an inner core of truth and substance that was bound to have its effect on the reader's mind. So sane and unpretentious a work seemed utterly fresh and delightful. It was free from rancor and self-righteousness. It had no axe to grind" (17).

What is *Religio*'s "inner core of truth and substance"? The first major theme of the book is, as noted above, Browne's assertion that one's religious belief is an entirely personal choice that others should respect. Such religious tolerance was almost unheard of in Europe during the 17th century, except to a limited extent in the Netherlands. In England, public practice of Catholicism was illegal; priests could be executed for saying Mass. Jews had long since been expelled from the country. The official Church of England condemned reformed Protestant churches, such as Presbyterianism and Puritanism, and the latter eagerly returned the favor. Arising in this context, *Religio Medici* may, in fact, be the earliest Western statement of tolerance and respect for religious beliefs that differ from one's own. Two years after its publication, Roger Williams, the founder of Rhode Island, published *The Bloody Tenet of Persecution for Cause of Conscience* (1644), an early defense of liberty of conscience; and John Locke's *A Letter Concerning Toleration*, often considered the font of Enlightenment teaching on liberty of conscience, did not appear in print until 1689 (18).

Although Browne concluded that no church "squares unto my conscience" as well as the Church of England (19), he said he would have no objection to entering another Christian church, including a Catholic one, and praying with the congregants (20). He judged that many Catholic dogmas were false beliefs, but he also appreciated the beauty of Catholic ritual and reckoned it had potential value for spirituality, if approached with the right attitude. Browne opposed any form of conflict in the name of religion, "Particular churches and sects usurp the gates of heaven, and turn the key against each other; and thus we go to heaven against each others' wills, conceits, and opinions, and, with as much uncharity as ignorance, do err" (21).

Browne's respect for religious diversity, remarkable though it was, did not extend beyond Christianity. He expressed admiration for the endurance and steadfastness of the Jews, but considered Judaism itself "contemptible and degenerate" (22). In his mind, the Jewish people had suffered persecution for 500 years "in a bad cause." As to Islam, Browne dismissed the "Turks," and especially the Koran, as full of "ridiculous errors in philosophy, impossibilities, fictions, and vanities beyond laughter..." (23). His blanket condemnation of Islam is especially ironic because Islamic societies had a history of being considerably more tolerant of others' religious practices than any Christian society at the time. In effect, Muslims actually practiced the tolerance that Browne preached.

Despite his negative comments about other monotheistic faiths, Browne made it clear that he did not reject the individual's right to believe them.

> I could never divide myself from any man upon the difference of opinion, or be angry with his judgment for not agreeing with me in that, from which perhaps within a few days I should dissent myself: I have no Genius to dispute in Religion, and have often thought it wisdom to decline them (24).
>
> Further, no man can judge another, because no man knows himself; for we censure others but as they disagree from that humour which we fancy laudable in ourselves, and commend others but for that wherein they seem to quadrate and consent with us (25).

In another place he wrote, "I cannot...condemn a man for such an error, or conceive why a difference of opinion should divide an affection..." (26). The scope of his tolerance for liberty of conscience was so broad that he even criticized Christian churches for burdening believers with too many rules and restrictions, thus making the pathway to salvation "far narrower than our Savior ever meant it" (27).

On a more secular plane, Browne also pronounced himself free of prejudice regarding national and cultural differences (28).

Religio Medici's second major theme is its demarcation between revealed religion and natural philosophy, that is, the 17th-century term for science. Browne's conception of science was by no means modern, but his commitment to skepticism and empirical observation was advanced for his time and in the spirit of his older contemporary Sir Francis Bacon whose *Novum Organum* (1620) helped lay the groundwork for the modern scientific method. From Browne's perspective, nature was one of the two "books" through which we can come to some understanding of God and his Divine Providence:

> For there is in this Universe a stair, or manifest Scale of creatures, rising not disorderly, or in confusion, but with a comely method and proportion (29).
>
> I hold there is a general beauty in the works of God, and therefore no deformity in any kind of species whatsoever: I cannot tell by what Logic we call a Toad, a Bear, or an Elephant, ugly, they being created in those outward shapes and figures which best express the actions of their inward forms (30).

Although Browne respected the book of nature in general, his personal interest in science seemed confined to human biology. As noted earlier, Browne was an early proponent of William Harvey's proof that Galen had been mistaken about the nature of the circulatory system. Later in life, Browne avidly followed the *Transactions of the Royal Society*, commenting favorably, for example, on Hammen and Leeuwenhoek's report in 1679 of their observing spermatozoa under the microscope (31). However, in the physical realm, Browne remained unwilling to question traditional concepts of astronomy and the physics. In *Religio* he dismissed the Copernican model, and in *Pseudodoxia Epidemica* he continued to take a detached, but skeptical, viewpoint toward heliocentricity (32). Moreover, although he attended the University of Padua, where Galileo's ideas were widely discussed, Browne never mentioned the great Italian astronomer.

The second book upon which Browne based his knowledge of divinity was, of course, the Bible. Like most Europeans in the 17th century, he believed that the Bible was "written by God," literally true in all its details (33). As such, statements in the Bible necessarily transcend the book of nature and, hence, must not be questioned. For example, Browne pronounced the stories of Genesis to be historical fact, even though critical examination revealed inconsistencies and contradictions. Consider the story of Noah's Ark. Browne wrote that reason leads us to question how so many creatures could fit into a vessel built to the specifications listed in Genesis. We might also question how the dove that didn't return to the Ark because it discovered dry land could have found a mate in a world where all the other doves had died. Furthermore, given recent knowledge of exotic New World fauna, reason might ask where llamas came from, or why didn't America have horses:

> How America abounded with beasts of prey, and noxious animals, yet contained not in it that necessary creature, a horse, is very strange.... How there be creatures there, which are not found in this triple continent, all must needs be strange unto us, that hold but one Ark, and that the creatures began their progress from the mountains of Ararat (34).

While these questions sound reasonable, Browne considers them off limits, since the Bible trumps observation and natural philosophy. God is not bound by reason, "I hold that God can do all things, how he should work contradictions I do not understand, yet dare not deny" (35).

COMPASSION AND MEDICINE

At the beginning of his religion of a physician, Browne asserted that lack of religion was "the scandal of my profession" (36). In a later section, he disavowed the many "sordid and unchristian desires" attributed to physicians, such as hoping for plagues and famines, presumably to stimulate business (37). Instead, he expressed the belief that medical practice was a natural extension of the moral life and not simply a trade or business. In fact, he seemed apologetic about charging his patients, especially when the treatment was not beneficial. For Browne, the physician's motivation is compassion for others that, when acted upon, also benefits the physician, "For by compassion we make others' misery our own, and so, by relieving them, we relieve ourselves also" (38). The good physician places his patient's interests before his own, "I desire rather to cure his infirmities than my own necessities; where I do him no good methinks it is scarce honest gain, though I confess, 'tis but the unworthy salary of our well-intended endeavors" (39).

Browne delighted in biological complexity, but was keenly sensitive to the fragility of life:

> Men that look no further than their outsides think health an appurtenance unto life, and quarrel with their constitutions for being sick; but I that have examined the parts of man, and know upon what tender filaments that fabric hangs, do wonder that we are not always so; and considering the thousand doors that lead to death do thank God that we can die but once (40).

In this context, he expressed what today we might call a holistic or biopsychosocial perspective on illness. For example, he believed that the physician can deal with some vices (for example, emotional problems or bad behavior) more effectively by physical means than clergy could relieve them by spiritual intervention, "I can cure vices by physic when they remain incurable by divinity, and shall obey my pills when they condemn their precepts" (41). Yet Browne also considered medical diseases more amenable to treatment than characterological problems (vices), "I can cure the gout or stone in some, sooner than divinity [can cure] pride or avarice in others" (42). Nonetheless, the effects of medicine are limited by the inevitability of death, "I boast nothing, but plainly say, we all labor against our own cure, for death is the cure of all diseases" (43).

While he marveled at the order and beauty of nature and believed that Divine Providence guides human history, Browne also considered the world an inferior place in which true health and happiness are impossible, "For the world, I count it not an inn, but a hospital, and a place, not to live, but to die in" (44). Our real home is heaven, which Browne viewed in both a Christian sense as union with God and a Platonic sense as the world of eternal forms, "The visible world is but a picture of the invisible" (45). Nonetheless, the man who wrote, "I conclude therefore and say, there is no happiness under (or as Copernicus would have it, above) the Sun..." (46), was a stable, productive, and presumably happy person who devoted his life to a world-affirming profession.

BROWNE'S BLOCKS

The disjunction between Browne's theology, which requires the world to be an unhappy place, and his human sense of value and enjoyment in life may seem contradictory in our secular age, but was probably invisible to him. Likewise, "his pre-Copernican astronomy, his belief in witches, and (acceptance of) the literal truth of the creation stories in Genesis" present difficulties for us (47). Like most people of his day, Browne believed in magic, spirits, and witches. He made a distinction between natural or traditional magic, which relies on "the honest effects of nature" (48) and can be learned and practiced by a person who is not possessed by the devil, and black or evil magic, which is only practiced by witches. The biblical authority for witchcraft is so strong, Browne stated, that to doubt its existence is tantamount to becoming an infidel or atheist (49). Later in his career, Browne put these beliefs into practice when he actually testified against two women on trial for witchcraft (50). When reminded of Browne's affirmations of witchcraft in *Religio*, Osler pointed out that "a man must be judged by his times and his surroundings..." (51).

Even more distressing are the statements of *Religio Medici* about woman, misogynous musings that, in light of Browne's subsequent life, may be more youthful bluster than stable belief. Given the literal truth of Genesis and its Christian interpretation, Browne concluded that "Man is the whole world, and the breath of God; woman the rib and crooked piece of man" (52). Because of her inferior status, he expressed doubt that he could love a woman with as much fervor as he could love a male friend, "I never yet cast a true affection upon a woman, but I have loved my friend as I do virtue, my soul, my God" (53). To Browne, the only useful function of the female gender is procreation, but he even questioned the value—that is, from a moral perspective—of sexual intercourse, since "I could be content that we might procreate like trees, without conjunction, or that there were any way to perpetuate the world without this trivial and vulgar act of coition; it is the foolishest act a wise man commits in all his life" (54).

This is a surely an unusual point of view for a vigorous 30-year-old man. Presumably, he learned greater appreciation for the opposite gender as he courted Dorothy Mileham and they began their long, happy marriage that resulted in 10 children. It is clear, though, as Osler acknowledged, that this most liberal of men "expressed himself very strongly against the method of the nature for the propagation of the race" (55, 56).

OSLER, BROWNE, AND THE RELIGION OF MEDICINE

Osler considered *Religio Medici* "stylistically beautiful, intellectually complex, profoundly tolerant, and, for him, a richly satisfying argument..." (57). Nonetheless, his appreciation for Sir Thomas Browne and his "religion of a doctor" was not simply intellectual approval, but rather an emotional—even spiritual—attachment. I believe he experienced what might be called a kind of "literary transference" upon encountering *Religio Medici*. Osler developed an image of Browne as a wise, priestly figure who pointed the way toward a new religion, a religion that Osler could passionately espouse (even though it differed greatly from the one Browne actually affirmed). Consequently, Osler idealized *Religio Medici* and touted its merits, while excusing its faults. To the great physician, *Religio Medici* functioned as a touchstone, a surrogate Bible, and its author became Osler's priest, big brother, and beloved mentor.

Although he initially intended to become a minister like his father, the young Osler soon abandoned traditional religious faith and committed himself to science and medicine. His 1905 lecture, "Science and Immortality," illustrates the respectful, but detached and skeptical, attitude the mature Osler demonstrated toward religious doctrines, like the soul and immortality (58). In his opinion, for the vast majority of people who believe in an afterlife, the belief has little influence on the way in which they live in the world. Nor, he argued, does religion have much influence on the way people die. Summarizing his observations on 500 dying patients, Osler claimed that the vast majority experienced peaceful deaths no matter whether they believed or not. According to him, only one in 500 experienced spiritual exaltation, 11 were apprehensive, and three felt terror or remorse (59). He concluded, "As a rule, man dies as he lived, uninfluenced practically by the thought of a future life" (60). Osler's observations, if not optimistic about spirituality at the end of life, were at least more sanguine than those of his 17th-century mentor, who contended that people generally become less virtuous as they age and approach death, "But age doth not rectify, but incurvate our natures, turning bad dispositions into worse habits, and (like diseases) brings on incurable vices; for every day as we grow weaker in age, we grow stronger in sin, and the number of our days doth make our sins innumerable" (61).

Nonetheless, Osler recognized that some people do experience a deep connection with the eternal, a connection they articulate in terms of resurrection, salvation, and union with God. In this relatively small group, immortality permeates daily life and forms the person's moral core. Osler considered mysticism a positive, albeit unusual, attribute. He recognized that spirituality may constitute "an asset in human life," but from his perspective as a scientist, the idea of consciousness without the brain didn't make sense:

> Why should he consider the, to him, unthinkable proposition of consciousness without a corresponding material basis? The old position, so beautifully expressed by Sir Thomas Browne, "Thus we are men and we know not how: there is something in us that can be without us and will be after us; though it is strange that it has no history what it was before us, nor cannot tell how it entered us," this old Platonic and orthodox view has no place in science (62).

Unlike Browne, who believed that God could "work contradictions," Osler could not accept the "old position." Thus, he was left with a quandary, recognizing as he did that "the emotional side to which faith leans makes for all that is bright and joyous in life... (and) the human heart has a hidden want which science cannot supply" (63).

Osler's personal solution was to turn medicine itself into a secular religion that he could affirm without reservation. In his lectures and essays, he summarized this view of medicine as a modern ministry, and he articulated moral and conceptual standards that considerably outstrip a sober assessment of traditional medical practice. As a minister's son, Osler brought "to the practice of medicine, medical education, and medical writing... the rich lode of Christian ideas of service... " (64). Moreover, the secular religion of medicine strongly echoed the themes of tolerance and individual responsibility so prominent in *Religio Medici* (65). Just as Sir Thomas Browne pioneered an inclusive vision of religion for his time, so his disciple would pioneer the inclusive ministry of medicine. Interestingly, subsequent generations of physicians and medical educators have converted Osler's professional life into the founding myth, and his writings into the sacred scriptures, of "Oslerianism," which is in some ways an extension of Osler's own medical ministry, but in other ways a distortion and glorification of the human and his beliefs.

FOR FUTURE PHYSICIANS

Not many of today's medical students and physicians are likely to find in *Religio Medici* a source of personal and professional inspiration, or to develop a close vicarious friendship with its author. While works of great literature may continue to inspire us for hundreds of years, Sir Thomas Browne's religion of a physician strikes the modern reader as primarily of historical interest and not a living testament that addresses the existential concerns of today. I suspect that even in Osler's time few students embraced

Religio Medici with as much passion as their teacher did, even though they may have been more likely to read classical literature than their 21st-century counterparts. Sir Thomas Browne, impressive physician though he was, no longer engages us as a stirring role model.

We live at a time when the moral compass of medicine is wavering. In response to serious concerns about how we teach the moral core of our profession (perhaps best articulated in Thomas Inui's report, "A Flag in the Wind" (66)), educators have rushed to adopt the concept of "professionalism" as an explicit theme of the medical curriculum (67). The content of this new curriculum in professionalism is controversial, ranging from approaches that focus on rules of propriety to more ambitious schemes that embrace the process of character formation (67, 68). The term "narrative professionalism" encompasses the notion that values and virtues of the good physician develop gradually as the student integrates and identifies with the stories of role model physicians (68). In addition to real-life preceptors and teachers, such narratives can include vicarious models, that is physicians and other healers who have written personal narratives, or about whom others have written. I suspect, too, that most of us have had the experience sometime in our lives of identifying strongly, even passionately, with a fictional physician we would like to emulate.

Reading such works may serve to broaden the student's range of role models, to enhance self-awareness, to stimulate social responsibility, and to expand and deepen the student's narrative competence, that is "the capacity to adopt others' perspectives, to follow the narrative thread of complex and chaotic stories, to tolerate ambiguity, and to recognize the several, often contradictory meanings of events that befall human beings" (69, 70). In sum, literary role models may engage and expand the student's moral imagination and contribute to professional identity (71). If Sir Thomas Browne's work affected the young William Osler in this way, the question arises: What physician stories or essays might have similar effects on contemporary medical students? In other words, what book or books might take the place of *Religio Medici* on a 21st-century version of the bedside reading list?

Osler's life and work provide an obvious starting point. His *Aequanimitas and Other Essays* occupies the #2 spot on Pai and Gursahani's suggested bedside library for the 21st century (72). Certainly iconic devotion to Osler permeates contemporary teaching about professional ethics and the "good doctor." However, as much as I admire the great Canadian physician, I wonder how many of today's medical students really "fall for" Osler's restrained and elegant style? How many take him to their hearts as a beloved mentor? I suspect Osler's own writings will never be able to occupy the emotional niche he envisioned for *Religio Medici*, and in this era of social and cultural diversity in medicine, I doubt whether any single book can.

When I look to my own experience, several literary physicians lay claim to being my teachers and guides. One who certainly deserves Osler's appellation "most liberal of men and distinguished of general practitioners" (73) is Anton Chekhov, known to the world primarily as a great author and dramatist. Yet Chekhov, who supported himself in Moscow University Medical School by selling his stories to newspapers and magazines, practiced clinical medicine through much of his literary career, and was particularly committed to public health and education. Though by no means wealthy, Chekhov devoted much of his time to providing free medical care for the rural poor and serving gratis as a district health officer. Consider, for example, this excerpt from an 1892 letter to his publisher, explaining why Chekhov could not join him on a trip to Vienna, "I have been busy being sole doctor of the Serpehovskovo District, and trying to catch cholera by the tail and organize health services. . . . I have in my district 25 villages, 4 factories, and a monastery. In the morning I receive patients, and in the afternoon go on house calls" (74). Chekhov never wrote a book comparable to *Religio Medici*, but reflected in his stories I visualize a humane, compassionate physician who inspires me and whose work I share with my students. *The Island of Sakhalin*, Chekhov's report of his 1890 public health investigation of the Russian prison colonies on Sakhalin Island, provides an explicit look at Chekhov as a medical role model, unmediated by fiction (75).

Another of my literary physicians is Albert Schweitzer, whose autobiography *Out of My Life and Thought* was published in 1931 (76). When I was a college student in the 1960s, Schweitzer was one of the most famous people on earth, renowned as a physician and humanitarian, but also a Renaissance figure who made significant contributions to theology, philosophy, and musicology. He was a heroic character who turned away from a secure, scholarly career to devote his life to practicing medicine in a remote corner of West Africa. In *Out of My Life and Thought*, written in his mid-50s, Schweitzer reflected on his belief that "I must not accept (my) happiness as a matter of course, but must give something in return for it" (77). Thus, he went back to medical school, trained in tropical medicine, and established a hospital at Lambaréné in Gabon, where he continued working until his death in 1965. While Schweitzer's reputation has suffered in recent decades because of his paternalism and reluctance to accept change, he remains for me a courageous and compassionate physician whose reverence for life is an inspiring ideal.

Paul Farmer presents a more contemporary version of a physician "who would cure the world." Tracy Kidder's *Mountains Beyond Mountains* is a journalistic biography of Farmer, the Harvard anthropologist and infectious disease specialist, who has devoted his life to crusading for improved treatment of resistant tuberculosis in Haiti, Peru, Russia, and countries around the world (78). Although not written by Farmer himself, *Mountains Beyond Mountains* contains reflective dialogue in which he reveals much about himself; for example, his commitment to improving health care in developing countries, despite obstacles and possible failure, "I have fought the long defeat and brought other people to fight the long defeat, and I'm not going to stop because we keep losing" (79).

William Carlos Williams and his *Autobiography*, first published in 1951, are also important to me (80). Like Sir Thomas Browne, Williams combined the roles of family physician and man of letters, in Williams' case as a world-class modernist poet and perceptive medical storyteller. The *Autobiography* paints a good picture of Williams' personal and professional beliefs. True to his famous aphorism, "no ideas but in things," he presents his views on concepts like virtue, duty, compassion, and empathy as anecdotes drawn from his practice, using a case-based approach that is likely more appealing to the physicians of today than Browne's elegant 17th-century paragraphs.

Robert Coles is another physician-writer whose work has been an important influence in my career. While he hasn't published an autobiography or testament of belief, many of his books reveal his passionate humanism and commitment to the moral life; *Lives of Moral Leadership* (81) and *The Call of Stories* (82) have been especially meaningful in my own life. *The Call of Stories* first introduced me to the power of literature as a factor in character development and to the concept of "moral imagination," which I believe lies at the center of ethical practice. Richard Selzer's work has also greatly enriched my concept of narrative professionalism, and his stories and essays are consistently appealing to medical students (83, 84). Probably the physician whose secular testament or "religion of a doctor" has contributed most to my understanding of healing and my love for the profession is Eric Cassell. His books, *The Healer's Art* and *The Nature of Suffering and the Goals of Medicine*, should be on any medical student's reading list (85, 86).

As I reflect on these and other role models, I recall a summary statement from Osler's essay on the author of *Religio Medici*, "Mastery of self, conscientious devotion to duty, deep human interest in human beings—these best of all lessons you must learn now or never—and these are some of the lessons which may be gleaned from the life and from the writings of Sir Thomas Browne" (87). That's what we are looking for. That's what we want to teach our students. That's the kind beloved mentor I hope all students and young physicians discover for themselves.

Shakespeare

Othello as a Study in Toxicology

Arnold Weinstein

I would like to believe that Osler found *Othello* fascinating as a virtual case study in the workings of jealousy. Yet, its still darker truths have to do with how one cunning person can *create* the ultimately murderous rage of another person. At the play's very center, Act III, Scene iii, we watch hypnotized, something on the order of a laboratory experiment in character-change. It is not accidental that Shakespeare has Iago refer to this operation in medical terms. "I'll pour this pestilence into his ear," says the Ensign, and the notion and effects of effective poison are displayed for us upfront. Please note that poison-in-the-ear is (also) about as brilliant a notion of *language*, especially of *lying*, as we are likely to come across. Lying words come into us as toxins, and work their will inside us. I should think Osler found the play's transmogrification of a hitherto balanced and honorable man fascinating if not horrifying. I will cite a number of the key passages in Act III, Scene iii, and comment on them as I go.

> OTHELLO.
> *Excellent wretch! Perdition catch my soul,*
> *But I do love thee! and when I love thee not,*
> *Chaos is come again* (III, iii, pp. 90–93) (1).

These beautiful lines from Othello to Desdemona are prophetic, indeed diagnostic, in ways that Othello cannot fathom. We see Renaissance idealism at its peak here, as love is granted the power of making or unmaking the world order. The poisoner Iago will undo the Moor, turning his love into crazed jealousy, and chaos will come again in the form of bloodshed and the slaughter of innocence. Now, let's see how Iago does it.

> IAGO.
> *I did not think he had been acquainted with her.*
> OTHELLO.
> *O, yes; and went between us very oft.*

IAGO.
Indeed!
OTHELLO.
Indeed! ay, indeed: —discern'st thou aught in that?
Is he not honest?
IAGO.
Honest, my lord!
OTHELLO.
Honest! ay, honest.
IAGO.
My lord, for aught I know.
OTHELLO.
What dost thou think?
IAGO.
Think, my lord!
OTHELLO.
Think, my lord! By heaven, he echoes me,
As if there were some monster in his thought
Too hideous to be shown (III, iii, pp. 99–108) (1).

Here we see the muscularity and economy of not only Shakespeare but also the human psyche as it goes about hatching feverish designs. Words— *honest, indeed, think*—twist and turn here, releasing their power, turning from question to statement to obsession, as this verbal ping-pong gets into ever higher gear. Jealousy is our species' most creative act: It takes the poor bits and pieces we know, and it fashions them into a masochistic torture-narrative. It is hardly metaphorical to term such activity "generative," and this passage discloses the "monster" itself about to be born. What kind of monsters do we either make or hide? One wonders if it is a question Osler posed.

Urged by Othello to come clean, to utter his thoughts, Iago tells us that our psyches are bestiaries:

> *Utter my thoughts? Why, say they are vile and false;—*
> *As where's that palace whereinto foul things*
> *Sometimes intrude not?* (III, iii, pp. 136–138) (1).

We are, I think, dead center. The human mind/heart, when sufficiently goaded, when sufficiently "poisoned," is no longer the palace of *Homo sapiens*, but rather a vile place teeming with animals. Shakespeare has been telling us for some time about this bad news. We recall that the play opens with Iago trying to start a riot in Venice, by yelling up to Brabantio that his daughter, Desdemona, has eloped with Othello. But he doesn't use the word "elope"; his language has more pith: "Your daughter and the Moor are now making the beast with two backs." I know of no stronger utterance in all of literature to denote sexual coupling. It—along with the madness and jealousy that can be engendered in us—takes out of the so-called human and into the animal realm. What is Iago's project, if not to transform Othello into a raging beast? This would confirm his view of Africans, as well as his cynical, quasi-Machiavellian view of human behavior and appetite.

I have to think Osler, the shrewd diagnostician, would also have noted the sheer sadistic pleasure that Iago experiences in the torture he's inflicting. Note how cunning he is, how well he knows where the weak spots are. Othello is a Moor, ergo, he is an outsider to Venice, ergo he can be persuaded he has no clue about the behavior of Venetian girls. Iago lessons him:

> Look to't.
> I know our country disposition well;
> In Venice they do let heaven see the pranks
> They dare not show their husbands; their best conscience
> Is not to leave undone, but keep unknown (III, iii, pp. 200–205) (1).

Iago is the guy who turns everything to his favor (he would have made a great lawyer): Desdemona displayed great courage by defying her father, but is this not, he asks Othello, a sign of her duplicity? We watch—and he watches—the Moor begin to writhe in pain. This is fun for him:

> IAGO.
> I see this hath a little dash'd your spirits.
> OTHELLO.
> Not a jot, not a jot.
> IAGO.
> Trust me, I fear it has.
> I hope you will consider what is spoke
> Comes from my love; but I do see you're mov'd
> (III, iii, pp. 205–208) (1).

Osler, who wrote so eloquently about the need of *equanimity* as the physician's crucial posture, must have been deeply moved by this spectacle of a good man being undone. Shakespeare is an unrivaled observer of the sheer mobility of human feeling, the way in which composure can yield to rage in mere seconds, when the right pressure is applied. And I think Osler would have recognized that the mind, when sick, when under the sway of neurosis or vicious manipulation, when poisoned, can go wild, can run off the charts. Iago is the genius of the play, and his great sport consists of toying with Othello's core beliefs, not unlike the way a cat toys with a mouse it has caught. Othello seeks to remain himself: He protests to his tormentor, "I do not think but Desdemona's honest," and the rejoinder functions in the way toxins do, or time-release capsules do: "Long live she so! and long live you to think so!" (III, iii, pp. 225–226). One actually hears the time-lapse in Iago's words: She is innocent...because you are gullible enough, deceived enough, to think her so. A terrible truth comes into focus: Our thinking makes our truths. If you influence my thinking, you shape what I construe as true. There is a rich emotional, even ideological payload in all this, concerning the malleability and vulnerability of all of us. We can all be brainwashed. Maybe that is how culture itself operates. Toxicology.

Iago's most potent wild card lies in taunting Othello's masculinity. The Moor acknowledges that he is "declin'd/Into the vale of years," and this matters when we consider Cassio as a ladies' man; we are meant to hear the sexual innuendo when Iago suggests that Cassio should "have his place" back, "For sure he fills it up with great ability" (III, iii, pp. 246–247). I said the animal is let loose in this play, and that is Othello's unsurvivable discovery about marriage itself: "O curse of marriage,/That we can call these delicate creatures ours,/And not their appetites" (III, iii, pp. 268–270). Othello will go the full route in his journey toward bestial violence. He will rage, he will collapse in seizure, he will mutter his desire for revenge as "I see that nose of yours, but not that dog I shall throw it to" (IV, i, pp. 141–142), he will conclude his welcoming of Lodovico to Cyprus with the exclamation, "Goats and monkeys!" (IV, i, p. 256). The poison has worked. He strikes his wife in Act IV. We already see the murderer he will become at the play's end.

Here, then, is a literary masterpiece I would like to imagine placed on Osler's bedside table. Reading or rereading Act III, Scene iii of *Othello* would probably not have been the best way for getting a good night's sleep, or for closing the day with venerable and reassuring meditations. Osler was not a toxicologist as such, but he was a student of human behavior, and he knew a great deal about the transformations that can take place in the human body and the human mind. He knew the physician's task consisted in gauging and interpreting these changes in soma and psyche; understanding these disorders could—should—lead to treating them. Little in literature can match either the rapidity or the ferocity of the human alterations depicted in Shakespeare's great play about jealousy. The toxic events of

Othello, the spectacle of one man driving another mad, strikes me as rich but disturbing fare for Osler and for medicine as a whole. We are invited to ponder the ills to which we are heir (as Hamlet might have said). Act III, Scene iii of *Othello* puts to rest any fond notions of "unchanging human nature" and gives notice that there can be no human mind "whereinto foul things/Sometimes intrude not."

Food for thought for Osler, for us all.

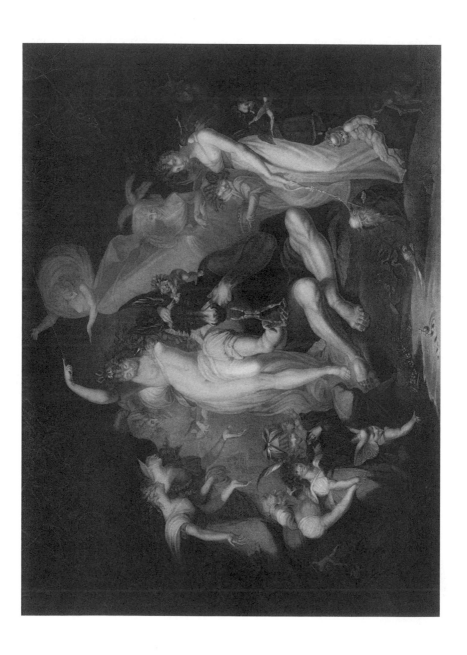

On Osler, Medicine, and the Comedy of Life:
A Midsummer Night's Dream

PAMELA BRETT-MACLEAN

Osler encouraged medical students to appreciate all aspects of life—the mundane, the tragic, and the comedic. Given this, it is not surprising that Osler was well versed in the collected works of Shakespeare, including the romantic comedy *A Midsummer Night's Dream*, one of Shakespeare's most popular works. Osler wrote:

> The comedy, too, of life will be spread before you, and nobody laughs more often than the doctor at the pranks Puck plays upon the Titanias and the Bottoms among his patients. The humorous side is really almost as frequently turned towards him as the tragic. Lift up one hand to heaven and thank your stars if they have given you the proper sense to enable you to appreciate the inconceivably droll situations in which we catch our fellow creatures (1).

Shakespeare's *A Midsummer Night's Dream* draws on many sources, including Chaucer's *Canterbury Tales*, *Plutarch's Life of Theseus*, Apuleius' *The Golden Ass*, and Ovid's *Metamorphoses* (2). Not surprisingly, the play follows a many-layered, convoluted, and farcical plotline, which strongly contributes to its comic effect.

A Midsummer Night's Dream portrays the interrelated stories of the four couples: Theseus and Hippolyta; Lysander and Hermia; Demetrius and Helena; and the royal fairy couple Oberon and Titania. The play begins with Theseus' (the Duke of Athens) announcement that he will marry the fair Hippolyta (Queen of the Amazon) in four days. Hermia wants to marry Lysander, but her father has chosen Demetrius for her, and asks for the right to dispose her to her death should she refuse. Hermia flees with Lysander into the forest outside of Athens to elope, after discussing her plans with her friend Helena. Helena, who had previously been betrothed to Demetrius, tells Demetrius about the plans hoping to win back his favor. Demetrius heads into the forest in pursuit of Hermia, Helena follows Demetria. Meanwhile, Oberon and Titania have also arrived in the forest to attend Theseus and Hippolyta's wedding. They argue about the orphan child Titania has adopted. When Titania refuses to give him the child, Oberon orders Puck (a fairy trickster figure) to obtain "love-juice" from Cupid that will make Titania fall in love with the first person she sees. Having observed Demetrius' cruel behavior toward Helena, he tells Puck to also anoint Demetrius with the love-juice. Puck obtains the potion, but first comes across Lysander and mistakenly applies the potion on him. As a result of this, Lysander falls in love with Helena, and abandons Hermia. Attempting to correct the situation, Oberon applies the potion on Demetrius. Both Demetrius and Lysander end up fighting over Helena, but she can only believe that they are mocking her. Puck places them all in a deep sleep.

Oberon then anoints Titania with the love potion while she is sleeping. Nick Bottom, a foolish, overconfident weaver, and other tradesmen called "the rude mechanicals" gather near Titania's forest bower to rehearse a play they plan on performing for Theseus and Hippolyta's wedding. Puck transforms Bottom's head to a donkey's head, and the actors flee. Upon awakening, Titania falls in love with Bottom, and lavishes him with attention. Soon after, Oberon removes the spell from Titania, and Oberon and Titania make up. Lysander's love for Hermia is restored, and Demetrius remains in love with Helena. A triple wedding is held in Athens, and the rude mechanicals (including Bottom, who has been transformed back to a human) perform a hilarious, fumbling rendition of the story of Pyramus and Thisbe from Ovid's *Metamorphoses*. As the play ends, Oberon and Titania offer fairy blessings to the newly married sleeping couples, and Puck asks the audience to remember the play as if it were only a dream:

> *If we shadows have offended,*
> *Think but this,—and all is mended,—*
> *That you have but slumber'd here*
> *While these visions did appear...* (3).

Theseus and Hippolyta play a relatively small role in this marriage-play. They appear at the beginning and the end of the play, mostly to signal the beginning of four days of celebration as they await their wedding day, and then a return to order and rationality that follows the magical night in the forest. It is Puck whose mischievous, child-like spirit pervades the action. Different devices, such as mistaken identity, magical potions ("love-juice"), a play-within-play, and wordplay of various kinds (irony, satire, puns, and so forth), are used to provoke both laughter and thoughtful reflection.

Every person who reads or experiences this play will have his own response to it. Some may not be overly positively receptive to the play. For example, there are themes that relate to male dominance and patriarchal order. Early on, Theseus states:

> Hippolyta, I woo'd thee with my sword,
> And won thy love doing thee injuries;
> But I will wed thee in another key,
> With pomp, with triumph, and with reveling (4).

Also recall that Hermia's father attempted to exert control over his daughter's choice of a husband. That Hermia succeeds in marrying Lysander, the man she loves, rather than the suitor chosen by her father, suggests that the play can also be viewed as a challenge to patriarchal rule.

There are few direct references to medicine in *A Midsummer Night's Dream*. The Fairy Queen Titania's barrenness may be viewed as "caused by and causative of her marital strife" as was the understanding of the day. Rather than look for direct medical allusions, I offer the following. I believe that some themes and observations that Osler might have reflected on include the importance of stories in our lives, positive possibilities of love and commitment, and engaging constructively with life.

The doubling of the fairy world and human world, as if each is the mirror version of the other, calls to mind the idea that we live our lives as stories and understand our lives through stories. Stories influence how we understand our lives. Stories offer the potential of transforming our lives, as alternate futures come into view. Osler in his farewell address in 1903 before leaving for England to take the position of Regius Professor of Medicine at the University of Oxford stated:

> Nothing in life is more glaring than the contrast between possibilities and actualities, between the ideal and the real. By the ordinary mortal, idealists are regarded as vague dreamers, striving after the impossible; but in the history of the world how often have they gradually molded to their will conditions most adverse and hopeless! (5).

What we dream and imagine then is intricately related to the making and shaping of our future. Our stories, even our imagined stories, can change our lives and our world.

Stories can also bring others into our lives, as we share our stories. *A Midsummer Night's Dream* is a transformation story that points to the positive potentials of love and marital commitment. The lovers are ultimately willing to commit to one another to create a new space for experiencing the world, for the benefit of both. It is not known when Osler first read *A Midsummer Night's Dream*. However, he began a new life story when he married his wife Grace at the relatively late age of 42. They are known to have enjoyed a strong, harmonious, and mutually supportive marriage together for many years, until Osler's death.

In relation to this and other aspects of Osler's life, it is not surprising that *A Midsummer Night's Dream* engaged his interest and imagination. An element of lightness winds its way through the play, and joyousness attends its resolution. Osler was a genial man who shared stories and jokes with colleagues and patients. He enjoyed a wonderful rapport with children. He had "a love of children and childhood and play and fantasy...that was reminiscent of no one so much as Lewis Carroll" (6). He frequently joined children in playing quiet and also riotous games, and telling them fantastic stories. Without trying to overstrain a connection, I believe that the joy Osler took in life relates to his commitment to optimism, and taking a constructive response to difficulties. After the loss of their beloved son Revere, he wrote: "We are both going to be brave, and take up what is left of life as if he were here with us" (6). I believe that Osler's commitment to life propelled him forward as he strived to realize the best he could offer in his relationships and in his work, for others and the world.

Shakespeare's *A Midsummer Night's Dream* offers a light but sophisticated treatment of serious human concerns—including the positive possibilities of stories, and what it means not merely just to live, but to live well. The period style and comedic focus of *A Midsummer Night's Dream* would appear to exclude it from present-day concerns of medicine; however, given the themes and emotional landscape of the play, it remains delightfully compelling. It reminds us of the positive possibilities available to us in going forward together.

The Play's the Thing:
Hamlet as a Foil for Reflective Practice

LYUBA KONOPASEK

It is a willful blindness, a sort of fool's paradise, not destroyed by a thought, but by the stern exigencies of life, when the "ministers of human fate" drag us, or—worse still—those near and dear to us, upon the stage. Then we become acutely conscious of human suffering, and of those inevitable stage accessories—doctor and nurse.

William Osler (1)

If all the world is indeed a stage, then physicians have much to gain through the study of drama. *The Globe Shakespeare* was Osler's "close companion" in his student days (2). Osler listed Shakespeare as one of the "saints of humanity" whom the medical student should "spend the last half hour of the day in communion with" (3) and considered Shakespeare to be "the greatest of the world's creators" (4). " 'Self-school'd, self-scann'd, self-honour'd, self-secure,' in heaven-sent moments he turned the common thoughts of life into gold" (5). What would have been Osler's prescription for us for the Bard's *Hamlet*?

The tragedy of Hamlet considers such eternal questions as uncertainty, bias, judgment, fallibility, and virtue. These themes are similarly essential to the practice of medicine, both in the processes of diagnosis and in the "theater" of interactions with patients and colleagues. Reading *Hamlet* may thus allow us to reflect more deeply upon our patients, our practice, and ourselves. Reflective practice in the context of care is one of the defining tenets of the modern medical professional (6). In addition, reflective practice outside of the patient encounter is useful for developing the "intellectual detachment" suggested by Osler as "a sort of separation from the vegetative life of the work-a-day world—always too much with us—which may enable a man to gain a true knowledge of himself and of his relations to his fellows" (7).

Osler strongly valued intellectual honesty and "his writings suggest at least four components: humility, skepticism, acknowledgements of the limits of truth, and the ability to tolerate the anxiety of uncertainty" (8). These themes resonate strongly throughout Hamlet. As the play's characters struggle with constant uncertainty, so the reader questions all she sees. In the first act, the Ghost of Hamlet's father tells Hamlet that Claudius, Hamlet's uncle, has murdered his father. Is the Ghost real or is Hamlet mad? Hamlet is willing to accept the Ghost as a real spirit saying:

> There are more things in heaven and earth, Horatio,
> Than are dreamt of in your philosophy 1.5.168–169 (8a).

However, Hamlet delays acting on the Ghost's directive to

> revenge his foul and most unnatural murder 1.5.25 (8a).

and kill Claudius. Why the delay? Perhaps it is Hamlet's uncertainty that stays his hand. What ghosts might the medical professional encounter? Are they the patients affected by our errors? Can our observations of a patient ever be objective? Osler suggests that we recognize that "absolute truth is hard to reach in all matters relating to our fellow creatures, healthy or diseased" (9). What is the implicit bias that we may bring to a patient encounter unaware of its impact on patient care? How does conflict of interest affect our own decision making? Hamlet prompts many of these difficult questions, often avoided in the bustle of daily clinical practice.

Like moths, Shakespearean scholars fly around the bright light of the question: What

> is rotten in the state of Denmark? 1.5.67 (8a).

Is it madness? If Hamlet is truly mad, then why only intermittently so? As Hamlet states,

> I am but mad north-north-west: when the wind is southerly I
> know a hawk from a handsaw...2.2.361–362 (8a).

Hamlet offers various approaches to diagnosis and discovery, from wild guessing to hypothesis testing. Osler was both a keen observer and a champion of the use of a methodical system in clinical diagnosis. Suspicion arises from observation. Something is not right, and so we must investigate further. In Hamlet, the queen's lack of suspicion about and possible complicity in Claudius' crime is unclear. Does she know? Was she involved? Does she even want to find out? How easy it can be to become derailed, turning a blind eye to some piece of history or finding that does not quite fit our diagnosis, makes us uncomfortable, or may prolong our day in the clinic. It is instructive that Hamlet doggedly pursues the truth of his father's death with method, if with a bit of madness. Empirically, he makes a plan to test his hypothesis through the public staging of a play, "The Mousetrap," to portray the events of the murder as told by the Ghost.

> Hamlet: *For murder, though it have no tongue, will speak*
> *With most miraculous organ, I'll have these players*
> *Play something like the murder of my father*
> *Before mine uncle: I'll observe his looks;*
> *I'll tent him to the quick: if he but blench,*
> *I know my course. The spirit that I have seen*
> *May be the devil: and the devil hath power*
> *To assume a pleasing shape; yea, and perhaps*
> *Out of my weakness and my melancholy,—*
> *As he is very potent with such spirits,—*
> *Abuses me to damn me: I'll have grounds*
> *More relative than this.—the play's the thing*
> *Wherein I'll catch the conscience of the king* 2.2.570–582 (8a).

Claudius does indeed react to the play, and the hypothesis is strengthened. We become part of the audience of "The Mousetrap" and thus discover the root cause of what is rotten in Denmark as confirmed by Claudius' confession in the next scene.

Osler suggests that we pursue the truth with diligence and a methodical manner. It is easy to jump to unfounded conclusions when overly influenced by experience. In attempting to diagnose the cause of Hamlet's madness, Polonius makes just this type of error and comes to premature closure in his diagnostic reasoning. Upon hearing that Ophelia has been rejecting Hamlet's love, Polonius assumes, with just this one piece of evidence and perhaps a little guilt for disrupting the relationship, that he has found the cause of Hamlet's erratic behavior.

> Pol.
> *What do you think of me?*
> King.
> *As of a man faithful and honourable.*
> Pol.
> *I would fain prove so. But what might you think,*
> *When I had seen this hot love on the wing,—*
> *As I perceiv'd it, I must tell you that,*

Before my daughter told me,— what might you,
Or my dear majesty your queen here, think,
If I had play'd the desk or table-book,
Or given my heart a winking, mute and dumb;
Or look'd upon this love with idle sight;—
What might you think? No, I went round to work,
And my young mistress thus I did bespeak:
"Lord Hamlet is a prince, out of thy sphere;
This must not be:" and then I precepts gave her,
That she should lock herself from his resort,
Admit no messengers, receive no tokens.
Which done, she took the fruits of my advice;
And he, repulsed,—a short tale to make,—
Fell into a sadness; then into a fast;
Thence to a watch; thence into a weakness;
Thence to a lightness; and, by this declension,
Into the madness wherein now he raves,
And all we wail for.
King.
Do you think 'tis this?
Queen.
It may be, very likely.
Pol.
Hath there been such a time,—I'd fain know that—
That I have positively said "Tis so,"
When it prov'd otherwise? 2.2.129–156 (8a).

Polonius lacks the "grace of humility" and the "quality of thoroughness," which Osler recommends for the clinician (10). How easy it is to succumb to this type of clinical reasoning when pattern recognition leads to a rapid, successful clinical diagnosis so much of the time. How do we as mature clinicians keep humility and an open mind as the foundation of our clinical wisdom? Osler wrote that "We, the doctors are so fallible, ever beset with the common and fatal facility of reaching conclusions from superficial observations, and constantly misled by the ease with which our minds fall into the ruts of one or two experiences," (11) and advised to be sure to recognize errors, learn from them, and avoid repeating them.

This above all,—to thine own self be true;
And it must follow, as the night the day,
Thou canst not then be false to any man.
Farewell: my blessing season this in thee! 1.3.78–81 (8a).

Osler bade us carry these same ideals. The study of *Hamlet* encourages the physician to "catch his own conscience." To grow as clinicians we must systematically reflect on the objectivity of our observations, the source of our motivations, and the wisdom of our actions. Just as Hamlet used "The Mousetrap" to study Claudius' reactions, so we can use *Hamlet* as the play within the play of our own lives and learn about ourselves.

This Pow'rful Rhyme:
Osler's Legacy and Shakespeare's Sonnets

MAUREEN RAPPAPORT

Sir William Osler was a hardworking, pragmatic physician who delayed marriage until the age of 42 and advised young medical students to do the same. He is often quoted as having said that "medicine is a jealous mistress" and "he who travels fastest travels alone." He did make a strong case to young physicians that they put their passions into "cold storage" as he had done (1). Why then did Osler recommend Shakespeare's sonnets, 154 lyrical love poems, as essential bedside reading in the education of young medical minds?

We know that Osler admired Shakespeare and called him "the greatest of the world's creators" (2). We know that Osler's first book purchase was a copy of Shakespeare's lexicon. And although Osler often quoted Shakespeare in essays and letters, he did not write specifically about the sonnets. Our challenge is to understand why Osler did not stop at Shakespeare's plays, with their insights on human nature, death, and immortality but included the sonnets in his list of great literature.

The opening couplet to sonnet 18 is probably the most famous among the sonnets, the most prone to Valentine-card abuse, yet one never tires of it. The highly structured form of the sonnet is not an explosive outpouring of emotion but a controlled, reasoned argument in which Shakespeare takes an analytic stance toward his experience and feelings. Helen Vendler, in her book, *The Art of Shakespeare's Sonnets* (3), asks, "What does a writer gain from working over and over, in one subgenre?" My brief answer is that Shakespeare learned to find strategies to enact feeling in form through 154 poems.

Osler, who valued efficiency, a highly structured life, imperturbability, and equanimity would have greatly admired the aesthetic challenge of writing 154 lyrical poems in sonnet form. And amid the form, rhyme, meter, imagery, and metaphor, Shakespeare manages to set up and resolve an argument.

Let's look at sonnet 18:

> Shall I compare thee to a summer's day?
> Thou art more lovely and more temperate:
> Rough winds do shake the darling buds of May,
> And summer's lease hath all too short a date:
> Sometime too hot the eye of heaven shines,
> And often is his gold complexion dimm'd,
> And every fair from fair sometime declines,
> By chance, or nature's changing course untrimm'd:
> But thy eternal summer shall not fade,
> Nor lose possession of that fair thou ow'st,
> Nor shall death brag thou wander'st in his shade,
> When in eternal lines to time thou grow'st,
> So long as men can breathe, or eyes can see,
> So long lives this, and this gives life to thee (4).

Read these lines out loud, copy them, read them aloud again, or best yet, memorize them. Committing these lines to memory is of more use to a medical student than memorizing the Krebs cycle. Poetry is a bodily art with the sounds of rhymes, full and half, internal and end line, such as in...*sometime* too hot the *eye* of heaven *shines*...sounds produced by each reader's breath through larynx, sounds that slow one down to enjoy the beauty of each word as well as the image evoked. Osler was a man of great passion. He loved practicing medicine and teaching medicine. He loved history and great literature, and as a young man he dared to follow his dream of writing a medical textbook that he completed like everything else in his life by being methodical and diligent. Osler was no doubt a workaholic. I would like to imagine that Shakespeare's beautiful sonnets fulfilled this young physician's yearning for something more than industry, diligence, and intellectual stimulation. While it is true that good poetry does not reveal itself easily and one must work at it, living with the lines of Shakespeare's sonnets on our tongues would continue to delight both our senses and spirits.

Some sonnets refer to disease and the approach to medical practice of that age, topics Osler surely valued given his interest in medical history.

> My love is as a fever longing still,
> For that which longer nurseth the disease;
> Feeding on that which doth preserve the ill,
> The uncertain sickly appetite to please.
> My reason, the physician to my love,
> Angry that his prescriptions are not kept,
> Hath left me, and I desperate now approve

Desire is death, which physic did except.
Past cure I am, now Reason is past care,
And frantic-mad with evermore unrest;
My thoughts and my discourse as madmen's are,
At random from the truth vainly express'd;
For I have sworn thee fair, and thought thee bright,
Who art as black as hell, as dark as night (5).

The physician, Reason, has left his patient because he didn't keep his prescription. It does not take a physician of Osler's caliber to find fault in this physician's behavior, and in Shakespeare's time, when a physician had nothing stronger than compassion in his pharmacy, he appears incompetent as well. Does the patient desire death or did Desire lead to death?

Consider the eternal issues of death and impermanence, and the subsequent quest for immortality. Physicians, like poets, work at this dark border of human existence and both Shakespeare and Osler understood the importance of leaving a legacy.

Not marble, nor the gilded monuments
Of princes, shall outlive this powerful rhyme;
But you shall shine more bright in these contents
Than unswept stone, besmear'd with sluttish time (6).

Shakespeare defeated "sluttish time" through his lover, kept young and beautiful forever in these sonnets, these *powerful* rhymes. Osler's great love was his work and as he told other physicians, "to carry on, though dead, the work he was interested in while living, is the nearest approach a man can make to cheating the great enemy" (7). Osler's greatest legacy, the *raison d'être* of this book, stemmed from his love of literature and his desire to keep the classics like Shakespeare's pow'rful rhymes alive forever. Osler bequeathed his vast library to McGill University:

> I like to think of my few books in an alcove of a fire-proof library of some institution that I love; at the end of an alcove an open fireplace and a few easy chairs, and on the mantelpiece an urn with my ashes and my bust or a portrait through which my astral self, like the Bishop of St. Praxed's, could peek at the books I have loved and enjoy the delight with which kindred souls still in the flesh would handle them (8).

Ten years ago, a burned-out female family physician wandered into McGill's Osler's Library for the first time. The light through stained glass windows, a walnut desk, a leather-studded armchair, invited me to select from among thousands of books a few volumes of prose and poetry and to sit for hours and read. In this way, Osler led me to a rich future in the medical humanities.

Instead of dreading one more day at the office, conflicts were shaped into narratives, a technique I was destined to share with medical students, kindred souls with nowhere else to place strong emotions evoked by what we witnessed daily on our rounds. Osler realized the importance of books for the health of a young physician's spirit, the wisdom of "art" nourishing cells not attained by intellect and almost a century after his death his "astral self" connected with my "kindred soul still in the flesh." I have Sir William Osler and the legacy of his library at McGill to thank for my healing.

> *His beauty shall in these black lines be seen,*
> *And they shall live, and he in them still green* (9).

ESSAIS
DE
MICHEL·SEIGNEVR
DE MONTAIGNE.

Cinquiesme edition, augmen
tee d'un troisiesme li-
ure et de six cens
additions aux
deux premiers.

A PARIS,
Chez ABEL L'ANGELIER,
au premier pillier de la grand
Salle du Palais.
Auec Priuilege du Roy.

Montaigne

Osler and Montaigne:
In Communion with the Saints of Humanity

LYNN C. EPSTEIN

Although over 250 years separate Montaigne's death and Osler's birth, there is much evidence to suggest that, had they met one another, there would have been strong, personal connections between them. I believe Montaigne would have been impressed with Osler's three personal ideals as outlined in his talk "L'Envoi,"

> I have had three personal ideals. One to do the day's work well and not to bother about to-morrow. It has been urged that this is not a satisfactory ideal. It is; and there is not one which the student can carry with him into practice with greater effect. To it, more than to anything else, I owe whatever success I have had to this power of settling down to the day's work and trying to do it well to the best of one's ability, and letting the future take care of itself.
>
> The second ideal had been to act the Golden Rule, as far as in me lay, towards my professional brethren and towards the patients committed to my care.
>
> And the third has been to cultivate such a measure of equanimity as would enable me to bear success with humility, the affection of my friends without pride and to be ready when the day of sorrow and grief came to meet it with the courage befitting a man (1).

Osler's respect for Montaigne is evidenced by his prominent place in Osler's bedside library and the way Osler refers to Montaigne's beliefs (2). Osler's lifework has helped to frame challenges for physicians in ways that endure, and that question the absolutes of medicine and of life. In a parallel fashion, Montaigne's philosophy and writings profoundly address the central tenets that govern our beliefs, ideas, and actions in life and in the domains of medicine.

As Osler said in *Aequanimitas*, his valedictory address at the University of Pennsylvania in 1889: "In seeking absolute truth we aim at the unattainable, and must be content with finding broken portions" (3). Aware that science must constantly update "facts," Osler strongly articulated the need to practice medicine as an art and to provide humane care for the sick. "The practice of medicine is an art, not a trade; a calling, not a business; a calling in which your heart will be exercised equally with your head" (4).

How did Montaigne find his way into Osler's bedside library? What compels us to add him to our own? Simply put, Montaigne's humble, "What do I know?" philosophy, together with his literary invention "the essay," created an enduring lens to review and to evaluate people, actions, events, and indeed life.

The French word *essais* literally means "attempts" or "trials." First published in 1580 in two small volumes, Montaigne's book created the essay literary form. Written in the first person, the text has countless references to Montaigne, to his family, and to his personal views, reflections, and experiences. In 1588, a new edition was published, which included a third book, plus other text additions.

In the dedication, Montaigne says he wrote the book for himself and that it is a self-portrait.

> Reader, thou hast here an honest book; it doth at the outset forewarn thee that, in contriving the same, I have proposed to myself no other than a domestic and private end. I have had no consideration at all either to thy service or to my glory. My powers are not capable of any such design. . . . Thus reader, myself am the matter of my book: there's no reason thou shouldst employ thy leisure about so frivolous and vain a subject. Therefore, farewell (5).

With this warning, Montaigne proceeds to portray himself as he talks about major aspects of the world: change, causality, the nature of man and the world, life, death, religion, and politics. Montaigne lived in a period of religious and political strife, which is reflected in his writings, in terms both of the subject matter and the way he explores it. One has to admire Montaigne's ability to cover controversial aspects of religion, war, torture, and injustice without unleashing a violent backlash. How does he do this? I believe it is Montaigne's self-effacing and apologetic tone that renders his doubts discreet. Similarly, his tendency to intertwine his personal feelings with his critiques, gives a subtle tone to his words.

Montaigne is not a "quick read," yet his writing is compelling and his text hard to put down. The tone of his writing seems to speak as much to himself as to the reader. His writing is both straightforward and intense, raising more questions than answers. In a similar fashion, his style leads to engagement

and the desire to read in larger time blocks. While raising issues and possible conclusions, he leaves topics open-ended and resists the temptation
to draw emphatic conclusions. Engaged readers will "try on" Montaigne's
answers, rereading passages, using thoughtful reflection to better understand
his points, and ultimately generating their own perspectives from the endless
questions raised by his writing.

Montaigne's motto, Que sais-je? (What do I know?), demonstrates how
he uses a play on words to make his points, a technique that Osler later used
to great advantage in his own writing and talks.

> The wisest man that ever was, when asked what he knew, replied "that
> he knew this much, that he knew nothing." He verified what has been
> said, that the greatest part of what we know is the least of what we do
> not know; that is to say, that even that same that we think we know is
> a portion, and a very small portion, of our ignorance (6).
>
> The Ignorant man who knows himself to be ignorant, who judges
> and condemns himself as ignorant, is not absolutely ignorant; to be
> that, he must be ignorant of himself (7).

On the subject of death, Montaigne writes:

Where death waits for us is uncertain; let us look for him everywhere.
The premeditation of death is the premeditation of liberty; he, who has
learned to die, has unlearned to serve. There is nothing of evil in life, for
him who rightly comprehends that privation of life is no evil: to know how
to die, delivers us from all subjection and constraint.

> Wherever your life ends, it is all there. The utility of living consists not
> in the length of days, but in the use of time; a man may have lived long,
> and yet lived but a little. It depends upon your will, and not upon the
> number of days, to have a sufficient length of life.
>
> "Every day travels towards death: the last only arrives at it." These
> are the good lessons our mother nature teaches.
>
> The first day of your birth starts you on the road to death (8).

On illness and physicians, Montaigne writes at length and critically:

> Would you like an example of the ancient controversy in medicine?
> First on the science or lack there of: Herophilus places the original
> cause of diseases in the humours; Erasistratus, in the blood of the
> arteries; Asclepiades, in the invisible atoms gliding though our pores;
> Alcmaeon, in the exuberance or deficiency of the bodily power; Diocles,
> in the inequality of the elements of the body, and in the quality of the
> air we breathe; Strato, in the abundance, crudity, and corruption of the
> food we take; and Hippocrates lodges it in the spirits.

There is a friend of theirs, whom they know better than I, who exclaims in this connexion, that the most important science we practice, as having charge of our health and preservation, is unfortunately the most uncertain and most confused, and is more disturbed by changes than any other (9).

On medicines:

> In the matter of drugs, he must know their weight, their strength, the place of their origin, their appearance, their age, and the right way to administer them; and he must know all the parts are to be proportioned and related to each other to create a perfect symmetry. Wherein if he makes the slightest error, if there is a single one of these springs that is twisted awry, it is enough to kill us (10).

He gives a lengthy, comical discourse on the conflicting advice and treatments given by physicians and the dangerous outcomes that result:

With regard to the variety and feebleness of the reasonings of this profession, they are more apparent than in any other:

> Aperients are beneficial to a man with the stone, because by opening and dilating the passages they help forward the sticky matter of which the gravel and calculi are formed and convey downward the matter that is beginning to collect and harden in the kidneys.
>
> Aperients are dangerous to a man with the stone, because by opening and dilating the passages they convey the matter that forms the gravel towards the kidneys, which by their nature are apt to seize upon it, so that they must necessarily arrest a great part of that which was carried to them.
>
> Moreover, if there happens to be some body that is a little too big to pass through all those narrows that still have to be passed in order to be expelled, that body, being stirred up by the aperient and thrown into those narrow channels, will stop them up and bring on a certain and very painful death.
>
> Their advice with regard to regimen is equally wobbly:
>
> It is a good thing to pass water frequently, for we know by experience that by allowing it to stagnate, the excrements and lees which form the matter of which the stone is built in the bladder, have time to settle.
>
> It is a good thing not to pass water frequently; for the heavy excrements it drags along with it will not be carried away without violence, as we see by experience that a swiftly rolling torrent sweeps and cleans the places it passes over much more effectually than a gently flowing and sluggish river (11).

After several additional examples, he goes on to say:

On the whole I honour the physicians; not in accordance with the precept, because they are necessary (for this text we may oppose another
where the prophet reproved king Asa for having recourse to a physician),
but for love of themselves, having met many honest and likeable men
among them. It is not them I attack, but their art; and I do not greatly
blame them for taking advantage of our folly, for the greater part of the
world does so. Many professions, both of greater and less repute than
theirs, are built up and rely upon the deception of the public (12).

Montaigne ends the chapter with a critique of the "evidence/proof" on
which physicians base their treatments.

Besides, supposing this proof to have been perfect, how many times
was it repeated? How often was this long bead-roll of chances and
coincidences strung anew, to infer a certain rule therefrom? Should it
be inferred, by whom? Among so many millions there will be but three
men who trouble about recording their experiments; will chance have
lighted upon just one of these three? What if another or even a hundred
others have had the contrary experiences? We might perhaps see some
daylight if all the reasonings and all the decisions of men were known
to us; but that three witnesses, and those three doctors, should lord it
over mankind is against reason. They would have to be chosen and
deputed by human nature, and declared our judges by express power
of attorney (13).

Imagine Osler's bemused response to Montaigne's satire on the pretentious-
ness of physicians and his comical play on the vagaries of medicine, the
gross remedies, and the weakness of "presumed" scientific methods and
findings.

Speaking at McGill College in Montreal in 1899, Osler advises students
to maintain a balance in their lives and recommends reading Montaigne to
lighten the load of pharmacology.

While medicine is to be your vocation, or calling, see to it that you
also have an avocation—some intellectual pastime which may serve to
keep you in touch with the world of art, of science, or of letters....For
the hard working medical student it is perhaps easiest to keep up an
interest in literature. Let each subject in your year's work have a corre-
sponding outside author. When tired of anatomy refresh your mind with
Oliver Wendell Holmes; after a worrying subject in physiology, turn to
the great idealists, to Shelley or Keats for consolation; when chemistry
distresses your soul, seek peace in the great pacifier, Shakespeare; and
when the complications of pharmacology are unbearable, ten minutes
with Montaigne will lighten the burden (14).

In a subsequent talk, "The Master-Word in Medicine," given at the University of Toronto in 1903, Osler tells students that "I propose to tell you the secret of life as I have seen the games played, and as I have tried to play it myself." He goes on to propose that the master-word, the "open-sesame to every portal...is *WORK*. Something to be achieved by cultivating system. Start at once a bed-side library and spend the last half hour of the day in communion with the saints of humanity." Montaigne's place in the library? "Montaigne will teach you moderation in all things, and to be 'sealed of his tribe' is a special privilege." (15)

The more one reads Montaigne, the more one understands Osler's fondness for him. Montaigne's words often overlap those of Osler as both question the concept of certainty, reject absolutism and dogma, and value self-knowledge, balance, and practicing what one believes. Osler, like Montaigne, cultivated a personal library, read extensively, and demonstrated his thoughtfulness in his writings, talks, and lifeworks.

Montaigne used personal observations to illustrate the nature of man and the meaning of life, as did Osler. His essays are at once about him and about all human behavior.

Marcus Aurelius

Osler and Marcus Aurelius: Philosophical Brothers

ALBERT HOWARD CARTER, III

I imagine Osler returning from work, having his supper, and looking for solace in the writings of Marcus Aurelius. What would nourish him in this slim volume and why would he recommend it to future readers in the field of medicine?

The modern English title, *Meditations*, is inaccurate, suggesting extended reveries or thought-out essays. The title of the lost Greek manuscript used for the first printed edition was, instead, *Eis heauton* or "To Himself," which would be a more accurate title—although still perhaps not his—for this collection of advice to himself, insights, and reflections. Although a Roman aristocrat and emperor, Marcus was educated in Greek philosophy and wrote this collection in Greek not in Latin. Some of the 488 entries are a page or two in length, but most are a handful of lines, and there is much repetition among them, as Marcus sought for the best expression and had new insights. Modern editions organize them into 12 books (probably the lengths of the original papyrus rolls) containing numbered chapters, so that an entry may be cited III.2, but such divisions are arbitrary. It's best to think of these as journal entries by a very thoughtful man, whose private explorations were never intended for publication as a book, much less a modern "classic." The first reward to Osler, I suggest, is an intimate look into the rich mind of a colleague who sought order through language to assess a chaotic world. Marcus could serve, across the centuries, as a kind of philosophical brother to him or to anyone in a stressful profession.

Indeed, Marcus affirms that physicians know the dangers of this world and the need for wisdom and authority:

> 3.13. As physicians have always their instruments and knives ready for cases which suddenly require their skill, so do thou have principles

ready for the understanding of things divine and human, and for doing everything, even the smallest, with a recollection of the bond which unites the divine and human to one another. For neither wilt thou do anything well which pertains to man without at the same time having a reference to things divine; nor the contrary (1).

8.15. Remember that as it is a shame to be surprised if the fig-tree produces figs, so it is to be surprised if the world produces such and such things of which it is productive; and for the physician and the helmsman it is a shame to be surprised if a man has a fever, or if the wind is unfavorable (1).

6.55. If sailors abused the helmsman, or the sick the doctor, would they listen to anybody else; or how could the helmsman secure the safety of those in the ship, or the doctor the health of those whom he attends? (1).

However gifted a physician Osler was, the scientific knowledge and medical tools of his day were limited, especially before the changes brought about by the Flexner report of 1910. Emperor Marcus also had difficulties in his professional life, including court intrigue and also plague and warfare. Marcus rarely mentions the troubles of his actual daily life, however, focusing instead on 1) the philosophical order of the world and 2) how his character should grow in concert with that world. For both men, the *Meditations* provides an escape to a purer and more orderly world. As Marcus wrote in 8.48: "The mind without passions is a fortress. No place is more secure. Once we take refuge there we are safe forever."

Many entries (and often the more interesting ones) are quite brief, like Zen koans:

6.36. Asia, Europe, are corners of the universe; all the sea a drop in the universe; Athos a little clod of the universe: all the present time is a point in eternity. All things are little, changeable, perishable. All things come from thence, from that universal ruling power either directly preceding or by way of sequence. And accordingly the lion's gaping jaws, and that which is poisonous, and every harmful thing, as a thorn, as mud, are after-products of the grand and beautiful. Do not then imagine that they are of another kind from that which thou dost venerate, but form a just opinion of the source of all (VII. p. 75) (1).

Some entries are a page or two in length, mini essays, and some are more specific, encouraging, even advising:

4.3. Men seek retreats for themselves, houses in the country, sea-shores, and mountains; and thou too art wont to desire such things very much. But this is altogether a mark of the most common sort of men, for it is in thy power whenever thou shalt choose to retire into thyself. For nowhere either with more quiet or more freedom from trouble does a man retire than into his own soul, particularly when he has within him such thoughts that by looking into them he is immediately in perfect tranquility; and I affirm that tranquility is nothing else than the good ordering of the mind. Constantly then give to thyself this retreat, and renew thyself; and let thy principles be brief and fundamental, which, as soon as thou shalt recur to them, will be sufficient to cleanse the soul completely, and to send thee back free from all discontent with the things to which thou returnest. For with what art thou discontented? With the badness of men? Recall to thy mind this conclusion, that rational animals exist for one another, and that to endure is a part of justice, and that men do wrong involuntarily; and consider how many already, after mutual enmity, suspicion, hatred, and fighting, have been stretched dead, reduced to ashes; and be quiet at last.—But perhaps thou art dissatisfied with that which is assigned to thee out of the universe.—Recall to thy recollection this alternative; either there is providence or atoms [fortuitous concurrence of things]; or remember the arguments by which it has been proved that the world is a kind of political community [and be quiet at last].—But perhaps corporeal things will still fasten upon thee. Consider then further that the mind mingles not with the breath, whether moving gently or violently, when it has once drawn itself apart and discovered its own power, and think also of all that thou hast heard and assented to about pain and pleasure [and be quiet at last].—But perhaps the desire of the thing called fame will torment thee.—See how soon everything is forgotten, and look at the chaos of infinite time on each side of [the present], and the emptiness of applause, and the changeableness and want of judgment in those who pretend to give praise, and the narrowness of the space within which it is circumscribed [and be quiet at last]. For the whole earth is a point, and how small a nook in it is this thy dwelling, and how few are there in it, and what kind of people are they who will praise thee (1).

This then remains: Remember to retire into this little territory of thy own, and above all do not distract or strain thyself, but be free, and look at things as a man, as a human being, as a citizen, as a mortal. But among the things readiest to thy hand to which thou shalt turn, let there be these, which are two. One is that things do not touch the soul, for they are external and remain immovable; but our perturbations come only from the opinion which is within. The other is that all these things which thou seest, change immediately and will no longer be; and constantly bear in mind how many of these changes thou hast already witnessed. The universe is transformation: life is opinion (1).

12.3. The things are three of which thou art composed: a little body, a little breathe, intelligence. Of these the first two are thine, so far as it is thy duty to take care of them; but the third alone is properly thine. Therefore if thou shalt separate from thyself, that is, from thy understanding, whatever others do or say, and whatever thou hast done or said thyself, and whatever future things trouble thee because they may happen, and whatever in the body which envelops thee or in the breath [life], which is by nature associated with the body, is attached to thee independent of thy will, and whatever the external circumfluent vortex whirls round, so that the intellectual power exempt from the things of fate can live pure and free by itself, doing what is just and accepting what happens and saying the truth: if thou wilt separate, I say, from this ruling faculty the things which are attached to it by the impressions of sense, and the things of time to come and of time that is past, and wilt make thyself like Empedocles' sphere.

"All round and in its joyous rest reposing"; and if thou shalt strive to live only what is really thy life, that is, the present,—then thou wilt be able to pass that portion of life which remains for thee up to the time of thy death free from perturbations, nobly, and obedient to thy own daemon [to the god that is within thee] (II. pp. 13, 17; III. pp. 5, 6; XI. p. 12) (1).

If you can cut yourself—your mind—free of what other people do and say, of what you've said or done, of the things that you're afraid will happen, the impositions of the body that contains you and the breath within, and what the whirling chaos seeps in from outside, so that the mind is freed from fate, brought to clarity and lives life on its own recognizance—doing what is right, accepting what happens and speaking the truth...then you can spend the time you have left in tranquility. And in kindness. And at peace with the spirit within you.

The underlying philosophy to the *Meditations* is Stoicism, developed by the Greeks but modified by the Romans to "a practical discipline—not an abstract system of thought, but an attitude to life," according to Hays (1a). But Marcus is wary of received wisdom:

5.10. Things are in such a kind of envelopment that they have seemed to philosophers, not a few nor those common philosophers, altogether unintelligible; nay even to the Stoics themselves they seem difficult to understand. And all our assent is changeable; for where is the man who never changes? Carry thy thoughts then to the objects themselves, and consider how short-lived they are and worthless, and that they may be in the possession of a filthy wretch or a robber. Then turn to the morals of those who live with thee, and it is hardly possible to endure even the most agreeable of them, to say nothing of a man being hardly able to endure himself. In such darkness then and dirt, and in so constant a flux both of substance and of time, and of motion and of things moved, what there is worth being highly prized, or even an object of serious pursuit, I cannot imagine. But on the contrary it is a man's duty to comfort himself, and to wait for the natural dissolution, and not to be vexed at the delay, but to rest in these principles only: the one, that nothing will happen to me which is not conformable to the nature of the universe; and the other, that it is in my power never to act contrary to my god and daemon: for there is no man who will compel me to this (1).

In general, though, Marcus believes that there is a specific force that holds everything together. While Hammond translates it as *reason* and Maxwell Staniforth (2) makes it *reason* or *universal reason*, Hays leaves it in the original Greek, *logos*, familiar to New Testament readers as "the Word" in the Gospel of John: "In the beginning was the word." The following entries affirm that the *logos* is in both external reality and in ourselves:

7.8. Let not future things disturb thee, for thou wilt come to them, if it shall be necessary, having with thee the same reason which now thou usest for present things (1).

7.9. All things are implicated with one another, and the bond is holy; and there is hardly anything unconnected with any other thing. For things have been coordinated, and they combine to form the same universe [order]. For there is one universe made up of all things, and one god who pervades all things, and one substance, and one law, [one] common reason in all intelligent animals, and one truth; if indeed there is also one perfection for all animals which are of the same stock and participate in the same reason (1).

7.11. To the rational animal the same act is according to nature and according to reason (1).

This line of thought provides a second reward to Osler, confirmation by Marcus that the world does indeed have a sensible order, despite its apparent chaos. And for a person with hardworking *logos*, there are always rewards.

7.59. Look within. Within is the fountain of good, and it will ever bubble up, if thou wilt ever dig (1).

This is Marcus at his most optimistic, and it has been reported that "[b]y most accounts, Osler was positive thinking personified" (3). Usually, by contrast, Marcus is realistic or even somewhat melancholic.

While the entry just cited uses water imagery positively, Marcus more often uses water to represent external threats and overwhelming change, as did Heraclitus, who is mentioned in 4.46. In *Meditations*, Aurelius advances a fatalism that does not permit utopian solutions:

> 9.29. The universal cause is like a winter torrent: it carries everything along with it. But how worthless are all these poor people who are engaged in matters political, and, as they suppose, are playing the philosopher! All drivellers. Well then, man: do what nature now requires. Set thyself in motion, if it is in thy power, and do not look about thee to see if any one will observe it; nor yet expect Plato's Republic: but be content if the smallest thing goes on well, and consider such an event to be no small matter. For who can change men's opinions? And without a change of opinions what else is there than the slavery of men who groan while they pretend to obey? Come now and tell me of Alexander and Philippus and Demetrius of Phalerum. They themselves shall judge whether they discovered what the common nature required, and trained themselves accordingly. But if they acted like tragedy heroes, no one has condemned me to imitate them. Simple and modest is the work of philosophy. Draw me not aside to insolence and pride (1).
>
> 12.14. Either there is a fatal necessity and invincible order, or a kind providence, or a confusion without a purpose and without a director (IV. 27). If then there is an invincible necessity, why dost thou resist? But if there is a providence which allows itself to be propitiated, make thyself worthy of the help of the divinity. But if there is a confusion without a governor, be content that in such a tempest thou hast in thyself a certain ruling intelligence. And even if the tempest carry thee away, let it carry away the poor flesh, the poor breath, everything else; for the intelligence at least it will not carry away (1).

Osler chose a similar passage (albeit in another translation) for an epigraph to his oft-cited essay *Aequanimitas*:

> Thou must be like a promontory of the sea, against which, though the waves beat continually, yet it both itself stands, and about it are those swelling waves stilled and quieted (4).

In this oft-read, oft-anthologized essay, Osler explains that Antoninus Pius (Marcus' adopted father) summed up his philosophy of life in the word aequanimitas, literally "an even or balanced mind or soul," which could control one's mind, emotions, and attitudes, no matter what the stresses. Michael Bliss styles this quality as "the right demeanor—the essence of medical cool" (5).

And how is the soul to gain such wisdom? Marcus frequently questions, advises, or exhorts his inner character:

10.1. Wilt thou, then, my soul, never be good and simple and one and naked, more manifest than the body which surrounds thee? Wilt thou never enjoy an affectionate and contented disposition? Wilt thou never be full and without a want of any kind, longing for nothing more, nor desiring anything, either animate or inanimate, for the enjoyment of pleasures? Nor yet desiring time wherein thou shalt have longer enjoyment, or place, or pleasant climate, or society of men with whom thou mayest live in harmony? But wilt thou be satisfied with thy present condition, and pleased with all that is about thee, and wilt thou convince thyself that thou hast everything, and that it comes from the gods, that everything is well for thee, and will be well whatever shall please them, and whatever they shall give for the conservation of the perfect living being, the good and just and beautiful, which generates and holds together all things, and contains and embraces all things which are dissolved for the production of other like things? Wilt thou never be such that thou shalt so dwell in community with gods and men as neither to find fault with them at all, nor to be condemned by them? (1).

10.8. When thou hast assumed these names, good, modest, true, rational, a man of equanimity, and magnanimous, take care that thou dost not change these names; and if thou shouldst lose them, quickly return to them. And remember that the term Rational was intended to signify a discriminating attention to every several thing, and freedom from negligence; and that Equanimity is the voluntary acceptance of the things which are assigned to thee by the common nature; and that Magnanimity is the elevation of the intelligent part above the pleasurable or painful sensations of the flesh, and above that poor thing called fame, and death, and all such things. If, then, thou maintainest thyself in the possession of these names, without desiring to be called by these names by others, thou wilt be another person and wilt enter on another life. For to continue to be such as thou hast hitherto been, and to be torn in pieces and defiled in such a life, is the character of a very stupid man and one over-fond of his life, and like those half-devoured fighters with wild beasts who, though covered with wounds and gore, still entreat to be kept to the following day, though they will be exposed in the same state to the same claws and bites. Therefore fix thyself in the possession of these few names: and if thou art able to abide in them, abide as if thou wast removed to certain islands of the Happy. But if thou shalt perceive that thou fallest out of them and dost not maintain thy hold, go courageously into some nook where thou shalt maintain them, or even depart at once from life, not in passion, but with simplicity and freedom and modesty, after doing this one [laudable] thing at least in thy life, to have gone out of it thus. In order, however, to the

remembrance of these names, it will greatly help thee if thou rememberest the gods, and that they wish not to be flattered, but wish all
reasonable beings to be made like themselves; and if thou rememberest
that what does the work of a fig-tree is a fig-tree, and that what does
the work of a dog is a dog, and that what does the work of a bee is a
bee, and that what does the work of a man is a man (1).

8.34. If thou didst ever see a hand cut off, or a foot, or a head, lying
anywhere apart from the rest of the body, such does a man make himself, as far as he can, who is not content with what happens, and sepa-
rates himself from others, or does anything unsocial. Suppose that thou
hast detached thyself from the natural unity,—for thou wast made by
nature a part, but now thou hast cut thyself off,—yet here there is this
beautiful provision, that it is in thy power again to unite thyself. God
has allowed this to no other part, after it has been separated and cut
asunder, to come together again. But consider the kindness by which
he has distinguished man, for he has put it in his power not to be
separated at all from the universal; and when he has been separated,
he has allowed him to return and to be united and to resume his place
as a part (1).

And in 11.18, he lists nine points for improving his inner self, concluding,
"Keep these nine points in mind, like gifts from the nine Muses, and start
becoming a human being. Now and for the rest of your life."

This, then, is the third reward, that the mind/soul/character can contin-
uously be improved, even if there are intractable obstacles, such as chaos,
discussed above, and mortality, described below. Let us give Marcus the last
word, lines that we can imagine Osler reading with much pleasure:

9.3. Do not despise death, but be well content with it, since this too
is one of those things which nature wills. For such as it is to be young
and to grow old, and to increase and to reach maturity, and to have
teeth and beard and gray hairs, and to beget and to be pregnant and
to bring forth, and all the other natural operations which the seasons
of thy life bring, such also is dissolution. This, then, is consistent with
the character of a reflecting man,—to be neither careless nor impatient
nor contemptuous with respect to death, but to wait for it as one of the
operations of nature. As thou now waitest for the time when the child
shall come out of thy wife's womb, so be ready for the time when thy
soul shall fall out of this envelope. But if thou requirest also a vulgar
kind of comfort which shall reach thy heart, thou wilt be made best
reconciled to death by observing the objects from which thou art going
to be removed, and the morals of those with whom thy soul will no
longer be mingled. For it is no way right to be offended with men, but

it is thy duty to care for them and to bear with them gently; and yet to remember that thy departure will not be from men who have the same principles as thyself. For this is the only thing, if there be any, which could draw us the contrary way and attach us to life,—to be permitted to live with those who have the same principles as ourselves. But now thou seest how great is the trouble arising from the discordance of those who live together, so that thou mayest say, Come quick, O death, lest perchance I, too, should forget myself (1).

Epictetus

The Enchiridion of Epictetus

MARIN GILLIS

The Stoic philosopher Epictetus was born between AD 50 and 60 in Hierapolis, Phrygia, then a Greco-Roman city and today Pamukkale in southwest Turkey. He began his life in slavery and suffered chronic ill health. Having been acquired by Epephrodites, a secretary to Emperor Nero and later Emperor Domitian, he moved to Rome. Epictetus was, despite his enslavement, permitted to study with Gaius Musonius Rufus, a Stoic philosopher in Rome. He was subsequently freed and taught philosophy until AD 95, when Domitian banished all philosophers from the Italian peninsula. He moved to Nicopolis, a political-economic center in northwest Greece, and established a philosophical school where he became known as a dedicated teacher whose reputation gained him students from elite families throughout the vast Roman Empire. He died in 135.

Like Socrates, Epictetus did not leave any writings. Or rather, like Socrates, we do not know if he ever wrote anything because we have no extant works. We know of his teachings through his pupil, Arrian (86–146), who became a very influential and respectable military leader, consul, and governor of Cappadocia under Emperor Hadrian. Arrian compiled two texts of Epictetus' lectures: *The Discourses*, four of the eight volumes of which are extant, and *The Enchiridion*, translated as the *Handbook* or the *Manual*, which contains excerpts and reworking of the major teachings found in the *Discourses*. *The Enchiridion* has never been out of print.

The Enchiridion is a kind of self-help book aimed at guiding the reader toward leading a good life. It is short, composed of 52 entries, mostly maxims meant to be reflected or meditated upon. It provides the reader with nontechnical thinking cues that invite him or her to reflect on how to deal with the anxieties of life and how, as an individual, to lead a good life.

Like most early philosophy, the maxims in *The Enchiridion* were not meant to be abstract exercises practiced only within the grounds of the academy; rather, the lessons were meant to inform all aspects of the student's life. Philosophy was a practice, a discipline in its true sense, the Stoic goal of which was a way to live with purpose, serenity, dignity, and social utility (1). *The Enchiridion* was accessible to all thoughtful persons, regardless of wealth, status, physical condition, or ability to obtain a tutor. It could be followed with one's reason as the guide. Philosophical education was thought to be a form of self-improvement. In this way, *The Enchiridion* is a perfect bedside companion for students.

The ethical question for Epictetus is how one should live a good life. He considered the good life one of *eudaimonia*, which is often translated as happiness. Happiness here is best understood not as a mood or state of mind, but rather as fulfillment or flourishing. For Epictetus, one is on the road to fulfillment as soon as one starts to bring one's actions and desires into harmony with the true nature of things. In particular, a person has to align one's actions and desires with one's essential nature. This means that to be happy one must develop one's potential to the fullest extent possible. In actualizing the potential of one's true essence, one becomes excellent. This idea of excellence, *arete*, is translated as virtue. So, the life of happiness is the life of virtue. To flourish, to be happy, one has to follow the natural order of things, and to live according to the nature of the world paying particular attention to the nature of the self.

Furthermore, Epictetus believed that it is incumbent on those who seek the good life to learn about the nature of the world and human beings. Epictetus was a rationalist and did not believe that events are determined by magic, sorcery, or the whims of the gods. His was a rational, created universe governed by knowable first principles, which he referred to as coming from the power of Zeus. Accordingly, these principles were thought to be divine. Since the nature of things is rational and knowable, the first order of business for the seeker of happiness is to use his or her reason to learn the nature of the world and the nature of the self. The road to happiness begins in self-reflective rational philosophical inquiry. The happy, fulfilled life, the life of virtue, is one of wisdom.

> It is a mark of want of genius to spend much time in things relating to the body, as to be long in our exercises, in eating and drinking, and in the discharge of other animal functions. These should be done incidentally and slightly, and our whole attention be engaged in the care of the understanding (Ench 41) (2).
>
> Keep in mind that you are merely an actor in a play which the Author has chosen. If the play is short, then it's short; if the play is

long, then it's long. If the Author chooses that you play a beggar, or a cripple, or a king, or a subject, your job is to act the part well. This is your only business—act your part well—for choosing what part you play belongs to another (Ench 17) (2).

It is also imperative for the good life to be dutiful in the roles one is fated to be in and not to be sidetracked from them.

> Consider when, on a voyage, your ship is anchored; if you go on shore to get water you may along the way amuse yourself with picking up a shellfish, or an onion. However, your thoughts and continual attention ought to be bent towards the ship, waiting for the captain to call on board; you must then immediately leave all these things, otherwise you will be thrown into the ship, bound neck and feet like a sheep. So it is with life (Ench 7) (2).

It is not the case that human life is governed totally by fate, that we are puppets. To be sure, one did not create the facts about oneself: one's birth, one's body, one's health, one's roles, or one's mortality. Individuals are, however, responsible for their own volition (sometimes translated as will), the capacity to make determinations or choices, and so can change course through rational self-reflection and self-discipline. One has volition and this volition is the essence of a human being. So, one does not have volition, one *is* essentially and by nature volition. For Epictetus, unhappiness and suffering comes from trying to direct that which is not in one's control, that is, the externals. One is unhappy when one makes false determinations. Happiness comes through concerning oneself only with that which is in one's control, the internals, making proper use of volition, and being unperturbed in the face of everything else.

> Those things within our power include opinions, goals, desires, and aversions, in other words, whatever affairs belong to us. Those things beyond our power include our bodies, property, reputation, and public office, that is, whatever does not properly belong to us (Ench 1) (2).
>
> Sickness is a hindrance to the body, but not to your ability to choose, unless that is your choice. Lameness is a hindrance to the leg, but not to your ability to choose. Say this to yourself with regard to everything that happens, then you will see such obstacles as hindrances to something else, but not to yourself (Ench 9) (2).

One learns how to control that which is in his or her proper domain and to execute proper volition through reflection. One's experience of anything always begins with impressions or ideas, or some kind of mental representation. The key is to find out which represent the real and true reality, including the good and proper human goals, and which are illusory, false promises. A wise person can make the distinction between what is really and truly worth pursuing from determining what are impossible desires.

> Work, therefore to be able to say to every harsh appearance, "You are but an appearance, and not absolutely the thing you appear to be." And then examine it by those rules which you have, and first, and chiefly, by this: whether it concerns the things which are in our own control, or those which are not; and, if it concerns anything not in our control, be prepared to say that it is nothing to you (Ench 1) (2).

If one tries to control that which is not controllable, for example, if one tries to avoid the reality of sickness or death, one will be frustrated.

> If you shun only those things which you can control, you will never acquire what you are averse to; but if you try to avoid sickness, or death, or poverty, you will eventually be miserable. Cease trying to avoid those things you have no power over, and apply your effort to those undesirable things which are in your power. For the present, restrain your desire. If you desire anything not within your power, you are sure to be disappointed (Ench 2) (2).

Again, one has to understand which things or enterprises they have control over and have true beliefs about them, in order not to lose their self.

> If you wish your children, and your wife, and your friends to live for ever, you are stupid; for you wish to be in control of things which you cannot, you wish for things that belong to others to be your own.... But, if you wish to have your desires undisappointed, this is in your own control. Exercise, therefore, what is in your control. He is the master of every other person who is able to confer or remove whatever that person wishes either to have or to avoid. Whoever, then, would be free, let him wish nothing, let him decline nothing, which depends on others else he must necessarily be a slave (Ench 14) (2).

We are free when we realize and act according to our nature, but slaves when we think that anything external, our bodies, status, and what people think about us determine anything real about us or that our volition can have anything to do with their existence. It is when we are slaves, and not free, that we are miserable. Being free is a proper, natural state of selves. We frustrate ourselves by trying to cause externals to act according to our volition. Folly will always ensue if we desire things outside the bounds of our rationality. However, when attending to things over which we have agency, leaving externals alone, we will be closer to *eudaimonia*.

...remember that if you ascribe freedom to things that are naturally dependent and take for yourself what belongs to others (such as your reputation), you will face obstacles, you will be full of regrets and unfulfilled wishes, and you will continually blame both the gods and men. But if you take for your own only that which properly is your own and regard what belongs to others as belonging to others, then you will never be coerced or restricted, you will not find fault with others, you will not blame others, and you will do nothing unwillingly; you cannot be hurt, you will have no enemies, you will suffer no harm...(Ench 1) (2).

Wisdom is anchored with knowledge of the true nature of reality. For Epictetus, the only good worth pursuing for the wise person is the life of virtue itself. The misfortunes human beings suffer result from mistaken beliefs about what the good life is, especially their beliefs about what will bring fulfillment and happiness. Human beings are born with the capacity to alleviate suffering though rationality and self-discipline, and through this method a good life may be led. Happiness is completely and only achievable by the individual; it cannot be found outside of oneself. So too with misery. Happiness depends on having proper perspectives and misery is a function of improper perspectives: one has control over these.

Men are disturbed, not by things, but by the principles and notions which they form concerning things. Death, for instance, is not terrible, else it would have appeared so to Socrates. But the terror consists in our notion of death that it is terrible. When therefore we are hindered, or disturbed, or grieved, let us never attribute it to others, but to ourselves; that is, to our own principles. An uninstructed person will lay the fault of his own bad condition upon others. Someone just starting instruction will lay the fault on himself. Someone who is perfectly instructed will place blame neither on others nor on himself (Ench 5) (2).

Remember that foul words or blows in themselves are no outrage, but your judgment that they are so. So when any one makes you angry, know that it is your own thought that has angered you. Wherefore make it your endeavor not to let your impressions carry you away. For if once you gain time and delay, you will find it easier to control yourself (Ench 20) (2).

The nature of the self for Epictetus is a free, autonomous volition, including our mental faculties, intentions, judgments, and convictions, our consciousness, and our character. Our nature is our ability to determine for ourselves, without the constraint of externals, that which is proper to us. Only in the domain of volition are we free, and this will be real and lasting freedom. When we are free, we are happy. We will experience only what we have agency over, our states of mind, and we will be unperturbed because we will lack any notion or desire to find externals in any other way than how we find them. This includes our bodies, our socioeconomic status, our material condition, and what anyone believes about our character. This also includes other externals such as the health and actions of our spouses and children or the political state of the world.

> Ask not that events should happen as you wish them to happen, but simply wish events to happen as they do happen, and you will be well (Ench 8) (2).

But our essential self is precarious because we live in a world where external things and wills are ever present and unless we are self-reflective and self-disciplined, we will identify with them, lose our freedom, and in so doing, become wretched.

Epictetus gives directives not only on how to avoid suffering, but also on what one should do in the midst of it. Times of anxiety are opportunities for growth, and therefore can be part of a life of happiness. Every trial is a time to strengthen our virtue.

> With every accident, ask yourself what abilities you have for making a proper use of it. If you see an attractive person, you will find that self-restraint is the ability you have against your desire. If you are in pain, you will find fortitude. If you hear unpleasant language, you will find patience. And thus habituated, the appearances of things will not hurry you away along with them (Ench 10) (2).

It is not surprising that people have turned to *The Enchiridion* in periods of personal suffering, despair, and stress. It is a resource for people who need to affirm human dignity and freedom amidst terrible, dehumanizing times, when one is publically slandered, imprisoned, enslaved, or tortured, suffering catastrophic material misfortune, experiencing agonizing physical or psychological pain, or grieving incalculable loss. Emperor Marcus Aurelius, whose reign was marked by incessant war, was not only a reader but also a commentator on Epictetus (see his *Meditations*). Recently, James Stockdale, who suffered seven and a half years of tortuous imprisonment in a North Vietnamese military prison during the Vietnam War, wrote that Epictetus helped him survive it.

Let us entertain the idea that a Stoic response is not the opposite of humanist or empathetic care. The Stoics did not advocate the removal of emotions, they believed we should cultivate proper emotions. It is better to be active and thoughtful in our interactions with the vagaries of life, not reactive and thoughtless. One cannot be an effective physician if one is overwhelmed by one's passions. The world of the physicians and other healthcare professionals, particularly in Osler's time, is one marked more so than others by embarrassing infirmity, suffering, and death: realities that evoke particularly strong emotional responses in all. And it is not just a matter of being in control as to not lose clinical competency that it is well to harness one's emotions. Self-control is also necessary for the physician in the clinical encounter. Betraying repugnance, horror, or grief, by word or by countenance, would seem to be in most instances detrimental to the person whose situation elicits such response. Further, it takes courage to be able to calmly discuss with a patient feared realities, like sickness, loss, or the futility of further curative treatment. Gentleness, calmness, and imperturbability would seem to be qualities that would do well for a compassionate caregiver (3).

Perhaps through Osler and the Stoics we have learned something important about the concept of empathy. And, as Epictetus would remind us, wisdom is anchored with knowledge of the true nature of reality.

Don Quixote

Sir William the Knight-Errant?
Osler Meets the Man of La Mancha

RONALD D. STEWART

There is good reason to ponder the "why" of the readings suggested for all medical students by Sir William Osler now that a century has passed since he first composed his list. We may view such a gesture by this great man of medicine as a natural expression of his profound commitment to good literature, but it is more than that. The gesture itself, insisting that medical students (and by extension practitioners of the art called medicine) should be steeped in literature and the classics, formed the cornerstone, or even the mortar, of his view of a balanced life in medicine and his quest for aequanimitas. With *the list*, Osler set out a challenge to his students and practitioners to accept a good dose of the classics as a *requirement* of a rewarding life in medicine. The fact that he created the list is ample evidence of his belief that the humanities should form a base for medical education and the practice of the art called medicine. But it is doubtful he would have anticipated a "curriculum" designed to marry elements of the humanities with medical education or that "humanities" would be treated as yet another "course" in the increasingly time-deficient life we foist on the modern medical student. Much more likely is that this great physician considered good literature and regular reading as the roots of a rich and rewarding *life*—especially a "medical" life—and not something to be "taught" or "separate." But it is the *content* of the list that tells us most of the man himself, his priorities in his vocation, and his profound insight into the human condition.

The list was composed and introduced by Dr. Osler in 1904 at a time during which he was beset by the demands of a growing popularity and renown among his students, peers, colleagues, and the lay public. Although it might be said he was happy in his vocation and seldom, if ever, lost the richness of the commitment to his calling, he found increasingly that his life was becoming decidedly unbalanced; he struggled to spend time with his loving wife Grace and his adored son, the nine-year-old Revere. His enormous responsibilities—as physician, teacher, administrator, writer, orator—were carried out in an age of domestic train travel and long overseas steamship voyages. Jetting across the Atlantic in a few hours was not contemplated even by the most wide-eyed dreamers; correspondence was formal, by handwritten letters—no click of the mouse sending instant messages into the ether of cyberspace. He yearned for some relief from the punishing professional pace in American medicine and he found it in the offer from Oxford to assume the mantle of Regius Professor of Medicine. His wife Grace cabled him in England a message expressing what both of them must have been feeling; "…better to go in a steamer than go in a pine-box" (1). His list of "required readings" then, came during the time of wrestling with the love of his work at Johns Hopkins against the background of a life that was decidedly unbalanced for, as he confessed in letters to friends, he was "…going down hill physically and mentally" (2). Could the "why" of the contents of Dr. Osler's "list" be best judged against the background of what was transpiring in his life?

To peruse his list of recommended volumes is to sweep through centuries of the wisdom, wit, philosophy, and history of the human race. Much of the list is expected; Osler was steeped in the classics and in the Bible as both literature and moral guide, and his knowledge of Latin and Greek was more than passing. Other than the question of why he composed the list in the first place is the more profound and less easily answered question: Why did he include the masterpieces he did? This question is more readily answered for some selections than for others. But one masterpiece on the list stands out as unique in the complexity of the reasons we might surmise for its inclusion: *Don Quixote de La Mancha*, which, in its original title, *El ingenioso hidalgo Don Quijote de la Mancha* (*The Ingenious Nobleman Don Quixote de la Mancha*) might well have been applied, figuratively at least, to the author of "The List." It might seem even more appropriate that such a title be applied today, aided by the passage of 90 years since his death in 1919 and the greater realization of the debt we owe to this giant of medicine. The questions that arise through a study of *Don Quixote de la Mancha* against the backdrop of the life, times, and achievements of Sir William Osler will be, then: *Did Sir William Osler see himself as a knight-errant in the style, if not madness of Don Quixote de la Mancha? Did the medical knight-errant emulate the great author? And might the wonderfully outlandish masterwork of Cervantes somehow reflect the life, philosophy, and character of his admirer Sir William Osler?*

The most obvious reason for Osler to include this remarkable work of 17th-century fiction was for its pure literary value and its place in the history of literature. Cervantes' parody is considered by most to be indeed a masterpiece and by some to be the greatest work of Western literature, or at the very least of its genre. That, then, would make it a worthy choice for *The List*.

More compelling and much more fanciful, perhaps, is the question as to how profoundly that great man of medicine might have been influenced by this masterpiece and therefore wished to expose his students to its lessons and philosophy. Did the Dr. Osler we have come to know as legend somehow see in Cervantes' work lessons worth communicating to the "modern" 1904-vintage medical student, and, by extension, to physicians then and now? Did he, perhaps, see himself, his vocation, and his life reflected in the noble intent, if not the deeds, of that brave knight-errant? Could he have seen the many defeats of that same knight-errant in his failure to win battles or overcome the obstacles that daily must have beset him? And could he have, in later life, seen in *Don Quixote* the parody and practical jokes foisted by himself on colleagues, the medical establishment and the public, in much the same way as did Cervantes in his creation of the whimsy and cleverness of the then 300-year-old masterpiece? If Cervantes, in his great work of literature, lived a double life through its pages, did not Sir William do the same in the pages of his correspondence and even the medical literature as he constructed the life of his alter ego, Egerton Yorrick Davis?

It has been said of *Don Quixote*, the novel, that its enduring magic arises from it being all things to all people. Most could see themselves as the brave knight, some might aspire to be Sancho Panza, his faithful sidekick, and some perceptive readers could "unpeel" the petals of this rose of literature, and, savoring each, revel in its scent of genius and see the masterwork of its author. Did Osler, then, at a time during which he was burdened by the demands of his busy life, professional and personal, see himself as a brave but perhaps unbalanced knight-errant, "unbalanced" in the sense of being overburdened by the demands of his eclectic work and obligations? Or perhaps he recognized in the land of the knight-errant familiar and sometimes hopeless struggles that he waged as a medical knight-errant against the foes of death, disease, deadlines, and demanding administrators well disguised as innocent windmills?

But for a man who based much of his philosophy on aequanimitas, literally, a balanced mind, it is ironic that one of the most prominent choices on his list builds its story around a gentleman with a decidedly unbalanced mind. But an examination of the full and storied life of William Osler would reveal that even that brilliant and very balanced medical mind could appreciate and enjoy the fantasy and delirium of one medieval knight-errant conceived, in part at least, as a brilliant "practical joke" by the mind of a literary genius. In truth, Cervantes was playing the joke on the creators of the extravagant and fashionable literature of the day, the church, authorities both high and low, and even on the humble reading public of his era; and he still casts his spell over us 400 years on, and has great fun doing it.

How well indeed might the William Osler we know have related to the parody and fun Cervantes was having! After all, had not young Willie Osler, schoolboy in the relative wilds of Upper Canada, "got the sack" from school because of practical joking? If truth be told, in our own day and age, young Willie might well have been disciplined, diagnosed or misdiagnosed, and promptly been either slotted into a special class or given a solid dose of some potion or other. Instead he was packed off to boarding school where he expanded his career in practical joking and actually found himself briefly in jail and then in court with his fellow-miscreants before a wiser, and, from some reports, more clever older brother successfully defended him (3). Despite his maturing years and grave responsibilities, despite his worldwide acclaim and respect of his peers and public, the good physician Osler not infrequently let loose the young Willie, still very much alive in the mature man of medicine, to pull a practical joke on many an unsuspecting soul, the medical community, or the public.

Could we not see in the elusive and wholly fictitious E. Y. Davis, Dr. Osler's alter ego, more than a hint of a Cervantes-like character galloping at will through the rather bleak, if not barren landscape of medical literature, or checking into inns with a mysterious damsel on his arm (the damsel was not amused by the joke, it appears) (4)? A case could be made that this same Dr. E. Y. Davis, who would publish accounts of fictitious medical marvels and thereby create some havoc in the medical press of the day and invite the wrath of this own "Dulcinea," was indeed Dr. William Osler's version of Don Quixote de la Mancha incarnate? Or might that great man of medicine be attempting to emulate the great Cervantes himself, not infrequently with similar disconcerting results, by writing his own romance peppered with fantastic stories, elaborate plots, invented characters, and laced with Rabelaisian humor. Witness the furor in the wake of Dr. Osler's farewell address to his Johns Hopkins' colleagues in February of 1905 in which he, in the spirit of his alter ego, suggested that there was a "fixed period" of achievement and productivity in a professional life, after which the gentleman (he exempted women in the proposal) might contribute most to society if he were dispatched promptly by means of chloroform (5). The press had a field day, and Dr. Osler had to react publicly to a misrepresentation of his intent. Once again, young Willie got loose. Could not a parallel be drawn to the frequent disastrous outcomes of the exploits of the knight-errant and his sidekick and foil Sancho Panza?

There is little doubt, of course, that the choice of *Don Quixote* reflected Osler's recognition of the work as the masterpiece of literature that it was. But the richness of his enjoyment of Cervantes' tale of the dreamy but mad knight-errant was no doubt increased with the author's tongue-in-cheek claim that far from being an invented character, Don Quixote de la Mancha was a real person. Indeed, if Sir William did not *pattern* his creation of E. Y. Davis after Cervantes' attempt to make Don Quixote de la Mancha real to his readers, he most certainly emulated the skill and daring of the author in the elaborate construction of the life, times, and peculiar gynecological and other medical interests of his alter ego. He could not help but appreciate the complex layers of the novel-within-a-novel-within-a-story in which the author was sometimes narrator, sometimes character, presenting much of the story through eyewitnesses with a commentary on the inadequacies of well-known, if not wildly renowned authors, and of course his competitors in the literary world of the day. Surely, if we examined the "life and times of E. Y. Davis" and their creation by that fertile medical mind we know as "Osler" we would be struck by the parallels with Cervantes' skill in detailing the life and times of *his* creation. Adding to the "joke," Cervantes describes a fictional conversation in the prologue suggesting that the tale of the knight needs no embellishments or exaggerations and declares his work to be one of the greatest simplicity, definitely in the style of the creator of one E. Y. Davis. The sweeping romance of that knight-errant, taken in its entirety, would have been no doubt recognized by Osler as a poke and jab, if not a lethal wound, to the novels of chivalry and exaggerated idealism so popular in the 16th and 17th centuries and beyond that, at the prejudices, power structures, morals, and mores of the society of Cervantes' time. With each stroke of his pen, Cervantes jousted at the literary and power-laden giants of his day (including the church), and, unlike his creation the honorable Don Quixote, he won those jousts by the sheer genius of his writing and clever construction and layering of his masterpiece. And literature was never quite the same.

One must leave to the imagination whether or not Sir William deliberately saw himself as another Cervantes in his creation of E. Y. Davis or as Don Quixote the knight-errant on the sometimes bleak landscape of medical practice and education. He might have been just an accidental tourist, and was merely letting loose the "young Willie" covered by the thin veneer of "maturity."

Much more likely, and by far the most reasonable assumption as to what might have moved him to recommend *Don Quixote de la Mancha* to medical students is, quite simply, that it was great literature. But surely to a discerning bibliophile as was he, this great landmark of literature was more than just "a good read." In its parody, Osler must have seen clear images of the many problems and challenges in the sometimes bleak landscape and the diverse set of characters inhabiting his world at Johns Hopkins and his medical world elsewhere. More evident (and perhaps much more fun) in the novel for him, however, might have been the brilliance of the Cervantes' camouflage of his real intent and philosophy that drives the story toward the "sanity" of its conclusion. "Camouflage" because the Censor appeared oblivious to the themes in the novel that 400 years on appear to us clearly as full-frontal attacks on the sacred cows of the power structures of the church and the government as well as institutional prejudices and even popular tastes in literature.

We cannot know when and how Osler was first introduced to the adventures of the knight-errant of La Mancha. But we can assume it was early in his life, whether in his home, the rectory of his Church-of-England cleric father, or in his early schooling during the times he was not expelled. We could be fairly certain that Cervantes' masterwork was on the curriculum for study, and therefore analysis, in both the public and the boarding schools attended by the young Osler. It could be argued that even the young Osler was laying down early a pattern for his life as a prankster, elaborately realized as the mature, seasoned man of letters and medicine, the Dr. Osler who let loose the "young Willie" in the form of frequent and often well-crafted jokes within a complicated "dual life"—the ruse of Dr. E. Y. Davis (4, 6).

But against the backdrop of any similarities one might concoct between Cervantes the literary joker and William Osler the medical joker must loom the fact that Osler surely saw the themes of Cervantes' work as the grand sweep of philosophy and transformative ideas that ushered in a new genre, if not a new age, of literature. Cervantes set out to do more than entertain and mock the mores of the time through the creation of a harebrained world of a mad devotee of romantic stories of medieval knights in shining armor. He set out to rewrite the rules, avoid the major consequences of angering the Censor, and change people's view of their world. He used humor, ridicule of the rules, institutions, and assumptions of society, and the evolution of character in his story to accomplish these lofty goals. Our latter-day Cervantes, Dr. Osler, using the same principle of humor, which, among other things, included hiding behind a Don

Quixote-like alter ego, strove to do the same. In his reading and study of this masterwork, Osler would have recognized the lessons and themes that Cervantes brought to light: The inward quest for what should be human values, the pain and loss of human existence—the stuff, often, of medicine—the need to respect others, their beliefs and customs, and his sympathy for those who are oppressed, disadvantaged, and yet who continue to strive in that human quest. These are, in the guise of humor and preposterous situations, the messages of the masterpiece, lessons that Osler no doubt wanted to convey to his students, to include them in their own "balanced" lives.

Looking over the broader panorama of *Don Quixote de la Mancha*, there is a gradual change in the knight-errant, and that evolution is sensed best, and is most pronounced, during Part II of the work. It is tempting, at the risk of being outrageously "literal" and entirely too fanciful, to suggest that the sweep of the story of the good but insane knight-errant, Don Quixote, parallels the evolution of the life of Sir William Osler. Part I of the Osler story was finished when he sailed from America, and perhaps out of sight of Dr. E. Y. Davis, to the academic plains of Oxford and his "castle," The Open Arms. Thus began Part II of his Quixote-like life and career, in which, as in the case of our knight-errant of some 300 years earlier, the figurative insanity of overwork and deception in the form of his alter ego, E. Y. Davis, all but ceased, and the reality of death struck not once, but twice: Once to his beloved son in 1917, and two years later to the medical knight-errant himself.

It is to be noted that with Osler's donning of the mantle of the Regius Professor of Medicine the former prominent role of E. Y. Davis, as perhaps Osler's Sancho Panza, faded from the scene. Perhaps E. Y. Davis *did* drown in the Lachine Rapids in 1884 or Sir William may have gotten the date wrong and he survived the turn of the century. The "young Willie" perhaps matured as well or at least was gagged to the point of not causing mayhem in the medical literature or alarm in the general public. Sir William began to settle into academic life in one of the most prestigious positions for any physician in the world, and set about welcoming, with the "Open Arms" students, colleagues and friends alike the world over.

Here then are the similarities between Osler and Cervantes: Find a calling, however mad it may seem, and pursue it with passion, loyalty, and purpose; live a life of character and careful caring; maintain persistence in the face of doubt or fear, and, above all, embrace hard work and aequanimitas. That is the legacy our own knight-errant left us and which still moves us today.

Selected Excerpts

Chapter VI

"Well," said the curate, "that and the second, third, and fourth parts all stand in need of a little rhubarb to purge their excess of bile, and they must be cleared of all that stuff about the Castle of Fame and other greater affectations, to which end let them be allowed the over-seas term, and, according as they mend, so shall mercy or justice be meted out to them; and in the mean time, gossip, do you keep them in your house and let no one read them" (7).

Chapter IX

I beg of your worship is to dress your wound, for a great deal of blood flows from that ear, and I have here some lint and a little white ointment in the alforjas. "All that might be well dispensed with," said Don Quixote, "if I had remembered to make a vial of the balsam of Fierabras, for time and medicine are saved by one single drop." "What vial and what balsam is that?" said Sancho Panza. "It is a balsam," answered Don Quixote, "the receipt of which I have in my memory, with which one need have no fear of death, or dread dying of any wound; and so when I make it and give it to thee thou hast nothing to do when in some battle thou seest they have cut me in half through the middle of the body—as is wont to happen frequently,—but neatly and with great nicety, ere the blood congeal, to place that portion of the body which shall have fallen to the ground upon the other half which remains in the saddle, taking care to fit it on evenly and exactly. Then thou shalt give me to drink but two drops of the balsam I have mentioned, and thou shalt see me become sounder than an apple" (7).

Chapter XI

Sancho did as he bade him, but one of the goatherds, seeing the wound, told him not to be uneasy, as he would apply a remedy with which it would be soon healed; and gathering some leaves of rosemary, of which there was a great quantity there, he chewed them and mixed them with a little salt, and applying them to the ear he secured them firmly with a bandage, assuring him that no other treatment would be required, and so it proved (7).

Chapter XLVII

"Well then," said the farmer, "this son of mine who is going to be a bachelor, fell in love in the said town with a damsel called Clara Perlerina, daughter of Andres Perlerino, a very rich farmer; and this name of Perlerines does not come to them by ancestry or descent, but because all

the family are paralytics, and for a better name they call them Perlerines; though to tell the truth the damsel is as fair as an Oriental pearl, and like a flower of the field, if you look at her on the right side; on the left not so much, for on that side she wants an eye that she lost by small-pox; and though her face is thickly and deeply pitted, those who love her say they are not pits that are there, but the graves where the hearts of her lovers are buried. She is so cleanly that not to soil her face she carries her nose turned up, as they say, so that one would fancy it was running away from her mouth; and with all this she looks extremely well, for she has a wide mouth; and but for wanting ten or a dozen teeth and grinders she might compare and compete with the comeliest. Of her lips I say nothing, for they are so fine and thin that, if lips might be reeled, one might make a skein of them; but being of a different colour from ordinary lips they are wonderful, for they are mottled, blue, green, and purple—let my lord the governor pardon me for painting so minutely the charms of her who some time or other will be my daughter; for I love her, and I don't find her amiss" (7).

Chapter L

My lord the duke wrote to me the other day to warn me that certain spies had got into this island to kill me; but up to the present I have not found out any except a certain doctor who receives a salary in this town for killing all the governors that come here; he is called Doctor Pedro Recio, and is from Tirteafuera; so you see what a name he has to make me dread dying under his hands. This doctor says of himself that he does not cure diseases when there are any, but prevents them coming, and the medicines he uses are diet and more diet until he brings one down to bare bones; as if leanness was not worse than fever (7).

Emerson

Osler and Ralph Waldo Emerson: The Humanity of Medicine

JERRY VANNATTA
SETH VANNATTA

Emerson's body of work is largely anchored in his first book-length essay, *Nature*, published in 1836. This work embodies a worldview best described as idealistic. Emerson believed in the reality of ideas that underlie, precede, and explain appearances. Emerson sees in all of nature profound laws that are the "final cause" or purpose of the universe. He writes in *Nature*:

> Nature, in its ministry to man, is not only the material, but is also the process and the result. All the parts incessantly work into each other's hands for the profit of man. The wind sows the seed; the sun evaporates the sea; the wind blows the vapor to the field; the ice, on the other side of the planet, condenses rain on this; the rain feeds the plant; the plant feeds the animal; and thus the endless circulations of the divine charity nourish man (1).

Because of Osler's childhood in a religious family, and because of his early childhood educational experiences, Emerson's idealism might well have appealed to him. Osler probably read Emerson's essays in his early adulthood, a time when he would have been open to a new way of understanding how the universe was organized, one, which stretched the limits and boundaries found in orthodox religion.

While still a young student, Osler was sent to the Weston school in rural Canada, which was run by an Anglican minister, William Arthur Johnson. Johnson exposed Osler to a sort of experiential learning in the woods, which served as a meaningful supplement to the traditional learning from books. This had a profound effect on the young Osler. From a lecture given many years later, he recalls those lessons:

Imagine the delight of a boy of an inquisitive nature to meet a man who cared nothing about words, but who knew about things—who knew the stars in their courses and could tell us their names, who delighted in the woods in springtime, and told us about the frog-spawn and the caddis worms, and who read us in the evenings Gilbert White and Kingsley's "Glaucus", who showed us with the microscope the marvels in a drop of dirty pond water, and who on Saturday excursions up the river could talk of the Trilobites and the Orthoceratites and explain the formation of the earth's crust (2).

Here we see "delight" in the young Osler's exposure to science as he was learning to unmask nature's secrets. Many of us understand the profound effect that a walk in the woods or a star gaze can have on us—the stillness, expansiveness, and dynamic processes of nature impress us and change our comportment toward her. The way science can reveal the laws that govern her only augments this romance. Emerson's idealism soared with this romantic spirit. Furthermore, the intelligence that pervaded *Nature* must have sparked Osler's curiosity and propelled him to dig deeper.

In addition to Johnson, Osler met the other most influential man in his young development, James Bovell, at Weston. Bovell was a physician who spent a portion of his week immersed in these explorations and observations of nature with Johnson and the students. Bovell taught Osler the utility and excitement of the microscope in exploring botany, microbiology, and parasitology, and later influenced the young Osler's career path, which veered away from theology toward medicine. Bovell had a lasting interest, one not lost on Osler, in the association of this new biology with theology.

But we find in Osler more than a pastoralist's love of the outdoors and a scientist's rigorous search for explanation. He was in many ways an early psychotherapist, and his musings in this seminal field tell us more about the relationship between Emerson's idealism and Osler's humanism. Teaching and practicing when the field of psychology was young and unorganized, Osler held that faith and hope were important in the healing process. He wrote in his essay, *Medicine in the Nineteenth Century*:

> Faith in us (the physician) faith in our drugs and methods, is the great stock in trade of the profession. In one pan of the balance, put the pharmacopoeias of the world [...]; in the other put the simple faith with which [...] the children of men have swallowed the mixtures these works describe, and the bulky tomes will kick the beam. It is the aurum potabile, the touchstone of success in medicine. As Galen says, confidence and hope do more good than physic—"he cures most in whom most are confident" (3).

Although Emerson is exploring nature as a metaphysical entity and Osler as a material or scientific one, Emerson's writing resonates with Osler's interests in a compelling way. They shared enticing biographical similarities. Both men were sons of Christian ministers. Emerson's father was a Unitarian minister in Boston; Osler's an Anglican minister in Canada. Emerson, for a time early in his career was also a Unitarian minister. Both men, therefore, would have found value in understanding of the universe through religious metaphors. However, both men developed doubts about this "religious" worldview. Emerson developed new metaphors and religious insights in *Nature*. Emerson's *Harvard Divinity School Address* (1838) articulated these insights and doubts in more detail. In this address, Emerson is critical of a religion (Christianity) that takes its truths from authority as opposed to reason. In his Divinity School Address, he states:

> Meantime, whilst the doors of the temple stand open, night and day, before every man, and the oracles of this truth cease never, it is guarded by one stern condition; this, namely; it is an intuition. It cannot be received at second hand (4).

Here, we find Emerson eschewing religious traditions, which rely on the authoritative transmission of religious insight in favor of the individual's immediate intuition of divinity. Emerson's religious views at the time were radical, but his radicalism was not marginalized entirely as the religious community was in need of novelty, especially as it confronted scientific worldviews, which were gaining more cultural momentum.

Osler, having chosen science as his life path, was in need of ideas and narratives to reconcile his religion with what was becoming a Darwinian world of science. Emerson's view that nature included man rather than excluded him—that all nature was enveloped by spirit and exuded beauty— would have provided Osler with a new way of understanding the study of man and his diseases. This new way painted the practice of science and medicine in an intensely normative hue. While a more guarded view of science focuses on the quest for objectivity and truth, untainted by the eccentricities of emotional and aesthetic considerations, the physician whose practice is inspired by Emerson sees medicine as the most humanistic of enterprises. The humanities and the sciences need not be separated any more than man and nature, mind and body, or physician and patient. Here, we see Emerson's writings paving the way to a humanism in the otherwise valueless world of scientific medicine. Perhaps it was Osler's hope that his students would heed these same insights, would propel medicine on a humanistic course, and would treat science and medicine as a value field.

Both men taught by lecture and the written word. Emerson taught best through his essays and poetry. Emerson's writings and lectures were aimed not at an institutional or group audience, but at the individual. Osler was at his best while on the sick wards teaching medicine to medical students. They were both highly sought-after lecturers. Both men also used aphorisms in their writing. Emerson immersed them in his essays, and at times taught almost exclusively from aphorisms that were meant to be self-evident statements—maxims of truth. Osler published a book of aphorisms as well (5).

In his essay *Self Reliance*, Emerson wrote:

> There is a time in every man's education when he arrives at the convic-
> tion that envy is ignorance; that imitation is suicide; that he must take
> himself for better, for worse, as his portion; that though the wide universe
> is full of good, no kernel of nourishing corn can come to him but through
> his toil bestowed on that plot of ground which is given to him to till (6).

Here Emerson demands that the individual must start from his own unique perspective and angle of vision. Osler also concentrated his lectures, essays, and aphorisms on the effect of the individual. In his essay on *Teacher and Student*, he quotes John Henry Newman:

> I say then, that the personal influence of the teacher is able in some sort
> to dispense with an academical system, but that system cannot in any
> way dispense with personal influence. With influence there is life, with-
> out it there is none; [...] An academical system without the personal
> influence of teachers upon pupils is an Arctic winter; it will create an
> ice-bound, petrified, cast-iron University, and nothing else (7).

Osler also hoped that his students and his profession at large would culti-
vate the ability to seek answers where there were none and to ask questions where tradition offered only uncritical and oversimplified customary prac-
tices. The ability for a medical physician to do this requires more than the experiential education one obtains on the wards and in the clinics. It requires the formation of a new habit, the habit of inquiry. Osler taught that students of medicine develop a "virtue of method," by which he meant a habit or virtue of thoroughness in study. He also taught the "art of detachment." By this art of detachment, Osler meant that the young, immature student should give up his childish ways and avoid the temptations of the young so as to concentrate on his professional preparation. Emerson offers that he should recognize that the time has come in their education to give up imitation, to quit relying on authority, and to ask the difficult questions. In medicine, this means asking "Where is the evidence? Why should I believe this to be true?" Emerson suggests that the true intellect trust his own abilities in the service

of becoming. Osler extends this suggestion to the case of becoming a self-aware, imaginative, creative, and empathic physician.

As self-evident truths, Emerson did not view his essays as simple life lessons in the spirit of a Benjamin Franklin. Instead, he considered them real in a philosophically robust way, in the way Plato considered "ideas" to be real. They were transcendent and universal. Consider the following examples from Emerson:

> Poetry liberates. Thought is also free (8).
> Creation is continuous. There is no other world; this one is all there is (8).
> The intuition of the moral sentiment is an insight of the perfection of the laws of the soul (9).

Published in a small book, *Counsels and Ideals and Selected Aphorisms* (10), William Osler listed similar maxims gleaned from his experience as a physician-educator. It is unclear whether or not Osler was consciously imitating Emerson in his use of aphoristic teaching. But similar to Emerson, he writes these as if they are real in a philosophically forceful way. Consider the following examples of Osler's aphorisms:

> But by the neglect of the studies of the humanities, which has been for too general, the profession, loses a very precious quality (11).
> Medicine is learned at the bedside, and not in the classroom (12).
> The dissociation of student and patient is a legacy of the pernicious system of theoretical teaching (13).
> Let us emancipate the student, and give him time and opportunity for the cultivation of his mind, so that in his pupilage he shall not be a puppet in the hands of others, but rather a self-relying and reflecting being (14).

The last of these aphorisms suggest to us that Osler took Emerson's essay *Self Reliance* to heart and possibly had it in mind when he recommended that his students read Emerson.

Osler's commitment to social activism seemed to flow naturally from his work in medicine. He taught students within the university, politicians in government, and the public in general by working diligently for social change in public health. He lectured, wrote, and agitated in Baltimore and later in England for public health changes that would control the spread of tuberculosis and typhus. It seems quite likely that Osler was hoping that medical students and practicing physicians would use their education and privileged knowledge to further the health and well-being of their individual patients and the general public.

Osler would have recommended Emerson's writings, especially the later essays regarding abolition, to medical students as examples of virtue ethics, which turn critical thought into action.

Emerson's life was permeated with tragedy, as his son, Waldo, died at age five from scarlet fever. A sense of fate pervaded the *Second Series* of essays and finds its most mature articulation in his essays, *Fate* and *Power*. Emerson writes that Nature is that negative power, a "tyrannous circumstance, [...] necessitated activity; violent direction" (15). The good physician must confront this mortality and the inevitability of pain and suffering in the lives of his patients. Osler shared in Emerson's suffering, having lost a son, his only child, in World War I. Osler wrote, learning of his son's death, "The Fates do not allow the good fortune that has followed me to go with me to the grave—and in a reference to Aristotle he ends, call no man happy 'til he dies' " (16).

Both men seem inspired by the Stoics, whose famous maxim compares the plight of men to that of dogs tied to a wagon. Our fate is inevitable, as we cannot resist the inevitable pace of the wagon's pull. But we can choose to run! It often takes time and scars of lived experience to learn the lessons of our own mortality. But in Emerson, we find these insights crystallized, and Osler might have wanted to communicate them to his students through Emerson's late essays.

Emerson was interested in genius and he represented the ideal of genius, the scholar who achieved greatness as "Man Thinking" who is informed by nature, inspired by books, and has the courage to act. Furthermore, this new American scholar would be bound by duties. Emerson elaborated:

> They are such as become Man Thinking. They may all be comprised in self-trust. The office of the scholar is to cheer, to raise, and to guide men by showing them facts amidst appearances...he must accept— how often!—poverty and solitude. For the ease and pleasure of treading the old road, accepting the fashions, the education, the religion of society, he takes the cross of making his own, and, of course, the self-accusation, the faint heart... (17).

Emerson tells us that the path of "Man Thinking" is a trying one, marked by the difficulties of poverty and solitude. Trusting in one's own angle of vision and pursuing intuited truth in the face of reactionary opposition is not for the fainthearted. But Emerson traveled this path. He charged the divinity students at Harvard to do the same by taking up an original relationship to the divine, and in doing so himself. Emerson poetically articulated an idealistic worldview in which theology speaks to the value and purpose found in lived experience. But this vision of *Nature* and this rejection of institutional dogma cast him out of the church and the university. Emerson pursued greatness from the outside.

In Osler, we do not find an outsider or an anti-institutional loner, but we do see someone with an imaginative vision for reform. Furthermore, Osler knew the path was difficult and bound by duty. He believed that the mission of medical education need be bound by the duties of "Man Thinking." In an address at McGill University Medical School in 1895, Osler outlines his thought on the duty of a medical university:

> What I mean by the thinking function of the university is the duty, which the professional corps owes to enlarge the boundaries of human knowledge. Work of this sort makes a University great, and alone enables it to exercise a wide influence on the minds of men (18).

Osler is referring to the environment that looks beyond the status quo—that asks the important questions. What if? How do we know? What is a better treatment or prevention? This type of thinking is creative, imaginative, and courageous. We find it in the genius and greatness of Emerson, and it is meant to inspire us to action.

But the pursuit of greatness and genius of "Man Thinking" registers as a moral duty as well. Osler extended Emerson's vision of man as a part of nature to see that the practice of medicine was an application of the new science on the natural state of man. But because medicine is a value field, it is a spiritual, interpersonal enterprise, whose successful practice demands that the practitioner be in empathy with the plight of the suffering patient. Therefore, education in the spirituality of man was as important as education in the physiology of the human body. Osler says in an address to medical students:

> Like art, Medicine is an exacting mistress, and in the pursuit of one of the scientific branches, sometimes, too, in practice, not a portion of a man's spirit may be left free for other distractions, but this does not often happen. On account of the intimate personal nature of his work, the medical man, perhaps more than any other man, needs that higher education of which Plato speaks,—"that education in virtue from youth upwards, which enables a man eagerly to pursue the ideal perfection" (19).

However, achieving genius and greatness of the ideal of "Man Thinking" does not entail the passive reception of the Platonic forms alone. It demands a lifelong devotion to drill and discipline. Both Emerson and Osler recommended to others that one should read primarily books of proven value. Although he was a voracious reader, Emerson was also critical of how one learned from books. In his lecture and essay, *The American Scholar*(20), Emerson discusses the danger of books:

> Hence, instead of Man Thinking, we have the bookworm. Hence the book-learned class, who value books, as such; not as related to nature and the human constitution, but as making a sort of Third Estate [20] with the world and soul. Hence the restorers of readings, [21] the emendators, [22] the bibliomaniacs [23] of all degrees. This is bad; this is worse than it seems.
>
> Books are the best of things, well used; abused, among the worst. What is the right use? What is the one end which all means go to effect? They are for nothing but to inspire [24].

Emerson is warning the scholar that books can inhibit original thinking—what he calls man's creative spirit and godlike quality. He is warning us that bibliomania is a poor substitute for "Man Thinking," the exercise and attention to original thought. He is praising the use of books only in the service of inspiration. Inspiration is meant to enhance the quality of thinking and enliven our spirit and soul.

Emerson cautioned that the scholar not be a mere specialist, that his curiosity not be bound by any narrowly conceived discipline. The specialist is a partial man, falling short of "Man Thinking." Furthermore, Emerson criticizes college education as being run by specialists who cater to the "mercantile interests of students" (20). The utilitarian nature of this specialization results in a moral decay as we confuse our ends. The special skills and knowledge content needed to earn a living or climb the corporate ladder trump the character building of self-knowledge. This does not suit Emerson's philosophy because for him, "character is higher than intellect" (21). Emerson criticized this failure of education in his day. He lamented that alongside the heavy preference for the teaching of facts and the exercise of the understanding in comparison and analysis came a deficiency in teaching the imagination. If the imagination were disregarded, so would be the practical and the moral (22).

Osler also expressed his delight in books as a necessary foundation for the experiential learning in the clinic. In an address at the opening of the Boston Medical Library, he echoed the Emersonian balance struck between bookish scholarship and pragmatic learning:

Books have been my delight these thirty years, and from them I have received incalculable benefits. To study the phenomenon of disease without books is to sail an uncharted sea, while to study books without patients is not to go to sea at all (25).

Scholarship in light of Emerson means reading for inspiration, appropriating others' ideas in an open and courageous spirit, learning experientially, and advancing one's profession by novel contributions. Perhaps Osler thought his students might intuit this wisdom by reading Emerson. And, as Emerson told us, we should read for inspiration.

Oliver Wendell Holmes

Osler at the Breakfast Table

BRIAN HURWITZ

Oliver Wendell Holmes is little read today, but his Breakfast-Table series became wildly popular with public and medical readerships alike as soon as it appeared in serial form in 1857. It appeared in the pages of *Atlantic Monthly*, a literary journal whose name Holmes had suggested to its first editor, James Russell Lowell. The setting for the series is a domestic Boston boardinghouse, where an autocrat expounds his thoughts to a group of fellow boarders—a schoolmistress, a divinity student, a young man called John and an ever-present landlady who initially is granted only a background presence in the dialogue: "I was going to say something about our boarders the other day when I got run away by my local reminiscences. I wish you to understand that we have a rather select company at the table of our boarding-house" (1).

> As coffee, tea and flapjacks are being consumed, the reader overhears a series of conversation pieces—genial exchanges concerning a multitude of topics, thoughts and anxieties "I feel sure that there is an Englishman somewhere precisely like myself." (I hope he does not drop his h's, for it does not seem to me possible that the Royal Dane could have remained faithful to his love for Ophelia, if she had addressed him as 'Amlet) (2).

In 1907, Leslie Stephen described Holmes as "a strange new sort of cultural spokesman," able to express himself as an autocratic voice "dictating the standards of Victorian gentility or as the author of multivoiced table-talk works that respond to every issue from a spectrum of opposing positions, avoiding singular conclusions, unsettling fixed standards, and challenging the old verities" (3). Snippets of recollections, aphorisms and anecdotes, and local and scientific news crowd together in table talk that is witty, imaginative, and quirky, and relayed in conversations that offer a heady mix of the personal, intellectual, abstract, and the unpredictable:

> I was just going to say, when I was interrupted, that one of the many ways of classifying minds is under the head of arithmetical and algebraical intellects. All economical and practical wisdom is an extension or variation of the following arithmetical formula: 2 + 2 = 4. Every philosophical proposition has the general character of the expression a + b = c. We are mere operatives, empirics, and egotists, until we learn to think in letters instead of figures...a divinity student lately come among us...abused his liberty on this occasion by presuming to say that Leibniz had the same observation—No, sir, I replied, he has not (4).

From the outset of what was to be a prolonged opportunity for readers to eavesdrop on the chatter and musings of a lively group of people from different walks of American life—"This table is a very long one. Legs in every Atlantic and inland city...legs everywhere, like a millipede or a banian-tree [*sic*]..." (5)—many of the characteristics of conversations that were later collected together (6) are immediately apparent: interruption in the midst of fluency, informed opinion volubly expressed and claim and counterclaim. The great theological question now heaving and throbbing in the minds of Christian men is this:

> No, I won't talk about these things now. My remarks might be repeated, and it would give my friends pain to see with what personal incivilities I should be visited. Besides, what business has a mere boarder to be talking about such things at a breakfast table? (7).

The Breakfast-Table series is the work of a "talkist" and it covers an extraordinary range of ideas and experiences that can neither be evoked nor classified easily: scenes with first loves, primal death and burial encounters, fantasies and dreams of heavenly conversations, déjà-vu experiences, remembrances of smells and sounds, of tending the sick as a medical student in Paris, and feelings engendered by being a child and lying to grown-ups. Such topics jostle for space with disquisitions about science, drama, and poetry:

> Scientific knowledge, even in the most modest persons, has mingled with it a something which partakes of insolence. Absolute, peremptory facts are bullies and those keep company with them are apt to get a bullying habit of mind;—not of manners, perhaps; they may be soft and smooth, the smile they carry has a quiet assertion in it...Take the man, for instance, who deals in the mathematical sciences. There is no elasticity in a mathematical fact; if you bring up against it, it never yields a hair's breadth; everything must go to pieces that comes in collision with it. What the mathematician knows being absolute,

unconditional, incapable of suffering question, it should tend, in the nature of things, to breed a despotic way of thinking. So of those who deal with the palpable and often unmistakable facts of external nature; only in a less degree....But mark this which I am going to say once and for all; If I had not force enough to reject a principle full in the face of the half dozen most obvious facts which seem to contradict it, I would think only in single file from this day forward (8).

The literary scholar, Peter Gibian, finds in these texts a vitality of thought that reflects simultaneously a parlor etiquette and the culture of outside meetings: "For mid-century Americans of all classes...outside the home and the workplace was a series of meetings centering around a highly developed network of talk communities: political clubs, reform associations, coffeehouse discussion groups, salons, Lyceums, debating societies, literary and philosophical societies, militias, trade associations, fire companies" (9). From such diverse gatherings the Breakfast-Table pieces arise; the result is writings that embody mid-19th-century American argument, digression, extemporary reactions, and rapid switches of mood that stand apart from the "monological sermon" (10) or formal lecture:

Talking is one of the fine arts,—the noblest, the most important, and the most difficult...It is not easy, at the best, for two persons talking together to make the most of each other's thoughts, there are so many of them....When John and Thomas, for instance, are talking together, it is natural enough that among the six there should be more or less confusion and misapprehension (11).

When the listeners around the table question reference to *six* interlocutors, the Autocrat explains that in any conversation between two people "six personalities" take part, in this case, three Johns—the real John known only to his Maker, John's ideal John, and Thomas' ideal John—and equivalently three Thomases. The participation of multiple selves in the speakers in these pieces helps us to make sense of the many voices at play in the Breakfast-Table texts (12)—prefiguring, perhaps, today's blogs and chat rooms.

Each chapter of the series ends with a poem—Holmes was well known for signing off his lectures and after-dinner talks with a poetic flourish (for which he was in much demand); he was, himself, more ambitious to be thought a poet than a physician, scientist, or teacher (13): "It has been as much from good nature as from vanity that I so often got up and jangled my small string of bells. I hold it to be a gift of a certain value to be able to give that slight passing spasm of pleasure which a few ringing couplets often cause, read at the right moment" (14). Chapter II of the *Autocrat* finishes with a poem "with corrections," half-transformed by a dialogue. The Autocrat had previously sent a poem to a committee to mark "a certain celebration...a festive and convivial occasion...[But] it seems the president of the day was what is called a "teetotaler" and a note was sent back "with slight alteration":

> *Come! Fill a fresh bumper,—for why should we go*
> *While the logwood still reddens our cups as they flow!*
> *Pour out the decoction still bright with the sun,*
> *Till o'er the brimmed crystal the dye-stuff shall run.*
> *The half-ripened apples their life-dews have bled;*
> *How sweet is the taste of the sugar of lead*
> *For summer's rank poisons lie hid in the wines!!!*
> *That were garnered by stable-boys smoking long-nines*
> *Then a scowl and a howl, and a scoff, and a sneer*
> *For all the strychnine and whiskey, and ratsbane and beer*
> *In cellar, in pantry, in attic, in hall,*
> *Down, down, with the tyrant that masters us all!* (15).

Oliver Wendell Holmes' life (1809–1894) touched every decade of the 19th century. The son of Abiel Holmes, a Calvinist clergyman, and his second wife, Sarah Wendell, who was from a well-known New York family, Holmes was born in Cambridge, Massachusetts, and educated at Phillips Academy in Andover and Harvard College. He traveled to Paris in 1833 to the École de Médecine, to study under Pierre Louis at La Charité and the Salpêtrière. On his return to Boston, Holmes became a leading proponent of the French clinical method and of Pierre Louis' medical philosophy. He gained his MD from Harvard and set up practice in Boston, becoming for 10 years Professor of Anatomy and Physiology at Dartmouth, then Parkman Professor of Anatomy and Physiology at Harvard, and the first Dean of its Medical School (1847–1853). Though not particularly successful in his own practice—it is said that well-healed Bostonians were reluctant to place themselves in the hands of a brilliant talker and versifier who appeared to lack due clinical sobriety—it was writing that brought him recognition in the eyes of his contemporaries and fame

> as a national character, even a national institution. For foreign visitors like William Thackeray, Charles Dickens, or Oscar Wilde, a meeting with the tiny, hyperactive, loquacious Holmes became as much a part of the standard North American tour as a visit to Niagara Falls. Well into the twentieth century, the Holmes name still stood in most

people's minds as a loaded, multivalent figure. Playing a variety of parts on the national stage, he came to be celebrated as spokesman for and representative personification of American achievements in two very different fields—medicine and literature—and was acclaimed both as a voice of gravity and of levity, a Sage and a Jester, a man of reason and an irrepressible humorist . . . [H]aving given Boston its still-current title as "Hub" of the universe, and having named and defined the "Brahmin caste" of intellectuals so often associated with that New England Center. Holmes also made himself the embodiment of widely-shared national aspirations to intellectual advancement (16).

Osler hailed Holmes as the most successful combination of physician and man of letters the world had ever seen (17), but what was it that attracted Osler to the Breakfast-Table series? He would very likely have chimed in with the Autocrat's view that "great minds are those with a wide span, which couple truths related to, but far removed from, each other" (18). Despite Osler's own commitment to the methods and explanatory power of pathology, he practiced as a clinical generalist for most of his life (19) and increasingly came to believe that the best guarantor of good practice and future medical progress were the values of a broad education:

> . . . Medicine is seen at its best in men whose faculties have had the highest and most harmonious culture. The Lathams, the Watsons, the Pagets, the Jenners, and the Gardners have influenced the profession less by their special work than by exemplifying those graces of life and refinements of heart which make up character . . . the Warrens, the Jacksons, the Bigelows, the Bowditches, and the Shattucks in Boston . . . Brahmins all, in the language of the greatest Brahmin among them, Oliver Wendell Holmes,—these and men like them have been the leaven which has raised our profession above the dead level of a business (20).

Osler shared Holmes' view of the inherent power of nature to heal disease and sympathized with Holmes' therapeutic caution, if not the profound skepticism wrongly attributed to him following his 1860 indictment that "if the whole *Materia Medica* as now used, could be sunk to the bottom of the sea, it would be all the better for mankind,—and all the worse for the fishes" (21). Osler greatly admired the prescience of Holmes' work on the contagiousness of puerperal fever that had appeared in *The New England Quarterly Journal of Medicine and Surgery* in 1843. In this paper, Holmes reviewed dozens of medical reports, testimonial letters, and case series published over a 70-year period, originating in America, Scotland, Ireland, England, and France, and achieved a remarkable synthesis from what then were understood to be mixed sources of evidence. He concluded: "It would seem incredible that any should be found too prejudiced or indolent to accept the solemn truth knelled into their ears by the funeral bells from both sides of the ocean—the plain conclusion that the physician and the disease entered, hand in hand, into the chamber of the unsuspecting patient" (22).

Holmes' drive to make sense of the multiplicity of sources he'd identified and to reason toward causes in the face of such diverse materials led him to devise a model systematic review in narrative terms:

> In the view of these facts it does appear a singular coincidence that one man or woman should have ten, twenty, thirty, or seventy cases of this rare disease following his or her footsteps with the keenness of a beagle, through the streets and lanes of a crowded city, while the scores that cross the same paths on the same errands know it only by name. It is a series of similar coincidences that has led us to consider the dagger, the musket, and certain innocent-looking white powders as having some little claim to be regarded as dangerous. It is the practical inattention to similar coincidences which has given rise to the unpleasant but often necessary documents called indictments, which has sharpened a form of the cephalotome sometimes employed in the case of adults, and adjusted that modification of the fillet which delivers the world of those who happen to be too much in the way while such striking coincidences are taking place (22).

In 1891, Osler met Holmes, at about the time Harvard was hoping to lure him away from Johns Hopkins and later recounted his impressions of the poet-physician to Lymen Powell, his literary assistant who was then helping to prepare the manuscript of the first edition of the *Principles and Practice of Medicine*. Osler's account of the meeting was later recalled by Powell: "I spent a day with him last week," my host remarked. "You know, he is far more than *Autocrat of the Breakfast Table*. He has had a great career in medicine. He has discovered things. Back in 1843 he ferreted out that puerperal fever was contagious, and as a result thousands of mothers have lived to bring their babies up. And he is such a boy in spite of his 82 years." Then Osler leaped to his feet with the spring of youth, walked swiftly back and forth across the room, flecking the ashes from his cigarette, and, in vivid imitation of his aged friend, made his visit live again before me. He even quoted Holmes: "Who says I am growing old? I am as young as any of you boys. Look at this—flinging his arms wildly around and stooping over until his fingers all but touched the floor" (23).

In Holmes' brilliance, playfulness, and vitality, Osler found a modern source of profound fun and meditation, which he wanted medical students both to share in and to draw on.

Old and New Testaments

Osler and the Bible

RITA CHARON

Why are the Old and New Testaments on Osler's list of 10? What would the Canadian son of an immigrant minister of the Church of England, himself seduced by the microscope away from a life in the ministry into a life in medicine *do* with the Bible? No doubt, he had studied the Bible extensively, if only as his father's son.

From scripture to Shakespeare to scientific scoop, the written word *gave* something to Osler, *put Osler through* something, as it does to us. The language a person feasts on not only satiates but also, more fundamentally, *constitutes* the self. Repeating the sentiments of T.S. Eliot and Keats and Wordsworth that poets are not people who make poems but rather are places where poems happen, magisterial literary critic and Biblical scholar Northrup Frye suggests that "[m]an makes words but there is also a sense in which words make him. It's not only that they condition him but that they transform his being" (1).

My methodological approach here to the Bible is to treat it as a text rather than as a statement of religious dogma. Taking the Bible as a work of literature, first of all, frees the reader to absorb its beauty before its precepts, to surrender to its art instead of to its laws. Several of the most eminent and authoritative of our contemporary literary scholars have written about scripture as literary text. Attention to the Bible as language and linguistic discourse forces a fresh and sharp attention to the Bible's genres, its diction, its figures of speech, its narrative strategies, and its rhetorical devices on top of its plots (2). Such attention repays the reader not only with a deep appreciation of the beauty of the text but, more fundamental to my point in this essay, also with a powerful and singular grasp on what the Bible does to its reader. The hypothesis advanced by such work is that the discursive, linguistic features of the text add to—or, more radically, enable—the transcendent features of sacred texts. How, I am in a somewhat convoluted way asking, does the Book of Isaiah or the Gospel of St. John reach its reader? What does it *do* to that reader? How can its inspiration and benediction and redemption come about in the course of its reader assimilating and metabolizing the words on its pages?

What interests me here is the state of attention required by close reading. Not only is there the text itself, first of all, but also the accrual of *all* the commentary, the interpretations, the rabbinical debates, the Midrash, and the *gloss*. If the biblical text is seen as the ground, then the entire historical and transhistorical experience of reading it and rereading it in view of prior readings weave a vast collectivity past and future, bridging times, languages, cultures, and continents. Not only for the faithful but also simply for its *readers*, this biblical text has erected, perhaps, the biggest tent in history under whose shelter we all crowd. British literary scholar Frank Kermode, who loves the Bible and writes often about scripture (when not writing about Shakespeare or modernist fiction), describes the Bible as the *ur*-canonical text that embodies the very relation of text to life:

> [Canonical works] are inexhaustibly full of senses only partly available to any previous reading, and the cumulative influence of tradition upon new readings is fitful and partial. Every verse is occultly linked, in ways to be researched, with all the others; the text is a world system. And since the canonical work is fixed in time but applicable to all time, it has figural qualities not to be detected, save at an appropriate moment in the future. Interpretations may be regarded not as modern increments but rather as discoveries of original meanings hitherto hidden; so that, together with the written text, these interpretations constitute a total object of which the text is but a part or version; an Oral Torah, or Oral Tradition, preserved by an apostolic institution, equal in authority and coeval with the written (3).

Beyond the recognition of the Bible as one among many canonical texts, Kermode glimpses the New Testament's emergence not from historical but from textual origins, making it *primarily* a work of words and secondarily a work of belief. He learns from biblical scholars and historians studying the development of Christian texts about how the evangelists perhaps wrote what became the Gospels. As early disciples of Jesus bent on having him recognized as the Messiah, they had to tell his story in a way that accorded with and fulfilled the prophecies of the Old Testament. And so, this version suggests, they carried around, on something like index cards, bits of text from the Old Testament that contained specific oracular predictions. In sermons and lectures, they could then "tell" the story of Jesus in a way that could be recognized as the answer to the prophecies of old. This collection of bits of text was called a *codex*. Perhaps more like a chapbook of poetry or a portfolio of loose-leaf papers, the codex was the basis for an eventual manuscript that became the Gospels. Unlike the roll of the Torah, in which the beginning is safely rolled away and hidden from view when one reads later portions of the text, the codex keeps all elements in play, provisional, even the old redactable for the sake of the new.

If the Bible, and perhaps even the world, can be treated as text, then "literature must be treated as literature" (4). The very literariness of books on a bedside table and of the extensively cataloged and *handled* books of the Osler Bibliotheca seem to prove the point that Osler treated his books as, well, literature—not only, that is to say, as information but also as story. As I turn to two scriptural texts singled out by Osler, one from the Old Testament and one from the New, be aware that I will treat them *as* literature so as to give us a chance to unearth what Osler himself might have *seen* in them. What are, one can ask, their narrative strategies? What are their genres, their dictions, their governing images, and their temporal scaffoldings? To what other texts do they allude? Compared to Homer, who represents a world illuminated, fully externalized, profoundly *knowable*, as if unfolding in the eternal present tense, the writer of the Book of Genesis leaves much to the reader to visualize. It represents an occluded world, a fraught world, a world of mystery and unknowability. Auerbach inspects the story of Abraham and Isaac, in which the voice of God that instructs Abraham to sacrifice his only son comes from nowhere. Abraham and Isaac's ensuing "journey is like a silent progress through the indeterminate and the contingent, a holding of the breath.... All [is] ... left in obscurity; the decisive points of the narrative alone are emphasized, what lies between is nonexistent; time and place are undefined and call for interpretation; thoughts and feeling remain unexpressed, are only suggested by the silence and the fragmentary speeches; the whole, permeated with the most unrelieved suspense and directed toward a single goal (and to that extent far more of a unity), remains mysterious and 'fraught with background'" (5). How does the reader pierce the darkness and imagine the sounds to fill the silences to reach the goal of such mysterious texts?

In 1875, Osler hospitalized a young Englishman he met socially who struck him as appearing ill. The young man died of smallpox in Montreal General Hospital three days later. Osler wrote a note of condolence to the young man's parents, telling them of their son's last days: "He was well aware of his dangerous state. He spoke to me of his home, and his mother, and asked me to read the 43rd chapter of Isaiah, which she had marked in his Bible. I spent the greater part of the morning talking and reading with him" (6). As a text from the Old Testament that directly entered into Osler's practice of medicine, this chapter seemed an apt choice for an extended close reading here.

In chapters 40–42 of Isaiah, a voice cries out to the heart of Jerusalem that the time of atonement has come to a close and that preparations can be made for the coming of Yahweh. The voice implores that its hearers prepare the valleys, the mountains, the cliffs, and the ridges for the glory of Yahweh. Conjuring up images that recur throughout the Old and New Testaments, Yahweh is figured as the shepherd feeding his flock, as he who measures mountains and seas, he who made the heavens and the stars in them, he who created the boundaries of the earth. By late in chapter 40, the auditor condenses from all inhabitants of Jerusalem to one of its inhabitants, Jacob. Jacob is singled out, without warning, as the representative or, perhaps, the personification of Israel. Remembering that Jacob was renamed Israel by God or God's surrogate after wrestling with the angel in Genesis 32, the reader now finds himself or herself reading at two levels at once—the biographical level of the Jacob known to be the grandson of Abraham, son of Isaac, twin brother of Esau (born grabbing the actual first-born Esau by the heel), he who tricked his way into primogeniture by "buying" the position from his brother and getting himself so blessed by the ailing and blind Isaac, the Jacob who is to become father of Joseph and Benjamin and their 10 half-brothers and, as a result, the immediate parent of the 12 tribes of Israel. And, at the same time, the reader reads at the allegorical level of the Jacob who stands for the entire land of, or culture of, or tradition of, or *promise* of Israel, the Jacob who, however flawed as a human, has achieved or attracted the eye of God and is drawn forth from a state of sin to the state of having been, through no desert of his own, chosen. If a reader can for whatever reason align himself or herself with Jacob (and who, being human, cannot?), then the call of the scripture simultaneously summons both action and a view beyond time—how do I, having been chosen, act and where will this choice take me?

Through a series of condensations and enlargements, Yahweh beckons to the man and that for which he stands—"Jacob, poor worm, Israel, puny mite"—to enter the position of the chosen, the redeemed. He turns Jacob into the threshing sled to "crush the mountains and turn the hills to chaff." He slakes parched Jacob's thirst by "making rivers well up on barren heights" and plants the barren desert with juniper and cedar trees, making of it a new Eden. This is all done so that the world will know of the might of Yahweh, that its inhabitants will see the future foretold by Jacob and

Israel. The historical king Cyrus, conflated with Jacob, is used as a figure for the Messiah along the way and "recognized" by Christian readers as also an oracular figure for Jesus. A long series of "songs of the servant of Yahweh" present a figure clothed in mystery—who *is* this servant of simultaneous submission and election, delighting his master while modest in his faithfulness, the appointed covenant of the people who lets the blind see and sets the captive free in the hymn of triumph and yet, in the next section, who himself is deaf and blind and trapped and hidden. The tension is held between the valor of the chosen Jacob and the ruin of Jacob before election, the difference being, simply, the imperial or even capricious will of Yahweh.

Chapter 43 of the Book of Isaiah

The liberation of Israel

23:043:001 But now thus saith the LORD that created thee, O Jacob, and he that formed thee, O Israel, Fear not: for I have redeemed thee, I have called thee by thy name; thou art mine.

23:043:002 When thou passest through the waters, I will be with thee; and through the rivers, they shall not overflow thee: when thou walkest through the fire, thou shalt not be burned; neither shall the flame kindle upon thee.

23:043:003 For I am the LORD thy God, the Holy One of Israel, thy Saviour: I gave Egypt for thy ransom, Ethiopia and Seba for thee.

23:043:004 Since thou wast precious in my sight, thou hast been honourable, and I have loved thee: therefore will I give men for thee, and people for thy life.

23:043:005 Fear not: for I am with thee: I will bring thy seed from the east, and gather thee from the west;

23:043:006 I will say to the north, Give up; and to the south, Keep not back: bring my sons from far, and my daughters from the ends of the earth;

23:043:007 Even every one that is called by my name: for I have created him for my glory, I have formed him; yea, I have made him.

23:043:008 Bring forth the blind people that have eyes, and the deaf that have ears.

23:043:009 Let all the nations be gathered together, and let the people be assembled: who among them can declare this, and shew us former things? let them bring forth their witnesses, that they may be justified: or let them hear, and say, It is truth.

23:043:010 Ye are my witnesses, saith the LORD, and my servant whom I have chosen: that ye may know and believe me, and understand that I am he: before me there was no God formed, neither shall there be after me.

23:043:011 I, even I, am the LORD; and beside me there is no saviour.

23:043:012 I have declared, and have saved, and I have shewed, when there was no strange god among you: therefore ye are my witnesses, saith the LORD, that I am God.

23:043:013 Yea, before the day was I am he; and there is none that can deliver out of my hand: I will work, and who shall let it?

23:043:014 Thus saith the LORD, your redeemer, the Holy One of Israel; For your sake I have sent to Babylon, and have brought down all their nobles, and the Chaldeans, whose cry is in the ships.

23:043:015 I am the LORD, your Holy One, the creator of Israel, your King.

23:043:016 Thus saith the LORD, which maketh a way in the sea, and a path in the mighty waters;

23:043:017 Which bringeth forth the chariot and horse, the army and the power; they shall lie down together, they shall not rise: they are extinct, they are quenched as tow.

23:043:018 Remember ye not the former things, neither consider the things of old.

23:043:019 Behold, I will do a new thing; now it shall spring forth; shall ye not know it? I will even make a way in the wilderness, and rivers in the desert.

23:043:020 The beast of the field shall honour me, the dragons and the owls: because I give waters in the wilderness, and rivers in the desert, to give drink to my people, my chosen.

23:043:021 This people have I formed for myself; they shall shew forth my praise.

23:043:022 But thou hast not called upon me, O Jacob; but thou hast been weary of me, O Israel.

23:043:023 Thou hast not brought me the small cattle of thy burnt offerings; neither hast thou honoured me with thy sacrifices. I have not caused thee to serve with an offering, nor wearied thee with incense.

23:043:024 Thou hast bought me no sweet cane with money, neither hast thou filled me with the fat of thy sacrifices: but thou hast made me to serve with thy sins, thou hast wearied me with thine iniquities.

23:043:025 I, even I, am he that blotteth out thy transgressions for mine own sake, and will not remember thy sins.

23:043:026 Put me in remembrance: let us plead together: declare thou, that thou mayest be justified.

23:043:027 Thy first father hath sinned, and thy teachers have transgressed against me.

23:043:028 Therefore I have profaned the princes of the sanctuary, and have given Jacob to the curse, and Israel to reproaches (6a).

When Osler read the section marked by his dying patient's mother, he was reading, perhaps, the words of an anonymous poet other than the prophet Isaiah (7). Structured in stanzas of line lengths varying from 2 to 22, the poetry emits from a first person speaker, Yahweh, as is proclaimed by the narrator who, in impresario-fashion, "presents" him: "Thus says Yahweh." Voiced predominantly in the present imperative, ("Do not be afraid" and "Bring forward the people that is blind, yet has eyes"), the monologue implies a public scene—as if this voice, amplified, fills Madison Square Garden or the Fertile Crescent or the new Eden.

This God who Speaks speeds among and so equates multiple contradictory acts. He comforts and assures the listener of his eternal presence and guardianship ("Should you pass through the sea, I will be with you/or through rivers, they will not swallow you up"); he boasts of the perceived value of his possession ("I give Egypt for your ransom/because you are precious in my eyes"); he lavishes freedom on his chosen people ("I will bring your offspring from the east,/and gather you from the west"). In rapid succession, he decries and neutralizes the competing idolaters who pretend to godhead, beating his breast, it seems, in haughty swagger, and then immediately shifts mode to protective militarism, recounting past deeds of demolishing enemies (notably the Pharaoh in the Red Sea). Nimbly, he again shifts register to warn against false nostalgia and instead to look ahead to "a new deed/even now it comes to light; can you not see it?" What he implores his listener to behold is the chosen land—where "wild beasts will honour me/ jackals and ostriches/because I am putting water in the wilderness/(rivers in the wild)/to give my chosen people drink." Chapter 43 closes in again another register, this one a homey, domestic quarrel as one might hear from a wronged wife or disappointed mother: "Jacob, you have not invoked me/ you have not troubled yourself, Israel, on my behalf." (You don't call, you don't write.) And yet, again, he shifts from complaint to reassurance—"But now listen, Jacob my servant/Israel whom I have chosen." Yahweh absolves the dilatory party, repeating the promises of sustenance, blessing, and future power while proclaiming at the end of the sequence as at its beginning that "I am the first and the last/there is no other God besides me."

The auditor shifts over the course of the poem—and therefore conflates—Jacob, Jerusalem, Israel, and all the chosen. Whoever is visualized as the actual "listener" or object of this rhetorical torrent is in turn bowled over, won over, shaken, *made anew* by the relentless harangue and the forgiving and beguiling intimacies of the passage. At once or at least in quick succession brought to his or her knees and elevated to the heavens, the listener proceeds through stages of accusation, confession, absolution, seduction, delight in the choosing eye of the suitor, awe at his power, and thanksgiving for the state of blessed election.

In the space of the 95 lines of the poem, it is as if no theme of importance is left out. Time, power, value, space, intent, and witness are all visited, much like keys struck on a keyboard. Similarly, affective states are not just cataloged but undergone by either speaker or listener—pride, gratitude, maternal brooding, jealous pouting, abjectness, fury, vengeance, loyalty, and fidelity. Time and space vibrate to provide a rhythmic beat to the poem's music—now, then, in the days of the Pharaoh, in the times of Cyprus, when the idolaters will be destroyed, when the chosen land becomes the new Eden. "No god was formed before me,/nor will be after me" locates the key of time squarely within the timeless prominence of the godhead—he who, in a manner of speaking, establishes and so can transcend time itself. The poem could use a GPS to keep track of the countries and continents hailed—Babylon, Chaldea, Egypt, the wilderness, the city walls, the prisons, the river valleys, the ocean, the desert as well as such intimate spaces as the sanctuary and the sacrificial altar. The cumulative effect of these percussive swings in time and space is to unseat the reader, to keep the reader on his or her toes, to exact an anxious state of uncertainty. In the presence of this god, one walks on eggs.

The formal elements of the poem provide clues to its power. The poet adopts parallel litanies that build density and force through amplifying repetition:

> *Should you pass through the sea, I will be with you;*
> *or through rivers, they will not swallow you up,*
> *Should you walk through fire, you will not be scorched*
> *and the flames will not burn you* (6a).

The repetition of this structure builds intensity until one doesn't even *need* the second or third or fourth installment in a sequence in order to be smitten with the power of the first. Similarly, the series of boasts nail the infinite ability of this godhead to *handle* anything thrown in his way.

For your sake I send an army against Babylon;
I will knock down the prison bars
and the Chaldaeans will break into laments
I am Yahweh, your Holy One
the creator of Israel, your king (6a).

Such rhetorical structures leave no room for doubt. This case for power, for fidelity, for redemption, and for love is closed.

As we read this section of the Old Testament, we imagine Dr. Osler reading aloud or, eyes closed, reciting by heart this familiar passage to his young patient succumbing to smallpox. However many times Osler had read this chapter of Isaiah before, he once again perhaps, there in Montreal General Hospital, experienced the power of this God, the redemption of having been chosen, the protection of the wide arms of God despite natural peril and human evil. Perhaps Osler, like many of us, could see himself in Jacob or *as* Jacob—however hapless and erring as a human being, a figure of dignity and stature in the eyes of a God. This stature confers duty, and perhaps Osler recognized even in the small secular gesture of having hospitalized this young man he met at lunch somewhere his own divine duty. Perhaps Osler wondered whether he were the servant of Yahweh—modest, obedient, and yet powerful against disease and captivity. My suggestion here is only that such text enters a reader, in the form of a codex, to buttress and to sharpen feelings already present, in this case of dutifulness, of having a calling, of being blessed with vocation and its attendant power. What might be called up by chapter 43 of Isaiah, especially in a person like Osler of discrimination and wide learning, is the duty toward the land and the people and the *good*, the sense of being singled out by the cosmic force that demonstrates its authority by showing off what it does in the natural and historical world. In a slightly convoluted but, I believe, widespread way, the reader of a text that emits from a figure of great power over earth and seas or at least over human history—God, the framers of the Constitution of the United States of America, Darwin, Freud, Hitler, Martin Luther King, or by a representative of a powerful institution—is beckoned to be enfolded within the destiny envisioned by that figure of power, aligns his or her own fate and efforts with the collective fates and efforts of all who recognize the cosmic power of the speaker. Particularly susceptible to such sway, persons of religion and of science heed the call of their leaders not only as personally compelling but also as collectively required. The person of faith *cannot* turn down the invitation to serve, if only because of the peril of hell to self and others. The person of science *cannot* turn away from the challenge to create knowledge, if only because of the hazards of ignorance to so many. Such forces might have underwritten Osler's response to scripture, exceeding the autobiographical pull on the son of an Anglican minister and achieving, by virtue of his position as a scientist, the status of a command that ontologically could not be defied.

In "The Art of Life," the 1913 Silliman Lecture to undergraduates at Yale, Osler points to a similar sentiment upon reading chapter 3 of the Gospel according to St. John:

> Do you remember that most touching of all incidents in Christ's ministry, when the anxious ruler Nicodemus came by night, worried lest the things that pertained to his everlasting peace were not a part of his busy and successful life? Christ's message to him is His message to the world—never more needed than at present: "Ye must be born of the spirit." You wish to be with the leaders—as Yale men it is your birthright—[to] know the great souls that make up the moral radium of the world. You must be born of their spirit, initiated into their fraternity, whether of the spiritually minded followers of the Nazarene or of that larger company, elect from every nation, seen by St. John (8).

Osler here focuses the power of scripture onto the lives of these college students, some of them no doubt destined for medicine. Speaking for Yale and, even more globally, for the life of the mind, Osler summons these young men to recognize their destiny as great men, to feel themselves personally chosen, or elected, first by Yale's leaders, then by the "great souls that make up the moral radium of the world," and, finally, through the agency of St. John, by Christ himself. A textual sleight of hand, as it were, enables Osler to make audible to these college kids the grandeur of admission to the ranks of the "elect from every nation." Heady business indeed for these young men, and instructive for us as we try to understand the writer's connection to the text he glosses.

In the Jerusalem Bible, the section of John that tells the story of Nicodemus is built generically as a chimera, in which the frame and plot appear as prose and the spoken word of Jesus as verse. This striking poetic form insists on dual planes for the giving and receiving of this account, placing by its very formal decisions the word of Jesus "above" ordinary talk. As a "leading Jew," the text implies, Nicodemus cannot risk attracting the attention of other Pharisees by his interest in this renegade preacher. Nicodemus therefore remains in partial darkness, having sought out the cover of night under which to approach Jesus with his questions of faith, while Jesus is not merely bathed in but is figured as the source of illumination. "Though the light has come into the world/men have shown they prefer/darkness to the light/because their deeds were evil."

The Gospel according to St. John, chapter 3, verses 1–21.

The conversation with Nicodemus

3:1 There was a man of the Pharisees, named Nicodemus, a ruler of the Jews:

3:2 The same came to Jesus by night, and said unto him, Rabbi, we know that thou art a teacher come from God: for no man can do these miracles that thou doest, except God be with him.

3:3 Jesus answered and said unto him, Verily, verily, I say unto thee, Except a man be born again, he cannot see the kingdom of God.

3:4 Nicodemus saith unto him, How can a man be born when he is old? can he enter the second time into his mother's womb, and be born?

3:5 Jesus answered, Verily, verily, I say unto thee, Except a man be born of water and of the Spirit, he cannot enter into the kingdom of God.

3:6 That which is born of the flesh is flesh; and that which is born of the Spirit is spirit.

3:7 Marvel not that I said unto thee, Ye must be born again.

3:8 The wind bloweth where it listeth, and thou hearest the sound thereof, but canst not tell whence it cometh, and whither it goeth: so is every one that is born of the Spirit.

3:9 Nicodemus answered and said unto him, How can these things be?

3:10 Jesus answered and said unto him, Art thou a master of Israel, and knowest not these things?

3:11 Verily, verily, I say unto thee, We speak that we do know, and testify that we have seen; and ye receive not our witness.

3:12 If I have told you earthly things, and ye believe not, how shall ye believe, if I tell you of heavenly things?

3:13 And no man hath ascended up to heaven, but he that came down from heaven, even the Son of man which is in heaven.

3:14 And as Moses lifted up the serpent in the wilderness, even so must the Son of man be lifted up:

3:15 That whosoever believeth in him should not perish, but have eternal life.

3:16 For God so loved the world, that he gave his only begotten Son, that whosoever believeth in him should not perish, but have everlasting life.

3:17 For God sent not his Son into the world to condemn the world; but that the world through him might be saved.

3:18 He that believeth on him is not condemned: but he that believeth not is condemned already, because he hath not believed in the name of the only begotten Son of God.

3:19 And this is the condemnation, that light is come into the world, and men loved darkness rather than light, because their deeds were evil.

3:20 For every one that doeth evil hateth the light, neither cometh to the light, lest his deeds should be reproved.

3:21 But he that doeth truth cometh to the light, that his deeds may be made manifest, that they are wrought in God (6a).

This discourse puts into play metaphors of dark and light, death and birth, and flesh and the spirit. Syntactically, the text relies more than once on conditional conjunctions that contrast opposites and imply judgment: "Unless a man is born through water and the Spirit/he cannot enter the kingdom of God" (v. 5) and "Though the light has come into the world/men have shown they prefer/darkness to the light" (v. 19). In both these conditional phrases, the Godlike positive (the light or the rebirth) is conjoined to the dreadful consequences of man's refusal to recognize it—banishment from the kingdom or relegation to the darkness. The conjunctions *unless* and *although* introduce near-punitive warnings that alert the reader that, if nothing else, this Jesus is a man to reckon with. This language implies power.

A drumbeat of metaphors represents a realm of light and birth and water and Spirit, dwelt in by those who have embraced Jesus and his teaching, while the realm of darkness and death and drought and the flesh is reserved for those too cowardly to step forward, over the threshold of baptism, into the light. Nicodemus reappears twice later in this Gospel, first as a thoughtful advocate of Jesus against the charges of other Pharisees and then, upon Jesus' death on the Cross, as the supplier of aloes and myrrh with which to embalm him. Such reappearance speaks to John's thematic of endurance, of the relation between birth and death, of the continuum of the temporal with the eternal, enacted most powerfully, within Christian iconography, by the incarnation. This minor figure of Nicodemus is one among the many literary devices that cohere the metaphors launched by John that make transparent the accruing meanings available to the attentive reader.

We can wonder at Osler's choice of Nicodemus' first appearance in the Gospel as the most "touching of all incidents" in the account of Jesus' work. What *is* it about this figure that appealed to Osler? The humble and cautious approach under cover of night, the fearful protection of reputation, the wariness that signals apprehension sound unlike the figure of

Osler abroad—powerful, assertive, decisive, and brave. Perhaps the loyalty despite apprehension appealed to him, the continued advocacy in more and more public ways that Nicodemus showed, the fidelity unto death demonstrated by providing the holy embalming herbs. If I wondered earlier in this essay about a parallel between Jacob and Osler, I again wonder at a parallel between Nicodemus and Osler. Texts *choose* their readers for reasons, and clearly this section of scripture beckoned to Osler. Was Osler worried about his own standing in the spiritual realm? Was Osler wondering about his access to the life of the spirit given all his engagement in the life of the flesh? Not unfamiliar with rites of baptism and passage into the sight of God, did Osler wonder, as he prepared to speak to this Yale crowd in a high-visibility academic performance, whether his secular success might threaten his spiritual salvation? Not idle questions, these are simply the train of thought of a reader trying to attentively inspect the tracks being made by another reader on a well-known text.

Compared to the so-called synoptic Gospels of Matthew, Mark, and Luke (synoptic meaning that they more or less agree among themselves), John's Gospel is more poetic, freer in its arrangement of events, more discriminating in the choices of what to report and what to withhold from his account. It is more, for want of a better word, *literary*. After Osler recommends to the Yale men the account of Nicodemus in the Silliman Lecture, he goes on to propose that the students read the Bible every day: "Begin the day with Christ and His prayer—you need no other. Creedless, with it you have religion; creed-stuffed, it will leaven any theological dough in which you stick. As the soul is dyed by the thoughts, let no day pass without contact with the best literature of the world. Learn to know your Bible, though not perhaps as your fathers did" (9). We see here such a masterful gathering up of ideas and images, positing a contradictory vision of a world in which there is progress (not as your fathers did), there is the eternal (you need no other), there is doubt (the creedless), there is faith (a soul colored by thoughts is still a soul), and there is judgment (the arrogance of the "best literature of the world"!).

The Old Testament and the New Testament join, as two among many, the texts that dyed the thoughts of Dr. William Osler. In the effort to appreciate the mind behind the medicine of this giant in our field, we try to pierce the darkness that envelops any person's thoughts. As we stand in the stacks of his *Bibliotheca*, experiencing the tensions and contrasts that snap out on its shelves, we understand that solutions to our problems are to be worked, not found. Living texts all, never closed on new readings, a codex forever fulfilling itself while redacting itself toward the future, we read—as we live—in open congress with all who have read before us and will read again.

Whether the arts of fiction and scripture merge with or abrade against the works of nature and science is never, for Osler, a question. With him, we move from the individual body, to its spirit, to its unity with that which is outside it, to its communion with others, and to its eventual union with its cosmos. As we sit attentively by the bedsides of our sick patients, let us too consume from our texts that which we savor, that which becomes us, and that which can heal.

Poets

Robert Burns

The Poetry of Robert Burns

PAUL S. MUELLER

One of Osler's ideals was "to do the day's work well and not to bother about to-morrow" (1). This ideal reflects Scripture ("Therefore do not worry about tomorrow... Each day has enough trouble of its own." [Matthew 6:34]) and Burns' famous poem, "To a Mouse." Burns was inspired to write the poem after turning up a nest of field mice with a plow:

> That wee bit heap o' leaves an' stibble,
> Has cost thee mony a weary nibble!
> Now thou's turn'd out, for a' thy trouble,
> But house or hald,
> To thole the winter's sleety dribble,
> An' cranreuch cauld!
> But, Mousie, thou art no thy lane,
> In proving foresight may be vain;
> The best-laid schemes o' mice an 'men
> Gang aft agley,
> An' lea'e us nought but grief an' pain,
> For promis'd joy!
> Still thou art blest, compar'd wi' me
> The present only toucheth thee:
> But, Och! I backward cast my e'e.
> On prospects drear!
> An' forward, tho' I canna see,
> I guess an' fear! (1a).

Despite the mouse's sudden predicament, "the present only toucheth" it and the mouse will "thole" (endure) and move on. The narrator, however, laments the mouse is better off than he is because of the narrator's preoccupation with the past ("I backward cast my e'e") and the future ("I guess an' fear!"). This perspective is consistent with Osler's: "...let the interest in the day's work absorb all of your energies, and the future...will look after itself" (2).

It is well-known that Osler admired equanimity. In a speech to students, Osler advised, "...accept in silence the minor aggravations, cultivate the gift of taciturnity and consume your own smoke with an extra draught of hard work, so that those about you may not be annoyed with the dust and soot of your complaint" (3). Likewise, Burns encouraged taciturnity. In letters to his brother, Burns writes, "...learn taciturnity. Let that be your motto. Though you had the wisdom of Newton or the wit of Swift, garrulousness would lower you in the eyes of your fellow-creatures" (4).

In "Man's Redemption of Man," Osler describes how advances in medicine have reduced suffering. However, Osler also acknowledges that man has great capacity for causing suffering: "...battle and murder, crimes unspeakable, tortures inconceivable, and the inhumanity of man to man has even outdone what appear to be atrocities in nature" (5). This statement directly refers to Burns' "Man Was Made to Mourn." In this poem, Burns has a conversation with a stranger:

> When chill November's surly blast
> Made fields and forests bare,
> One ev'ning, as I wander'd forth
> Along the banks of Ayr,
> I spied a man, whose aged step
> Seem'd weary, worn with care;
> His face furrow'd o'er with years,
> And hoary was his hair.
> Many and sharp the num'rous ills
> Inwoven with our frame!
> More pointed still we make ourselves,
> Regret, remorse, and shame!
> And man, whose heav'n-erected face
> The smiles of love adorn,—
> Man's inhumanity to man
> Makes countless thousands mourn! (1a).

"Man's inhumanity to man makes countless thousands mourn" is a modern proverb. Indeed, for the Oslers, it foreshadowed a tragedy to come. The Oslers' only son, Edward Revere Osler, served in the British army during World War I. On 29 August 1917, Lt. Osler was mortally wounded by a shell that dropped in his company's midst. Despite heroic efforts, "Revere" died the next day. The Oslers were crushed by Revere's death. Upon hearing the news, Osler wrote, "...the dreaded message came. One may hope 'the seen arrow slackened its flight'...A sweeter laddie never lived...We are heart broken, but thankful to have the precious memory of his loving life" (6). Osler's words recall "A Mother's Lament for the Death of Her Son," which Burns wrote to commemorate a young soldier:

> *Fate gave the word, the arrow sped,*
> *And pierc'd my darling's heart;*
> *And with him all the joys are fled*
> *Life can to me impart.*
> *By cruel hands the sapling drops,*
> *In dust dishonour'd laid;*
> *So fell the pride of all my hopes,*
> *My age's future shade.*
> *The mother-linnet in the brake*
> *Bewails her ravish'd young;*
> *So I, for my lost darling's sake,*
> *Lament the live-day long.*
> *Death, oft I've feared thy fatal blow.*
> *Now, fond, I bare my breast;*
> *O, do thou kindly lay me low*
> *With him I love, at rest!* (1a).

Osler was a lifelong advocate of public health. During World War I, the American Red Cross conducted a study that linked trench fever to the louse, which in turn resulted in prompt delousing of the troops. In a review of the report, Osler writes, "One of the great shocks of the Great War has been that lousiness and the itch have had such an innings. We had become clean enough, at least in this country and America, to forget the enormous capabilities of the louse. The fate of armies has been decided through the devastation of diseases transmitted through it.... Burns puts a truer feeling in his famous poem "To a Louse": "Ye ugly, creepin, blastit wonner, Detested, shunn'd by saunt an' sinner. The reports of the English and American commissions should help enforce effective regulations...against the 'crowlin ferlies' that have done so much damage" (7). Indeed, "To a Louse" is regarded as one of Burn's masterpieces. He wrote the poem after spying a louse on a lady's bonnet at church:

> *Ha! whaur ye gaun, ye crowlin ferlie?*
> *Your impudence protects you sairly;*
> *I canna say but ye strunt rarely,*
> *Owre gauze and lace;*
> *Tho', faith! I fear ye dine but sparely*

On sic a place.
Ye ugly, creepin, blastit wonner,
Detested, shunn'd by saunt an' sinner,
How daur ye set your fit upon her—
Sae fine a lady?
Gae somewhere else and seek your dinner
On some poor body.
I wad na been surpris'd to spy
You on an auld wife's flainen toy;
Or aiblins some bit dubbie boy,
On's wyliecoat;
But Miss' fine Lunardi! fye!
                         How daur ye do't?
O wad some Power the giftie gie us
To see oursels as ithers see us!
It wad frae mony a blunder free us,
An' foolish notion:
What airs in dress an' gait wad lea'e us,
An' ev'n devotion! (1a).

Stories of Osler's exemplary bedside manner are legion. During the 1918 influenza pandemic, Osler made frequent house calls to see patients, including young Janet, who was dying. Knowing the end was near, Osler made a final visit:

> The most exquisite moment came one cold, raw, November morning...he mysteriously brought out from his inside pocket a beautiful red rose carefully wrapped in paper, and told how he had watched this last rose of summer growing in his garden and how the rose had called out to him as he passed by, that she wished to go along with him to see his little lassie. That evening we all had a fairy tea-party, at a tiny table by the bed, Sir William talking to the rose, his "little lassie" and her mother in a most exquisite way; and presently he slipped out of the room just as mysteriously as he had entered it, all crouched down on his heels; and the little girl understood that neither fairies nor people could always have the colour of a red rose in their cheeks, or stay as long as they wanted to in one place, but that they nevertheless would be very happy in another home and must not let the people they left behind, particularly their parents, feel badly about it: and the little girl understood and was not unhappy (8).

This touching story is reminiscent of Burns' poem, "A Rose-bud, by My Early Walk" and is a tender note upon which to close:

A Rose-bud by my early walk,
Adown a corn-enclosed bawk,
Sae gently bent its thorny stalk,
All on a dewy morning.
Ere twice the shades o' dawn are fled,
In a' its crimson glory spread,
And drooping rich the dewy head,
It scents the early morning.
Within the bush her covert nest
A little linnet fondly prest;
The dew sat chilly on her breast,
Sae early in the morning.
She soon shall see her tender brood,
The pride, the pleasure o' the wood,
Amang the fresh green leaves bedew'd,
Awake the early morning.
So thou, dear bird, young Jeany fair,
On trembling string or vocal air,
Shall sweetly pay the tender care
That tents thy early morning.
So thou, sweet Rose-bud, young and gay,
Shalt beauteous blaze upon the day,
And bless the parent's evening ray
That watch'd thy early morning (1a).

John Keats

The Poetry of John Keats, Immortal Apothecary-Poet

DAVID J. ELPERN

On the 100th anniversary of the poet's birth, Osler delivered an oration on Keats to the Johns Hopkins Historical Club (1). He begins with: "We have the very highest authority for the statement that 'The lunatic, the lover, and the poet/Are of imagination all compact'" (2). Six years earlier, Osler wrote, "Literature has often been enriched by those who have deserted medicine for the muses. But to drink deep draughts at Pierian springs unfits and when the thirst is truly divine should unfit a man for the worrying rounds of practice. It is shocking to think had Goldsmith secured the confidence of the old women in Bankside, Southwark, we should probably never have known the Vicar, Olivia or Tony Lumpkin. Still worse, to think of what we should have lost had Keats passed on from a successful career at Guy's to obtain even a distinguished position as a London Surgeon! Happily, such men soon kick free from the traces in which the average doctor trots to success" (3).

First as an apprentice to a surgeon, then as a dresser at St. Thomas' and Guy's Hospitals in London, Keats spent a total of six years in medical training. Six years of a life that spanned less than 26 years. What the world would have lost had his health improved and had he embraced medicine!

At age 20, while still a medical student, Keats wrote "On first looking into Chapman's Homer," a poem that resonated with Osler and is included in most anthologies of English poetry.

> *Much have I traveled in the realms of gold,*
> *And many goodly states and kingdoms seen;*
> *Round many western islands have I been*
> *Which bards in fealty to Apollo hold.*
> *Oft of one wide expanse had I been told*
> *That deep-browed Homer ruled as his demesne:*
> *Yet did I never breathe its pure serene*

Till I heard Chapman speak out loud and bold:
Then felt I like some watcher of the skies
When a new planet swims into his ken;
Or like stout Cortez, when with eagle eyes
He stared at the Pacific—and all his men
Looked at each other with a wild surmise—
Silent, upon a peak in Darien (5).

Keats spent seven years in medical studies. He nursed his mother and then his brother, Tom, as they were dying from tuberculosis. He knew full well what his chronic pharyngitis, cough, and hemoptysis augured. As a young man in his 20s, as one with much to experience and with a "teeming brain" he saw his days foreshortened in this sonnet:

When I have fears that I may cease to be
Before my pen has glean'd my teeming brain,
Before high piled books, in charact'ry,
Hold like rich garners the full-ripen'd grain;
When I behold, upon the night's starr'd face,
Huge cloudy symbols of a high romance,
And feel that I may never live to trace
Their shadows, with the magic hand of chance;
And when I feel, fair creature of an hour!
That I shall never look upon thee more,
Never have relish in the faery power
Of unreflecting love;—then on the shore
Of the wide world I stand alone, and think,
Till Love and Fame to nothingness do sink (6).

How poignant this! How nakedly honest! Words from the heart of one of the world's most gifted bards on looking into the void.

Osler quotes Lowell, "We reward the discoverer of an anesthetic for the body and make him a member of all the societies, but him who finds a nepenthe for the soul we elect into the small Academy of the Immortals" (4).

Keats did not attend Oxbridge nor any prestigious university. His gift came from a singular soul; a mystery we can but contemplate. Yet, his posthumous gift to us is among the dearest we as a culture have received from our luminaries in the annals of humanity.

Presciently, on his deathbed, Keats asked his physician, "How long is this posthumous life of mine to last?" Keats may have understood that it would endure until the last sentient person picks up an anthology of the world's great poetry. John Keats, dead at age 25 of phthisis, is with the Immortals. His translations of the world he witnessed resonate with us today and stand as monuments to the human spirit.

Ode on a Grecian Urn

Thou still unravish'd bride of quietness,
Thou foster-child of Silence and slow Time,
Sylvan historian, who canst thus express
A flowery tale more sweetly than our rhyme:
What leaf-fringed legend haunts about thy shape
Of deities or mortals, or of both,
In Tempe or the dales of Arcady?
What men or gods are these? What maidens loth?
What mad pursuit? What struggle to escape?
What pipes and timbrels? What wild ecstasy?

Heard melodies are sweet, but those unheard
Are sweeter; therefore, ye soft pipes, play on;
Not to the sensual ear, but, more endear'd,
Pipe to the spirit ditties of no tone:
Fair youth, beneath the trees, thou canst not leave
Thy song, nor ever can those trees be bare;
Bold Lover, never, never canst thou kiss,
Though winning near the goal—yet, do not grieve;
She cannot fade, though thou hast not thy bliss,
For ever wilt thou love, and she be fair!

Ah, happy, happy boughs! that cannot shed
Your leaves, nor ever bid the Spring adieu;
And, happy melodist, unwearièd,
For ever piping songs for ever new;
More happy love! more happy, happy love!
For ever warm and still to be enjoy'd,
For ever panting, and for ever young;
All breathing human passion far above,
That leaves a heart high-sorrowful and cloy'd,
A burning forehead, and a parching tongue.

Who are these coming to the sacrifice?
To what green altar, O mysterious priest,
Lead'st thou that heifer lowing at the skies,
And all her silken flanks with garlands drest?
What little town by river or sea-shore,
Or mountain-built with peaceful citadel,

Is emptied of its folk, this pious morn?
And, little town, thy streets for evermore
Will silent be; and not a soul, to tell
Why thou art desolate, can e'er return.

O Attic shape! fair attitude! with brede
Of marble men and maidens overwrought,
With forest branches and the trodden weed;
Thou, silent form! dost tease us out of thought
As doth eternity: Cold Pastoral!
When old age shall this generation waste,
Thou shalt remain, in midst of other woe
Than ours, a friend to man, to whom thou say'st,
"Beauty is truth, truth beauty,—that is all
Ye know on earth, and all ye need to know" (7).

To paraphrase Pope:

A little Keats is a paltry thing—
Drink deeper, hear the poet sing (8).

X.
To one who has been long in city pent,
'Tis very sweet to look into the fair
And open face of heaven,—to breathe a prayer
Full in the smile of the blue firmament.
Who is more happy, when, with hearts content,
Fatigued he sinks into some pleasant lair
Of wavy grass, and reads a debonair
And gentle tale of love and languishment?
Returning home at evening, with an ear
Catching the notes of Philomel,—an eye
Watching the sailing cloudlet's bright career,
He mourns that day so soon has glided by:
E'en like the passage of an angel's tear
That falls through the clear ether silently (9).

Masters of the Story

MIDDLEMARCH

A
STUDY OF PROVINCIAL LIFE

BY

GEORGE ELIOT

VOL. I.

WILLIAM BLACKWOOD AND SONS
EDINBURGH AND LONDON
MDCCCLXXI

George Eliot

Dr. Osler and Dr. Lydgate:
George Eliot's *Middlemarch*

CLAIRE HOOKER

At the time George Eliot wrote *Middlemarch*, the boundaries between history and fiction like those between science and romance, or medicine and various arts (1) were still blurred (2). We, who are the heirs of that era, have insisted upon distinguishing the soberly factual nature of history from the unhampered fantasies of fiction. Yet, there are occasions when we must admit that the multifaceted emotional and sensuous grasp of an era or a character that a good novelist can evoke may be at least as insightful as scholarly history. Eliot offers us this Gestalt-like experience, for she is unsurpassed in the ability to set her characters, with all their uniqueness of traits and doubts and actions and dreams, within the relentless current of the society that shaped them. And our compassion for them is increased by this broader and many-layered conception of them.

When *Middlemarch* was published to instant acclaim in 1871–1872, William Osler was in the midst of his medical education. *Middlemarch* was and is famous for its finely tuned portrayal of Dr. Lydgate, one of its two leading protagonists, and thus this "history" of a fictional physician may tell us something of what was passing in young Osler's heart and mind. And Osler was hardly unique in identifying with Lydgate, as his own note on the novel suggests: "If [he] was to ask the opinion of a dozen medical men upon the novel in which the doctor is best described . . . the majority will say, 'Middlemarch' " (3).

How could Osler not have helped identifying with Lydgate? Lydgate embodies the loftiest ideals and the happiest balances associated with medicine—working for social good rather than personal profit, combining intellectual activity with emotional and social engagement. Few student physicians then or now would like to admit to lesser ambitions. Additionally, the young Osler and the young Lydgate had many things in common: Like Lydgate, Osler was driven by intellectual passion (and one fortuitously stumbled upon, since the education of neither could have evoked it, and both were indifferent students as boys); like Lydgate, Osler similarly harbored hopes of building a "reputation" as a scientific discoverer; like Lydgate, he could not earn a living in research, and had to integrate his intellectual ambitions with his professional life. And, although leaving the bench for the bedside initially depressed him (4), like Lydgate, Osler is known for his care for his patients as unique individuals.

Consider the interest—perhaps the shock of identification—with which he must have read Eliot's famous introductory portrait of Tertius Lydgate:

> He was one of the rarer lads who early get a decided bent and make up their minds that there is something particular in life which they would like to do for its own sake, and not because their fathers did it. Most of us who turn to any subject with love remember some morning or evening hour when we got on a high stool to reach down an untried volume, or sat with parted lips listening to a new talker, or for very lack of books began to listen to the voices within, as the first traceable beginning of our love. Something of that sort happened to Lydgate. He was a quick fellow, and when hot from play, would toss himself in a corner, and in five minutes be deep in any sort of book that he could lay his hands on: if it were Rasselas or Gulliver, so much the better, but Bailey's Dictionary would do, or the Bible with the Apocrypha in it. Something he must read, when he was not riding the pony, or running and hunting, or listening to the talk of men. All this was true of him at ten years of age; he had then read through "Chrysal, or the Adventures of a Guinea," which was neither milk for babes, nor any chalky mixture meant to pass for milk, and it had already occurred to him that books were stuff, and that life was stupid. His school studies had not much modified that opinion, for though he "did" his classics and mathematics, he was not pre-eminent in them. It was said of him, that Lydgate could do anything he liked, but he had certainly not yet liked to do anything remarkable. He was a vigorous animal with a ready understanding, but no spark had yet kindled in him an intellectual passion; knowledge seemed to him a very superficial affair, easily mastered: judging from the conversation of his elders, he had apparently got already more than was necessary for mature life. Probably this was not an exceptional result of expensive teaching at that period of short-waisted coats, and other fashions which have not yet recurred. But, one vacation, a wet day sent him to the small home library to hunt once more for a book which might have some freshness for him: in vain! unless, indeed, he took down a dusty row of volumes with

gray-paper backs and dingy labels—the volumes of an old Cyclopaedia which he had never disturbed. It would at least be a novelty to disturb them. They were on the highest shelf, and he stood on a chair to get them down. But he opened the volume which he first took from the shelf: somehow, one is apt to read in a makeshift attitude, just where it might seem inconvenient to do so. The page he opened on was under the head of Anatomy, and the first passage that drew his eyes was on the valves of the heart. He was not much acquainted with valves of any sort, but he knew that valvae were folding-doors, and through this crevice came a sudden light startling him with his first vivid notion of finely adjusted mechanism in the human frame. A liberal education had of course left him free to read the indecent passages in the school classics, but beyond a general sense of secrecy and obscenity in connection with his internal structure, had left his imagination quite unbiased, so that for anything he knew his brains lay in small bags at his temples, and he had no more thought of representing to himself how his blood circulated than how paper served instead of gold. But the moment of vocation had come, and before he got down from his chair, the world was made new to him by a presentiment of endless processes filling the vast spaces planked out of his sight by that wordy ignorance which he had supposed to be knowledge. From that hour Lydgate felt the growth of an intellectual passion.

. . . [H]is his scientific interest soon took the form of a professional enthusiasm: he had a youthful belief in his bread-winning work, not to be stifled by that initiation in makeshift called his 'prentice days; and he carried to his studies in London, Edinburgh, and Paris, the conviction that the medical profession as it might be was the finest in the world; presenting the most perfect interchange between science and art; offering the most direct alliance between intellectual conquest and the social good. Lydgate's nature demanded this combination: he was an emotional creature, with a flesh-and-blood sense of fellowship which withstood all the abstractions of special study. He cared not only for "cases," but for John and Elizabeth, especially Elizabeth (5).

One of the delights of reading *Middlemarch* is its great pleasure in science—from the metaphors wrought from science that give breadth and illumination to the characters, to the intellectual depth a lay reader gains from the sudden attempt to recall and compare how blood circulates or paper serves instead of gold, a kind of theorizing that does not enter into the general tenor of one's life. As readers we feel how Eliot's era (beginning with Lydgate in 1829, and reaching its zenith with Osler) was revolutionized and captivated by science. Osler himself must have felt the reverberations of shock and excitement of the discoveries outlined in the novel—the impact

of the stethoscope and microscope and the opening up of the science of
pathology in consequence—and felt himself still connected to the intellectual events that animated Lydgate, to whom he was a scientific heir:

> Perhaps that was a more cheerful time for observers and theorizers
> than the present; we are apt to think it the finest era of the world when
> America was beginning to be discovered, when a bold sailor, even if
> he were wrecked, might alight on a new kingdom; and about 1829 the
> dark territories of Pathology were a fine America for a spirited young
> adventurer. Lydgate was ambitious above all to contribute towards
> enlarging the scientific, rational basis of his profession. The more he
> became interested in special questions of disease, such as the nature of
> fever or fevers, the more keenly he felt the need for that fundamental
> knowledge of structure which just at the beginning of the century had
> been illuminated by the brief and glorious career of Bichat, who died
> when he was only one-and-thirty, but, like another Alexander, left a
> realm large enough for many heirs. That great Frenchman first car-
> ried out the conception that living bodies, fundamentally considered,
> are not associations of organs which can be understood by studying
> them first apart, and then as it were federally; but must be regarded as
> consisting of certain primary webs or tissues, out of which the various
> organs—brain, heart, lungs, and so on—are compacted, as the vari-
> ous accommodations of a house are built up in various proportions of
> wood, iron, stone, brick, zinc, and the rest, each material having its
> peculiar composition and proportions. No man, one sees, can under-
> stand and estimate the entire structure or its parts—what are its frail-
> ties and what its repairs, without knowing the nature of the materials.
> And the conception wrought out by Bichat, with his detailed study
> of the different tissues, acted necessarily on medical questions as the
> turning of gas-light would act on a dim, oil-lit street, showing new con-
> nections and hitherto hidden facts of structure which must be taken
> into account in considering the symptoms of maladies and the action
> of medicaments. But results which depend on human conscience and
> intelligence work slowly, and now at the end of 1829, most medical
> practice was still strutting or shambling along the old paths, and there
> was still scientific work to be done which might have seemed to be
> a direct sequence of Bichat's. This great seer did not go beyond the
> consideration of the tissues as ultimate facts in the living organism,
> marking the limit of anatomical analysis; but it was open to another
> mind to say, have not these structures some common basis from which
> they have all started, as your sarsnet, gauze, net, satin, and velvet
> from the raw cocoon? Here would be another light, as of oxy-hydrogen,
> showing the very grain of things, and revising all former explanations.

Of this sequence to Bichat's work, already vibrating along many currents of the European mind, Lydgate was enamoured; he longed to demonstrate the more intimate relations of living structure, and help to define men's thought more accurately after the true order. The work had not yet been done, but only prepared for those who knew how to use the preparation. What was the primitive tissue? In that way Lydgate put the question—not quite in the way required by the awaiting answer; but such missing of the right word befalls many seekers. And he counted on quiet intervals to be watchfully seized, for taking up the threads of investigation—on many hints to be won from diligent application, not only of the scalpel, but of the microscope, which research had begun to use again with new enthusiasm of reliance. Such was Lydgate's plan of his future: to do good small work for Middlemarch, and great work for the world (6).

The parallels between the physicians do not end here. Like Lydgate, Osler was conscious of wanting to place his profession on a more scientific basis; like Lydgate (and in the manner of scientifically ambitious medical students of the era), he traveled to Europe, had his outlook revolutionized by scientific developments there, and returned to a provincial home with a zeal for reforming medical education and practice along scientific lines. Perhaps Lydgate's resolves even came to inform his own:

> There was another attraction in his profession: it wanted reform, and gave a man an opportunity for some indignant resolve to reject its venal decorations and other humbug, and to be the possessor of genuine though undemanded qualifications. He went to study in Paris with the determination that when he provincial home again he would settle in some provincial town as a general practitioner, and resist the irrational severance between medical and surgical knowledge in the interest of his own scientific pursuits, as well as of the general advance: he would keep away from the range of London intrigues, jealousies, and social truckling, and win celebrity, however slowly, as Jenner had done, by the independent value of his work. For it must be remembered that this was a dark period; and in spite of venerable colleges which used great efforts to secure purity of knowledge by making it scarce, and to exclude error by a rigid exclusiveness in relation to fees and appointments, it happened that very ignorant young gentlemen were promoted in town, and many more got a legal right to practice over large areas in the country. Also, the high standard held up to the public mind by the College of which gave its peculiar sanction to the expensive and highly rarefied medical instruction obtained by graduates of Oxford and Cambridge, did not hinder quackery from having an excellent time

of it; for since professional practice chiefly consisted in giving a great many drugs, the public inferred that it might be better off with more drugs still, if they could only be got cheaply, and hence swallowed large cubic measures of physic prescribed by unscrupulous ignorance which had taken no degrees. Considering that statistics had not yet embraced a calculation as to the number of ignorant or canting doctors which absolutely must exist in the teeth of all changes, it seemed to Lydgate that a change in the units was the most direct mode of changing the numbers. He meant to be a unit who would make a certain amount of difference towards that spreading change which would one day tell appreciably upon the averages, and in the mean time have the pleasure of making an advantageous difference to the viscera of his own patients. But he did not simply aim at a more genuine kind of practice than was common. He was ambitious of a wider effect: he was fired with the possibility that he might work out the proof of an anatomical conception and make a link in the chain of discovery....

He was not going to have his vanities provoked by contact with the showy worldly successes of the capital, but to live among people who could hold no rivalry with that pursuit of a great idea which was to be a twin object with the assiduous practice of his profession. There was fascination in the hope that the two purposes would illuminate each other: the careful observation and inference which was his daily work, the use of the lens to further his judgment in special cases, would further his thought as an instrument of larger inquiry. Was not this the typical pre-eminence of his profession? He would be a good Middlemarch doctor, and by that very means keep himself in the track of far-reaching investigation. On one point he may fairly claim approval at this particular stage of his career: he did not mean to imitate those philanthropic models who make a profit out of poisonous pickles to support themselves while they are exposing adulteration, or hold shares in a gambling-hall that they may have leisure to represent the cause of public morality. He intended to begin in his own case some particular reforms which were quite certainly within his reach, and much less of a problem than the demonstrating of an anatomical conception. One of these reforms was to act stoutly on the strength of a recent legal decision, and simply prescribe, without dispensing drugs or taking percentage from druggists. This was an innovation for one who had chosen to adopt the style of general practitioner in a country town, and would be felt as offensive criticism by his professional brethren. But Lydgate meant to innovate in his treatment also, and he was wise enough to see that the best security for his practicing honestly according to his belief was to get rid of systematic temptations to the contrary (7).

No portrait of a physician could be more endearing! Now, as then, many young physicians combine exalted intellectual ambitions with selfless, absorbed dedication in their work. Eliot reminds us of how noble such a manner of living is, with continually broadening mental horizons and the satisfactions of humanistic interaction and social good in one's daily work. But having reminded us of the preciousness of intellectual activity, Eliot invites us to speculate on the potential for Lydgate's success:

> We are not afraid of telling over and over again how a man comes to fall in love with a woman and be wedded to her, or else be fatally parted from her. Is it due to excess of poetry or of stupidity that we are never weary of describing what King James called a woman's "makdom and her fairnesse," never weary of listening to the twanging of the old Troubadour strings, and are comparatively uninterested in that other kind of "makdom and fairnesse" which must be wooed with industrious thought and patient renunciation of small desires? In the story of this passion, too, the development varies: sometimes it is the glorious marriage, sometimes frustration and final parting. And not seldom the catastrophe is bound up with the other passion, sung by the Troubadours. For in the multitude of middle-aged men who go about their vocations in a daily course determined for them much in the same way as the tie of their cravats, there is always a good number who once meant to shape their own deeds and alter the world a little. The story of their coming to be shapen after the average and fit to be packed by the gross, is hardly ever told even in their consciousness; for perhaps their ardor in generous unpaid toil cooled as imperceptibly as the ardor of other youthful loves, till one day their earlier self walked like a ghost in its old home and made the new furniture ghastly. Nothing in the world more subtle than the process of their gradual change! In the beginning they inhaled it unknowingly: you and I may have sent some of our breath towards infecting them, when we uttered our conforming falsities or drew our silly conclusions: or perhaps it came with the vibrations from a woman's glance.
>
> Does it seem incongruous to you that a Middlemarch surgeon should dream of himself as a discoverer? Most of us, indeed, know little of the great originators until they have been lifted up among the constellations and already rule our fates. But that Herschel, for example, who "broke the barriers of the heavens"—did he not once play a provincial church-organ, and give music-lessons to stumbling pianists? Each of those Shining Ones had to walk on the earth among neighbors who perhaps thought much more of his gait and his garments than of anything which was to give him a title to everlasting fame: each of them had his little local personal history sprinkled with small

temptations and sordid cares, which made the retarding friction of his
course towards final companionship with the immortals. Lydgate was
not blind to the dangers of such friction, but he had plenty of confidence in his resolution to avoid it as far as possible: being seven-and-
twenty, he felt himself experienced ... (8).

Osler saw Lydgate as both an example and a warning, writing that "the
warning in his case is plain—not to marry a fool with a pretty face!" and
adding, "Would that the Lydgates existed only in fiction!" (9). But to take
this view of the novel is to miss both its lesson and its intelligent complexity.
Lydgate loses his way as a result of his marriage, yes—but his marriage is
the further result of the "spots of commonness" that Eliot reminds us even
men of genius possess in their makeup.

> Among our valued friends is there not some one or other who is a little
> too self-confident and disdainful; whose distinguished mind is a little
> spotted with commonness; who is a little pinched here and protuber-
> ant there with native prejudices; or whose better energies are liable to
> lapse down the wrong channel under the influence of transient solicita-
> tions? (10).

In Lydgate, she tells us:

> that distinction of mind which belonged to his intellectual ardor, did
> not penetrate his feeling and judgment about furniture, or women, or
> the desirability of its being known (without his telling) that he was
> better born than other country surgeons (11).

Lydgate's commonplace prejudices about women, combined with his native
tender-heartedness, marries him to—well, Osler's description of her as "a
fool" loses the compassionate unfaltering insight that Eliot shows and that
physicians might ideally aspire to in their relations with their patients (and
others). It is the character of Rosamund's foolishness that is important, and
she is not so much a fool as a woman of intense egoism, with entirely worldly
ideas and ambitions, for whom Lydgate is merely a constellations of signs
that initially fit him for the chief role in her preconceived romance. In these
days where "reflective practice" is promoted, Eliot's work should inspire us
to scrutinize our own prejudices as thoroughly as possible. Osler himself,
among other things a man infected with notions of the importance of the
British Empire, was not free of them, though none cost him his career.

That Lydgate should find himself struggling to keep his grand aims in
view while increasingly hampered by his marriage and by financial difficulties that come to prey daily on his mind to the exclusion of science may
be the inevitable result of his character (both his faults and his virtues)

combined with the misconceptions and anxieties of the uneducated and prejudiced social milieu in which he lives and works. But the joylessness that pervades his life is no less poignantly described:

> Lydgate's discontent was much harder to bear: it was the sense that there was a grand existence in thought and effective action lying around him, while his self was being narrowed into the miserable isolation of egoistic fears, and vulgar anxieties for events that might allay such fears.... Only those who know the supremacy of the intellectual life— the life which has a seed of ennobling thought and purpose within it— can understand the grief of one who falls from that serene activity into the absorbing soul-wasting struggle with worldly annoyances (12).

The web of his difficulties eventually leads Lydgate to a moment of moral weakness and consequently to a situation that could cost him his professional life. He fails to fully investigate a death because he does not wish to question the financial benefactor on whom he has become wholly reliant. Modern investigators of clinical ethics and of lapses in medical professionalism will appreciate, as Osler undoubtedly did, the sympathetic complexity and subtle shades of gray with which Eliot describes this and other moral crises faced by the characters of *Middlemarch*. Lydgate's case is neither simply bad or illegal, but rather enmeshed in both the social context of the event and in the whisperings of his own heart and conscience. When the death occurs, he is conscious that he had recommended a treatment that, in keeping with his dedication to scientific innovation, was at odds with that of his fellow practitioners (for those interested, it was to shockingly *withhold* alcohol [then considered a great fortifier of the ill] from one suffering delirium tremens); that the outcome was in any case uncertain; and that there was little to be gained by offending either his benefactor by instituting an inquiry, when the outcome could not be changed.

> That was the uneasy corner of Lydgate's consciousness while he was reviewing the facts and resisting all reproach. If he had been independent, this matter of a patient's treatment and the distinct rule that he must do or see done that which he believed best for the life committed to him, would have been the point on which he would have been the sturdiest. As it was, he had rested in the consideration that disobedience to his orders, however it might have arisen, could not be considered a crime, that in the dominant opinion obedience to his orders was just as likely to be fatal, and that the affair was simply one of etiquette. Whereas, again and again, in his time of freedom, he had denounced the perversion of pathological doubt into moral doubt and had said— "the purest experiment in treatment may still be conscientious: my

business is to take care of life, and to do the best I can think of for it. Science is properly more scrupulous than dogma. Dogma gives a charter to mistake, but the very breath of science is a contest with mistake, and must keep the conscience alive." Alas! The scientific conscience had got into the debasing company of money obligation and selfish respects (13).

Physicians today will easily relate to the ways in which political and social pressures can influence both treatment decisions and the ways in which we rationalize our actions. Perhaps more importantly for the medical humanities, they, like other readers, will be uncomfortably compelled as Eliot reveals how immoral actions come into being. Very few people intend to act in a manner that is simply deceptive or base, as she writes of Mr. Bulstrode the banker, Lydgate's benefactor:

> He did not measure the quantity of diseased motive which had made him wish for Lydgate's good-will, but the quantity was none the less actively there, like an irritating agent in his blood. A man vows, and yet will not cast away the means of breaking his vow. He was simply a man whose desires had been stronger than his theoretic beliefs, and who had gradually explained the gratification of his desires into satisfactory agreement with those beliefs (14).

Lydgate—who, like another character in the novel and indeed, like us all—is not unmixedly adorable, has had mixed reviews over the years, sometimes being deplored as a kind of fool and buffoon himself (15). Yet, I find a potent heroism in the actions he manages to take at the times when he is most conscious of loss and failure. Some of these actions are prompted by his chosen role as Healer, which remains the centrally defining impulse of his life. In the worst crisis, he acts first as a physician:

> Bulstrode, after a moment's hesitation, took his hat from the floor and slowly rose, but he grasped the corner of the chair so totteringly that Lydgate felt sure there was not strength enough in him to walk away without support. What could he do? He could not see a man sink close to him for want of help. He rose and gave his arm to Bulstrode, and in that way led him out of the room; yet this act, which might have been one of gentle duty and pure compassion, was at this moment unspeakably bitter to him. It seemed as if he were putting his sign-manual to that association of himself with Bulstrode, of which he now saw the full meaning as it must have presented itself to other minds. He now felt the conviction that this man who was leaning tremblingly on his arm, had given him the thousand pounds as a bribe, and that somehow the treatment of Raffles had been tampered with from an evil

motive...Poor Lydgate, his mind struggling under the terrible clutch of this revelation, was all the while morally forced to take Mr. Bulstrode to the Bank, send a man off for his carriage, and wait to accompany him home (16).

Similarly, Lydgate struggles constantly to maintain the heartbeats of his marriage, as Eliot poignantly describes:

It was as if a fracture in delicate crystal had begun, and he was afraid of any movement that might make it fatal. His marriage would be a mere piece of bitter irony if they could not go on loving each other...The first great disappointment had been borne: the tender devotedness and docile adoration of the ideal wife must be renounced, and life must be taken up on a lower stage of expectation, as it is by men who have lost their limbs. But the real wife had not only her claims, she had still a hold on his heart, and it was his intense desire that the hold should remain strong. In marriage, the certainty, "She will never love me much," is easier to bear than the fear, "I shall love her no more" (17).

And we who live in the age of divorce may yet appreciate that there is both honor and admirable self-sacrifice in his choosing to make his life by placing Rosamund's happiness above any other concern.

In fact, throughout the novel, Eliot explores what moral failure and moral achievement might mean, and shows these to be measured, not simply by outcomes or even actions, but by an individual's struggle to overcome concern for self. The grand moments of the novel do not, after all, come from intellectual achievement, but from the achievement of selflessness. This is as true for the other characters as for Lydgate, for our capacity for ruining our own best purposes through our mistakes, illusions, and egoism is a central theme of the novel:

An eminent philosopher among my friends, who can dignify even your ugly furniture by lifting it into the serene light of science, has shown me this pregnant little fact. Your pier-glass or extensive surface of polished steel made to be rubbed by a housemaid, will be minutely and multitudinously scratched in all directions; but place now against it a lighted candle as a centre of illumination, and lo! the scratches will seem to arrange themselves in a fine series of concentric circles round that little sun. It is demonstrable that the scratches are going everywhere impartially and it is only your candle which produces the flattering illusion of a concentric arrangement, its light falling with an exclusive optical selection. These things are a parable. The scratches are events, and the candle is the egoism of any person now absent (18).

But—to echo the novel—why always Lydgate? I am doing physicians a dis-service by concentrating so exclusively on him, when the book tells the histories of another protagonist and three additional leading characters, sup-ported by four major figures and a host of minor ones. Each places humor-ous insight and benevolent analysis at the service of the humanistic reader. The same themes are woven through these twined histories: The ardent desire to work selflessly toward the social good struggling against the fetters of social convention; the difficulties and delights of finding a vocation, and of working in a modest plodding daily way at it in the service of larger ends; the wearing pressures and self-restraint imposed by marriage; the internal struggles of scholarship; and the importance of looking beyond our immedi-ate desires.

Osler loved Eliot's lightly dropped analogies and the poetry she infused into her observations of daily humdrum existence. That Osler often referred to or quoted her is testimony to the ways her observations had been caught and woven into his own life, and to the transient sense of grasping the ineffable—the fabric of existence, the meaning of our lives—that she pro-vides. Osler became the physician that Lydgate started out to be—and who knows but that it was the whispered repetition of Lydgate's story in his inmost heart that held him firmest to his purpose and encouraged him along the way.

Charles Dickens

Charles Dickens: *A Tale of Two Cities*

AUDREY SHAFER

Osler shared his admiration of Dickens' writings with others. As the founding president of the McGill Medical Society, he selected works of Dickens for literary readings at the Society's meetings (1). Osler briefly mentions Charles Dickens and the chronicle of his 1842 journey, *American Notes: For General Circulation*, in a biographical essay of Dr. Elisha Bartlett (*An Alabama Student*, 1908) (2). Yet Osler's most famous attribution vis-à-vis Dickens concerns a fictional work, *The Posthumous Papers of the Pickwick Club* (better known as *The Pickwick Papers*), the novel which launched Dickens' career. The character "Joe the fat boy" (3) was described by Osler and others as possessing the attributes of what later became known as obstructive sleep apnea and the Pickwickian Syndrome, including the triad of obesity, hypersomnolence, and signs related to chronic alveolar hypoventilation (4).

During Osler's medical training at McGill, despite the Province of Quebec's Anatomy Act, bodies for dissection were still being obtained illegally (5). The "resurrection men" portrayed by Charles Dickens in *A Tale of Two Cities*, particularly in the form of Mr. Jerry Cruncher, and the graveyard scene in which Mr. Cruncher's son, young Jerry, is tormented by the sight of his father and cronies' nefarious doings, provide a clue to why, of all of Dickens' works, *A Tale of Two Cities* was chosen by Osler to be included in the *Bibliotheca*. Osler's only comment on entry #4722, page 426 is the terse Mr. Cruncher, "resurrectionist" (6).

I prefer to think, however, the choice of Dickens as a recommended author lies more with an admiration of Dickens' exquisite prose, his unique brand of Victorian morality, and his observational acuity. To read Dickens, particularly when one is not obliged due to a looming deadline for a school expository essay, is to savor the words, dialogue, and narrative momentum. It is to meet, admire, despise, and delight in the many characters spun from the imagination of Dickens. The power and heft of the opening and closing of *A Tale of Two Cities* included in the excerpts below have led to these words entering not only into the canon of Western literature, but also popular culture.

The boy Dickens was forced to work in a blacking factory while his parents were held in debtor prison. These experiences gave Dickens a sympathy for the poor and downtrodden illustrated in his prose and demonstrated by his philanthropy, such as his support for Urania Cottage ("Home for Fallen Women") and Great Ormond Street Hospital for Children. In *A Tale of Two Cities*, the themes of sacrifice, loyalty, friendship, virtue and vice, and conflict and love emerge from Dickens' compassionate and perceptive eye.

A Tale of Two Cities continues to be a source of literary and intellectual discovery. For instance, the depiction of Dr. Alexandre Manette has recently been analyzed as an accurate portrayal of posttraumatic stress disorder (7).

Excerpts:

A Tale of Two Cities by Charles Dickens

Book the First—Recalled to Life

I The Period

IT WAS THE BEST OF TIMES, it was the worst of times, it was the age of wisdom, it was the age of foolishness, it was the epoch of belief, it was the epoch of incredulity, it was the season of Light, it was the season of Darkness, it was the spring of hope, it was the winter of despair, we had everything before us, we had nothing before us, we were all going direct to Heaven, we were all going direct the other way—in short, the period was so far like the present period, that some of its noisiest authorities insisted on its being received, for good or for evil, in the superlative degree of comparison only.

There were a king with a large jaw and a queen with a plain face, on the throne of England; there were a king with a large jaw and a queen with a fair face, on the throne of France. In both countries it was clearer than crystal to the lords of the State preserves of loaves and fishes, that things in general were settled for ever.

It was the year of Our Lord one thousand seven hundred and seventy-five (6).

III The Night Shadows

A WONDERFUL FACT TO REFLECT UPON, that every human creature is constituted to be that profound secret and mystery to every other. A solemn consideration, when I enter a great city by night, that every one of those darkly clustered houses encloses its own secret; that every room in every one of them encloses its own secret; that every beating heart in the hundreds of thousands of breasts there, is, in some of its imaginings, a secret to the heart nearest it! Something of the awfulness, even of Death itself, is referable to this. No more can I turn the leaves of this dear book that I loved, and vainly hope in time to read it all. No more can I look into the depths of this unfathomable water, wherein, as momentary lights glanced into it, I have had glimpses of buried treasure and other things submerged. It was appointed that the book should shut with a spring, for ever and for ever, when I had read but a page. It was appointed that the water should be locked in an eternal frost, when the light was playing on its surface, and I stood in igno- rance on the shore. My friend is dead, my neighbour is dead, my love, the darling of my soul, is dead; it is the inexorable consolidation and perpetuation of the secret that was always in that individuality, and which I shall carry in mine to my life's end. In any of the burial-places of this city through which I pass, is there a sleeper more inscrutable than its busy inhabitants are, in their innermost personality, to me, or than I am to them? (6).

V The Wine-Shop

A LARGE CASK OF WINE had been dropped and broken, in the street. The accident had happened in getting it out of a cart; the cask had tumbled out with a run, the hoops had burst, and it lay on the stones just outside the door of the wineshop, shattered like a walnut-shell.

All the people within reach had suspended their business, or their idle- ness, to run to the spot and drink the wine. The rough, irregular stones of the street, pointing every way, and designed, one might have thought, expressly to lame all living creatures that approached them, had dammed it into little pools; these were surrounded, each by its own jostling group or crowd, according to its size. Some men kneeled down, made scoops of their two hands joined, and sipped, or tried to help women, who bent over their shoulders, to sip, before the wine had all run out between their fingers. Others, men and women, dipped in the puddles with lit- tle mugs of mutilated earthenware, or even with handkerchiefs from women's heads, which were squeezed dry into infants' mouths; oth- ers made small mud-embankments, to stem the wine as it ran; others, directed by lookers-on up at high windows, darted here and there, to cut off little streams of wine that started away in new directions; others devoted themselves to the sodden and lee-dyed pieces of the cask, lick- ing, and even champing the moister wine-rotted fragments with eager relish. There was no drainage to carry off the wine, and not only did it all get taken up, but so much mud got taken up along with it, that there might have been a scavenger in the street, if anybody acquainted with it could have believed in such a miraculous presence. . . .

The wine was red wine, and had stained the ground of the narrow street in the suburb of Saint Antoine, in Paris, where it was spilled. It had stained many hands, too, and many faces, and many naked feet, and many wooden shoes. The hands of the man who sawed the wood, left red marks on the billets; and the forehead of the woman who nursed her baby, was stained with the stain of the old rag she wound about her head again. Those who had been greedy with the staves of the cask, had acquired a tigerish smear about the mouth; and one tall joker so besmirched, his head more out of a long squalid bag of a nightcap than in it, scrawled upon a wall with his finger dipped in muddy wine-lees—BLOOD.

The time was to come, when that wine too would be spilled on the street-stones, and when the stain of it would be red upon many there (6).

Book the Second—The Golden Thread

XIII The Fellow of No Delicacy

He [Sydney Carton] put her hand to his lips, and moved towards the door.

"Be under no apprehension, Miss Manette, of my ever resuming this conversation by so much as a passing word. I will never refer to it again. If I were dead, that could not be surer than it is henceforth. In the hour of my death, I shall hold sacred the one good remembrance and shall thank and bless you for it that my last avowal of myself was made to you, and that my name, and faults, and miseries were gently carried in your heart. May it otherwise be light and happy!"

He was so unlike what he had ever shown himself to be, and it was so sad to think how much he had thrown away, and how much he every day kept down and perverted, that Lucie Manette wept mournfully for him as he stood looking back at her.

"Be comforted!" he said, "I am not worth such feeling, Miss Manette. An hour or two hence, and the low companions and low habits that I scorn but yield to, will render me less worth such tears as those, than any wretch who creeps along the streets. Be comforted! But, within myself, I shall always be, towards you, what I am now, though outwardly I shall be what you have heretofore seen me. The last supplication but one I make to you, is, that you will believe this of me."

"I will, Mr. Carton."

"My last supplication of all, is this; and with it, I will relieve you of a visitor with whom I well know you have nothing in unison, and between whom and you there is an impassable space. It is useless to say it,

I know, but it rises out of my soul. For you, and for any dear to you, I would do anything. If my career were of that better kind that there was any opportunity or capacity of sacrifice in it, I would embrace any sacrifice for you and for those dear to you. Try to hold me in your mind, at some quiet times, as ardent and sincere in this one thing. The time will come, the time will not be long in coming, when new ties will be formed about you ties that will bind you yet more tenderly and strongly to the home you so adorn the dearest ties that will ever grace and gladden you. O Miss Manette, when the little picture of a happy father's face looks up in yours, when you see your own bright beauty springing up anew at your feet, think now and then that there is a man who would give his life, to keep a life you love beside you!"

He said, "Farewell!" said a last "God bless you!" and left her (6).

XIV The Honest Tradesman

"Father," said Young Jerry, as they walked along: taking care to keep at arm's length and to have the stool well between them: "what's a Resurrection-Man?"

Mr. Cruncher came to a stop on the pavement before he answered, "How should I know?"

"I thought you knowed everything, father," said the artless boy.

"Hem! Well," returned Mr. Cruncher, going on again, and lifting off his hat to give his spikes free play, "he's a tradesman."

"What's his goods, father?" asked the brisk Young Jerry.

"His goods," said Mr. Cruncher, after turning it over in his mind, "is a branch of Scientific goods."

"Persons' bodies, ain't it, father?" asked the lively boy.

"I believe it is something of that sort," said Mr. Cruncher.

"Oh, father, I should so like to be a Resurrection-Man when I'm quite growed up!"

Mr. Cruncher was soothed, but shook his head in a dubious and moral way. "It depends upon how you dewelop your talents. Be careful to dewelop your talents, and never to say no more than you can help to nobody, and there's no telling at the present time what you may not come to be fit for." As Young Jerry, thus encouraged, went on a few yards in advance, to plant the stool in the shadow of the Bar, Mr. Cruncher added to himself: "Jerry, you honest tradesman, there's hopes wot that boy will yet be a blessing to you, and a recompense to you for his mother!" (6).

Book the Third—The Track of a Storm

XV The Footsteps Die Out For Ever

ALONG THE PARIS STREETS, the death-carts rumble, hollow and harsh. Six tumbrils carry the day's wine to La Guillotine. All the devouring and insatiate Monsters imagined since imagination could record itself, are fused in the one realisation, Guillotine. And yet there is not in France, with its rich variety of soil and climate, a blade, a leaf, a root, a sprig, a peppercorn, which will grow to maturity under conditions more certain than those that have produced this horror. Crush humanity out of shape once more, under similar hammers, and it will twist itself into the same tortured forms. Sow the same seed of rapacious license and oppression over again, and it will surely yield the same fruit according to its kind. . . .

There is a guard of sundry horsemen riding abreast of the tumbrils, and faces are often turned up to some of them, and they are asked some question. It would seem to be always the same question, for, it is always followed by a press of people towards the third cart. The horsemen abreast of that cart, frequently point out one man in it with their swords. The leading curiosity is, to know which is he; he stands at the back of the tumbril with his head bent down, to converse with a mere girl who sits on the side of the cart, and holds his hand. He has no curiosity or care for the scene about him, and always speaks to the girl. Here and there in the long street of St. Honore, cries are raised against him. If they move him at all, it is only to a quiet smile, as he shakes his hair a little more loosely about his face. He cannot easily touch his face, his arms being bound. . . .

The clocks are on the stroke of three, and the furrow ploughed among the populace is turning round, to come on into the place of execution, and end. The ridges thrown to this side and to that, now crumble in and close behind the last plough as it passes on, for all are following to the Guillotine. In front of it, seated in chairs, as in a garden of public diversion, are a number of women, busily knitting. On one of the fore-most chairs, stands The Vengeance, looking about for her friend.

As The Vengeance descends from her elevation to do it, the tumbrils begin to discharge their loads. The ministers of Sainte Guillotine are robed and ready. Crash! A head is held up, and the knitting-women who scarcely lifted their eyes to look at it a moment ago when it could think and speak, count One.

The second tumbril empties and moves on; the third comes up. Crash! And the knitting-women, never faltering or pausing in their Work, count Two.

The supposed Evremonde descends, and the seamstress is lifted out next after him. He has not relinquished her patient hand in getting out, but still holds it as he promised.

He gently places her with her back to the crashing engine that constantly whirrs up and falls, and she looks into his face and thanks him.

"But for you, dear stranger, I should not be so composed, for I am naturally a poor little thing, faint of heart; nor should I have been able to raise my thoughts to Him who was put to death, that we might have hope and comfort here to-day. I think you were sent to me by Heaven."

"Or you to me," says Sydney Carton. "Keep your eyes upon me, dear child, and mind no other object."

"I mind nothing while I hold your hand. I shall mind nothing when I let it go, if they are rapid."

"They will be rapid. Fear not!" . . .

She goes next before him is gone; the knittingwomen count Twenty-Two.

"I am the Resurrection and the Life, saith the Lord: he that believeth in me, though he were dead, yet shall he live: and whosoever liveth and believeth in me shall never die."

The murmuring of many voices, the upturning of many faces, the pressing on of many footsteps in the outskirts of the crowd, so that it swells forward in a mass, like one great heave of water, all flashes away. Twenty-Three.

THEY SAID OF HIM, about the city that night, that it was the peacefullest man's face ever beheld there. Many added that he looked sublime and prophetic.

"It is a far, far better thing that I do, than I have ever done; it is a far, far better rest that I go to than I have ever known" (6).

Sir Arthur Conan Doyle

Osler and The Sherlock Holmes Stories

Thomas P. Duffy

Holmes is a little too scientific for my tastes—it approaches to cold-bloodedness. I could imagine his giving a friend a little pinch of the latest vegetable alkaloid, not out of malevolence, you understand, but simply out of a spirit of inquiry in order to have an accurate idea of the effects. To do him justice, I think that he would take it himself with the same readiness. He appears to have a passion for definite and exact knowledge. (Arthur Conan Doyle, *A Study in Scarlet*.)

It is somewhat a shame that Arthur Conan Doyle and William Osler were not part of one another's lives or at least not serious correspondents sharing the details of their personal and professional lives with one another. They had so much in common with similar backgrounds, rearing, and life trajectories. Both received classical educations with a healthy mix of scholarship and athletics under the close supervision of clergy. They were Victorian gentlemen and physicians with only a decade separating their births. Osler's Canadian medical schooling at Toronto and McGill was a model and extension of the education that Doyle received at the University of Edinburgh. Their circles almost certainly overlapped in professional realms and both men were aware of one another's writings. Osler was offered but rejected the prestigious Chair of Medicine at Edinburgh prior to his appointment as the Regius Professor at Oxford. Doyle made numerous lecturing trips to America where his popularity would have come to the notice of Osler. At a later period in Osler's life, he does allude to Conan Doyle's involvement with spiritualism but Sherlock Holmes does not make an appearance in his many lectures or conversations. They were both physicians but their professional paths diverged early on when Conan Doyle stopped practicing medicine and began his very successful life as a detective novelist.

They lived their lives on different continents but Osler was a frequent visitor to London (it was believed to be his favorite city) and lived in Oxford as the Regius Professor; Doyle had a lifelong infatuation with the Wild West and Americana. A fitting and important intersection in their lives occurred in the person and writings of a third author-physician, Oliver Wendell Holmes, who remained an inspiring presence for both men throughout their lives. Early in his medical career, Oliver Wendell Holmes had made an original scientific observation recognizing puerperal fever as an infectious disease, a discovery that saved countless women's lives. In spite of the medical repute and guaranteed prominence this discovery afforded him in medical circles, he left medicine for a writing career and went on to achieve even greater prominence as the author of such literary works as "The Chambered Nautilus" and "The Autocrat of the Breakfast Table." His career and the choices he made were the subject of an essay that Osler wrote for the January 1889 issue of the *Montreal Medical Journal*. The article grappled with a question that Osler must have asked of himself; which face of the coin, the arts or the sciences, represents the acme of accomplishment and fulfillment for an individual who is gifted as both writer and physician? It was Osler's belief, delivered in his characteristic Latinate oratorical style, that "to drink deep draughts at Pierian (the home of the Muses) springs unfits, and when the thirst is truly divine should unfit, a man for the worrying rounds of practice." The creative life of the physician ill serves the needs of patients while the needs of the patients may ill serve the flights of imagination necessary for creative writing. Osler's counsel was that while it may be well for a physician to have pursuits outside his profession, "it is dangerous for them to be too absorbing."

Osler cited Oliver Wendell Holmes, the Autocrat of the Breakfast Table, as the most conspicuous example of success in both fields although doctoring and writing were pursued sequentially at different periods in Holmes' life. Osler was curious as to how Holmes had successfully resolved this difficult choice between the pen and the stethoscope. He asked Holmes for his thoughts regarding this matter and what he identified as the challenges and rewards of the divergent pathways of his life choices. Holmes' reply must have come as a surprise to Osler who never wavered in his devotion to medicine and whose life was always inextricably defined by medicine. Holmes thought otherwise; he believed that his poetry "filled him with a better feeling, the highest state of mental exaltation which had ever been granted to him." A literary life gave him an even more noble satisfaction than the lifesaving labor of medicine and the beginning conquest of a major infectious disease. This was unlikely the answer that Osler anticipated, but it was a decision that would have filled Conan Doyle with delight since he made the same choice as Oliver Wendell Holmes to be a writer early in his medical career. Stories written during all-too-frequent lulls in his medical practice initially allowed Doyle to supplement his meager medical profits and to discover his gift for the craft of writing. He left the practice of medicine to swim in Osler's Pierian springs, in the same waters that brought great fulfillment to his predecessor Oliver Wendell Holmes. In a telling fashion, he demonstrated his admiration and affection for him by organizing a wreath-laying ceremony at Holmes' grave in Boston shortly after his death. Osler later participated in a similar tribute at the grave of Pierre Louis in Paris, the father of the clinical method in medicine who started the tradition in medicine that defined Osler's life in the profession. Those grave-side ceremonies paid testimony to the different life choices, aspirations, and commitments of Osler and Arthur Conan Doyle.

Holmes began his hold on Conan Doyle with the reading of Holmes' essays during Doyle's stint as ship surgeon on a West Africa voyage. His reverence for the man remained firm throughout his life with his admission that he had never so known and so loved a man whom he had never seen. It was likely that this profound admiration for a fellow physician and man of letters led Conan Doyle to give Sherlock Holmes his name. This literary baptism would make this surname more renowned for a British detective than the Boston Brahmin from whom it was copied. But it was another physician, Dr. Joseph Bell, upon whom the character of Sherlock Holmes was almost certainly based. While a medical student at the University of Edinburgh, Conan Doyle witnessed and learned the art of diagnosis from Dr. Bell who was one of the foremost medical teachers in Edinburgh when this city was the epicenter of medicine throughout the world. Bell deserved the epithet of "Renaissance" man with wide-ranging interests in and outside medicine. He had received an education in the classics that was near identical to the education that Conan Doyle had received (and similar to Osler's education at Trinity). He chose Conan Doyle to be his clerk in his surgical clinic, perhaps responding to a person who resonated with himself. There the future physician observed Bell's skills in medical diagnosis that would become the centerpiece of Sherlock Holmes' fame as a brilliant scientific detective. These same skills defined Osler's life and fame. Both Sherlock and Osler used their artful skills and craft to solve solutions to crime or disease. Sherlock's exploits as a scientific detective would have natural appeal for a man like Osler who created his own fictional alter ego, the prankster E. Y. Davis. Sherlock with his commanding panache was the perfect counterweight to the classical figures in the books that occupied Osler's night table.

The Holmes series resonated with Osler for another, more seductive, reason. Part of the mystique that has grown up around Sherlock Holmes is the blurring of his fictional being with a real person. Sherlock Holmes clubs throughout the world engage in this whimsical subterfuge and ersatz biographies add to the legend that Sherlock was a living character. This phenomenon is further exaggerated by a blurring of the line between the character and exploits of Sherlock Holmes and those of his creator, Arthur Conan Doyle. It becomes unclear where the authorial line of Doyle stops and the fictional character of Holmes starts. Arthur Conan Doyle is Sherlock Holmes and in a startling and eerie fashion, Sir William Osler would have recognized himself as an alter ego to the scientific consulting detective and diagnostician. Osler's Victorian restraints could be thrown off as he entered the foggy, London world of Sherlock Holmes. E. Y. Davis could move beyond childhood pranks and the devilish side of Osler could find release in the exploits of Sherlock Holmes. Adding to the seduction is how perfectly Osler embodied those qualities that Holmes believed were necessary to qualify as a "super" detective.

The skills involved in super detection were described by Holmes in his less than complementary assessment of his French counterpart, Detective du Villard, and his Scotland Yard colleagues in *A Study in Scarlet*. The three components necessary for the successful detective (and, by extension, for a physician) were knowledge, the power of observation, and the ability to reason by induction (1). Holmes was careful to define what kind of knowledge a detective must command. It was not that of the academic scholar and certainly not that of the dilettante. Holmes' knowledge was extensive and wide-ranging but it was not encyclopedic; he was purposely selective and idiosyncratic in his knowledge base. On the one hand, he possessed knowledge of the ashes and stubs of particular brands of cigars and cigarettes—a knowledge that might suggest a smoker's identity and indicate his presence at the site of a crime.

> He had even smoked there. I found the ash of a cigar, which my special knowledge of tobacco ashes enables me to pronounce as an Indian cigar. I have, as you know, devoted some attention to this, and written a little monograph on the ashes of 140 different varieties of pipe, cigar, and cigarette tobacco.
>
> *The Boscombe Valley Mystery* (2)

He recognized the particular color of earth coating a shoe that permitted him to surmise from where an individual suspect had traveled. On the other hand, he was purposely deficient in several areas of knowledge that he considered peripheral to a detective's work. In *A Study in Scarlet*, Holmes' ignorance is described as being "as remarkable as his knowledge. Of contemporary literature, philosophy, and politics, he appeared to know next to nothing."

Osler also had extensive knowledge in specific areas; he commanded medicine, classics, and bibliography but demonstrated little interest in theater, arts, or contemporary literature. He is described as not knowing of Walt Whitman when asked to see him in consultation; "he felt that Whitman's poetry was not for his pampered palate, accustomed to Plato, and Shakespeare and Shelley and Keats." Immersion in his musty archives filled with the classics and medical historiography may have prevented Osler from venturing into Whitman or Holmes' world. Both Osler and Conan Doyle acted as though there needed to be a division of knowledge into worthy or unworthy categories and this determined what facts were retained or forgotten. Holmes describes the brain as being like an attic with a large but not unlimited capacity to store facts; any new idea may necessitate displacement of other facts from the finite housing space available in the brain.

> I consider that a man's brain originally is like a little empty attic, and you have to stock it with such furniture as you choose...the skilful workman is very careful indeed as to what he takes into his brain-attic. He will have nothing but the tools which may help him in doing his work, but of these he has a large assortment, and all in the most perfect order....It is of the highest importance, therefore, not to have useless facts elbowing out the useful ones.
>
> *A Study in Scarlet* (3)

This belief may have had its origin for Holmes in the schooling that his creator Conan Doyle had received as a young man and may also explain his seemingly uncanny ability to retrieve the smallest details surrounding his clients' lives. Doyle's early education was in an English Jesuit boarding school where he was rigorously schooled in the classics and Latin and Greek languages on the model of medieval scholasticism. An additional year was spent in another Jesuit boarding school in Austria where he learned German and French. He describes translating Cicero into German in one of his frequent letters to his mother who had been educated in French boarding schools. Sherlock's observation that the brain is like an attic could have had its source in Doyle's schooling by the Jesuits. His teachers may have instructed him in a memory technique that has been part of Jesuit didactics for centuries (4). This technique involves envisioning the contents of the brain as occupying rooms in an imaginary house. One takes a mental walk through the rooms of this house and links facts-to-be remembered with specific items of furniture in the rooms. One recalls these stored facts by repeating the journey through the rooms and connecting the facts with the objects displayed. Sherlock describes a similar wandering in the housing of his brain in the act of recalling information from the attic of his mind. Sherlock's creator may have developed his superior memory by erecting homes with capacious rooms that initially housed Latin and Greek vocabulary but subsequently became the housing for the details important for a detective's work.

Osler's curriculum at Trinity College included the same classical emphasis as Doyle's schooling although Osler's early passion for biology resulted in a heavier emphasis upon natural science. His Latin Prose Composition books are initially filled with Latin phrases but they soon give way to detailed descriptions of biologic specimens. Memorization and concentration were skills and habits that were finely honed, praised, and rewarded for both men. The skills involved in learning languages would have advantaged both of them in the tasks of diagnosing and detecting in addition to facilitating learning of the medical vocabulary. These tasks have been likened to the process of translation where ideas and concepts from one language are translated into a second language. In medicine, the signs and symptoms of the patient are translated into the language of disease and illness; a similar configuration exists for the detective's readings of the clues of a case. The original contents of their attics were Latin and Greek words that were later replaced by medical and crime vocabulary. Those exercises in translating schoolboy languages were excellent rehearsals for the translational demands of diagnosis and detection. The neural networks and connections possessed a plasticity that was easily reconfigured for the new but not different demands of their subsequent careers.

Medicine was the career initially chosen both by Osler and Conan Doyle and their medical knowledge had a common source. They were schooled in the Edinburgh medical tradition with a firm commitment to the centrality of the patient's story and physical examination as the key to all medical diagnosis and learning. It was Osler's famous dictum that "it is a safe rule to have no teaching without a patient for a text and the best teaching is that taught by the patient himself." "Medicine is learned by the bedside and not in the classroom." It was this commitment to the importance of access to patients as texts that led Osler to believe that his greatest accomplishment had been the creation of a medical training program where students were admitted to the ward. This philosophy echoed Doyle's mentor, Dr. Joseph Bell, who believed that physicians had to be not only learned but also immensely attentive to all of the features of a patient. Diagnosis, he taught, was made not just by visual observation but by the employment of all of one's senses. His dictum was to not just look at a patient but feel him, probe him, listen to him, and even smell him. The similarity of Bell's stance vis-à-vis the patient and Sherlock Holmes' methods in solving a crime forcibly demonstrates the provenance of much of Conan Doyle's oeuvre. His remarkable command of arcane knowledge was displayed in his recognition of a tattoo's origin in *The Red Haired Man*:

> The fish that you have tattooed immediately above your right wrist could only have been done in China. I have made a small study of tattoo marks and have even contributed to the literature of the subject. That trick of staining the fishes' scales of a delicate pink is quite peculiar to China. When, in addition, I see a Chinese coin hanging from your watch chain, the matter becomes even more simple.
>
> *The Red Haired Man* (5)

Holmes possessed knowledge in rich amounts as an essential component of the trinity of attributes of the skilled detective or clinician. The second requirement is the skill of observation, the ability to recognize what escapes others, to observe what others merely see. This skill is magnified immensely when it is coupled with knowledge of what to look for and what the subject or object should look like. Analysis of the methods used by gifted clinicians, such as Osler at the bedside, reveals that the most important skill in assigning a patient to a disease category is so-called pattern-recognition. The physician elicits the details of a patient's illness and identifies any abnormalities on physical exam. The physician uses this data to retrieve from his large storehouse of previous patient encounters an image of a patient who demonstrates the findings found in the patient in question. The constellation of remembered signs and symptoms in the patient is the hook that allows the clinician to make the connection and the correct diagnosis. The trove of stored clinical pictures makes the link possible between the patient in question and a specific patient from the past. The clinical repertory performs an additional important function for the experienced diagnostician. Since he has witnessed the particular constellation of disease findings in a previous patient, he is aware of what constitutes the picture of a specific disease and what elements characterize a suspected illness. He relies not only upon what is present but also recognizes that when certain features are absent, a particular diagnosis is no longer tenable. This was the basis for Sherlock's solving the crime where the dog failed to bark in the night. "That was the curious incident," remarked Sherlock Holmes in *The Retired Colourman*. It was the absence of the dog's barking that was the important clue to the crime's perpetrator.

The skilled clinician and detective must train their eyes and other senses to attentively gaze upon the portrait or canvas of the patient and his surroundings in the act of diagnosing and detecting. Both would be advantaged if they had mastered a technique originally developed in the late 19th century by an Italian physician, Giovanni Morelli; this was a technique likely known to Conan Doyle who was a frequent museumgoer and the son of an artist. The so-called Morelli method was originally a technique used for correct authentication and attribution of old master paintings. It remains an important method that is still used today to help distinguish originals from copied paintings. Morelli recognized that the obvious characteristics of a painter's style, the so-called major details, are most easily copied by a forger. One needs focus upon the minor details, those least significant in the style typical of the painter's own school—the fingernails, ear lobes, and the shapes of fingers and toes (6). Morelli, anticipating Sherlock Holmes, identified the ear peculiar to Botticelli and other artists and using this method made several new attributions throughout Europe. An Italian art historian, Enrico Castelnouva, has drawn a parallel between the Morelli method and those used by Sherlock Holmes to discover clues unnoticed by others. A striking example of this parallel is contained in Holmes' *The Cardboard Box*:

> He paused, and I was surprised, on glancing round to see that he was staring with singular intentness at the lady's profile. Surprise and satisfaction were both for an instant to be read upon his eager face.... As a medical man, you are aware, Watson, that there is no part of the body which varies so much as the human ear. In last year's Anthropological Journal you will find two short monographs from my pen upon the subject. I had, therefore, examined the ears in the box with the eyes of an expert and had carefully noted their anatomical peculiarities. Imagine my surprise, then, when on looking at Miss Cushing I perceived that her ear corresponded exactly with the female ear which I had just inspected. There was the same shortening of the pinna, the same broad curve of the upper lobe, the same convolution of the inner cartilage.
>
> *The Cardboard Box* (7)

Holmes considered attention to details as one of the most significant detective skills.

> Never trust to general impressions, my boy, but concentrate yourself upon details.
>
> *A Case of Identity* (8)

> By an examination of the ground I gained the trifling details which I gave to that imbecile Lestrade, as to the personality of the criminal.

But how did you gain them? (9). You know my method. It is founded upon the observation of trifles.

The Boscombe Valley Mystery (10)

This echoes a truism in medicine where the secret to a diagnosis is often in the details. Illness is described as announcing itself in small parentheses; it is in examining the patient for the minor detail and listening to the patient for the minor clue that the seasoned clinician arrives at the correct diagnosis. One of Osler's diagnostic coups was an excellent example of this ability. He is described as making a diagnosis of situs inversus on simple examination of a naked man. The diagnosis of this condition where there is a reversed position of the body organs was based on Osler's recognition that the man's right testicle was lower than the left, a subtle finding that is at variance with the normal positioning of the testes. This acumen required not only attention to detail but also the knowledge that only a rare clinician commands. Osler had described the cardiac manifestations of situs inversus in a scientific publication; this was likely the hook that prepared him to discern a finding that would certainly escape others.

Knowledge and observation are the basis from which the detective and physician must infer the proper conclusions. This skill of inference, which Sherlock Holmes and William Osler unquestionably possessed, requires an ability to reason not only forward, what will be the effect down the line of certain actions, but also to reason backward to identify what has given rise to the present situation. It is sometimes an intuitive leap but it is more than guesswork (11). Sherlock warns that one must eliminate all other possibilities for a crime before indicting a final cause. It also necessitates not leaping to a false conclusion on the basis of inadequate evidence, the so-called trigger phenomenon in clinical reasoning that is a frequent cause of errors in diagnosis.

It is a capital mistake to theorize before one has data. Insensibly one begins to twist facts to suit theories, instead of theories to suit facts.

A Scandal in Bohemia (12)

The process requires more than simple adherence to the rules; it requires a leap beyond the rules and some individuals like Osler and Sherlock Holmes appear particularly gifted in this regard. It is elementary for Sherlock Holmes but one needs ask what is this gift that he possessed and demonstrated with such bravado?

Cognitive psychologists have popularized the concept of the so-called Theory of Mind or mindfulness to describe the human ability to draw inferences from others' behaviors or statements. This mental activity permeates all of our interactions with others. It is so basic that its existence was overlooked or ignored in the past. It has more recently received attention because of its absence in autistic children. Its absence is thought to be the major reason for the marked social interactive difficulties of such children. It is as though they cannot read the text of their daily encounters. Gifted clinicians and detectives with heightened mindfulness on the other hand would have perfect pitch for analyzing clues, for interpreting signs, and for reading emotions. Mindfulness cultivates an empathetic stance of putting oneself in the patient or victim's shoes. It becomes a trip to one's curiosity so that the physician or detective may ask a critical question that would otherwise go unasked.

> You'll get results...by always putting yourself in the other fellow's place, and thinking what you would do yourself. It takes some imagination, but it pays.
>
> *The Retired Colourman* (13)

It is an ability that can be learned and perfected although some individuals appear to have a greater facility in this regard. This is the gift that Sherlock Holmes (and William Osler) may have possessed in disproportionate amounts, which positioned them to find elementary what others found difficult or impossible to interpret. Sherlock had it; Watson was not so gifted. This was a major source of Sherlock's friendly, successful intimidation of the frequently flustered physician.

Sherlock demonstrated his extraordinary ability to read another's thoughts when he described to Watson what he had surmised in gazing upon his dozing face.

> "What is this, Holmes?" I cried. "This is beyond anything which I could have imagined."...But I have been seated quietly in my chair, and what clues can I have given you.
>
> "You do yourself an injustice. The features are given to man as the means by which he shall express his emotions, and yours are faithful servants."
>
> "Do you mean to say that you read my train of thoughts from my features?"
>
> "Your features, and especially your eyes."
>
> *The Resident Patient* (14)

In *The Boscombe Valley Mystery*, he uses the appearance of a man's beard to describe his shaving habits and military neatness. He uses this analysis "as a trivial example of observation and inference. Therein lies my métier, and it is just possible that it may be of some service in the investigation that lies before us."

Knowledge, observation, and reasoning constituted the trinity of skills and abilities that Sherlock Holmes considered necessary for the gifted detective. Osler would have added hard work as an essential foundation for this trinity and the finding of pleasure in this work. Holmes echoed these sentiments with his frequent acknowledgment that his work was not only the source of pleasure but also the cause of mental exaltation.

Osler also identified his trinity of qualities that help guarantee success as a physician: the art of detachment, the virtue of method, and the quality of thoroughness. Just as Osler possessed the qualities of a super detective, Holmes possessed the trinity that Osler posited as necessary for the physician. Method and thoroughness were central to Holmes' success as a detective and he was firmly committed to detachment as an essential component of his detective wares. In *The Sign of Four*, Holmes states "It is of the first importance," he said, "not to allow your judgment to be biased by personal qualities. A client is to me a mere unit—a factor in a problem."

Holmes bias is a more exaggerated form of detachment than Osler's fabled aequanimitas and his recommendation of detached-concern in the physician–patient relationship. Sherlock was content to behave somewhat like an automaton; his well-advertised misogyny has been attributed to his fear that any emotional engagement with a woman would threaten his mental powers and concentration. Osler was certainly not of the same mind and had a loving marriage that lasted for several decades. Osler's detachment was more tempered; it was his advice to remain detached but not to the point of aloofness, and to stay concerned but not to the point of anxiety. Careful attention to this tension in Osler's life fostered his acquanimitas; it was not a posture that seemed to suit Sherlock's way of life.

The reach and influence of both Osler and Doyle continue to the present. Osler's *The Principles and Practice of Medicine* became the Bible of medical knowledge for generations of physicians; Conan Doyle's fictional detective has continued to enchant more and more generations of readers, young and old, with tales of evil men and dastardly events. The sources of their gifts and accomplishments are many but certainly there is a common fount for their lively minds and imaginations. Both men were omnivorous readers and bibliophiles throughout their lives. Osler bequeathed a listing of a bedside library for physicians that was mainly composed of "classical" authors. Doyle dallied in the same pastures; Holmes was never without his book of Petrarch poems, a behavior that would have endeared him to Osler. But Doyle's eminence as a writer of detective-fiction might lead his readers to assume that his command and breadth of literature were limited to this genre, that his literary tastes were lightweight and not on the exalted plane of Osler's readings. It is not well known that he authored a book, *Through the Magic Door*, which is a delightful broad-ranging tour of his favorite authors and stories. His choices are richer in variety than Osler's; they include the classics but also more modern authors, such as Sir Walter Scott, Rudyard Kipling, and, of course, Oliver Wendell Holmes. His favorite detective (upon whom he modeled Holmes) was Inspector Dupin, a creation of Edgar Allen Poe. Cowboys and Indians enchanted him throughout his life and Bret Harte's short stories of the gold rush were favorites. Echoing his own life and his service in the Boer War, adventure stories of Arctic and Antarctic exploration, and Napoleon's military memoirs took up a large amount of space on his bookshelf. It is surprising that Doyle was as well-read as Osler even though Osler was so learned as to be chosen President of the British Philosophical Society. The explanation for Doyle's breadth in literature may reside in the choice he made earlier in his life. Doyle chose to become a writer and it is a truism that no one writes well who doesn't read well. Osler, on the other hand, never strayed from the path and calling of medicine—he was a serious reader but the majority of his texts were the stories and bodies of his patients. He heeded his own advice that the patient is the most important text for the physician, accompanied by reading in medicine and the great classical texts of his bedside library. He was firm in his belief throughout his life that, "To study the phenomena of disease without books is to sail an uncharted sea; while to study books without patients is not to go to sea at all."

In Harvey Cushing's moving eulogy for Osler, he takes solace in imagining that Osler's spirit has now encountered the spirits of the illustrious men of medicine—Linacre, Harvey, and Sydenham—old and young, of former and modern times. It would seem fitting for that circle to be expanded to include everyone's favorite detective, Arthur Conan Doyle. Not only would there be sharing of his books and stories, but a whole new generation of detecting and diagnosing could also take place. Who knows what intrigue and schemes will be unearthed under the grand dome of Hopkins?

Sarah Orne Jewett

The Country Doctor and His Imperturbable Apprentice

LIVA H. JACOBY

We know Sir William Osler as having been a formidable mentor much like Dr. Leslie, the doctor in *A Country Doctor* by Sarah Orne Jewett. Osler would have appreciated and enjoyed an apprentice like Anna Prince, the young heroine of the story. Nan, as she is called, is portrayed as an eager student of the practice and art of medicine as well as a passionate advocate of the profession as a true calling. The love with which Anna relates to medicine and the characteristics that she embodies echoes that of Osler.

Early in the story, the reader is introduced to the therapeutic behavior of a physician when Nan's mother, Adeline, succumbs to tuberculosis in her mother's house. As Dr. Leslie enters the house " ...the benefaction of his presence is felt by everyone." Those present realize that "there is something singularly self-reliant and composed about him; one feels that he was the wielder of great powers over the enemies, disease and pain...." This portrayal of the comforting doctor reflects Osler's ideal of imperturbability as "a divine gift, a blessing to the possessor, a comfort to all who come in contact with him" (1). Conveying the notion of this healing power of the medical practitioner to today's physicians and students is something that Osler would have deemed essential. At a time when the medical profession is criticized for losing this significant trait, Jewett's *A Country Doctor* remains a compelling story to rekindle the passion for healing among doctors.

We come to know Dr. Leslie and Nan as residents of Oldfields, a small town in Maine during the late 1800s. Dr. Leslie has been the doctor for the townspeople and the surroundings for several decades. Nan, the orphan of a young couple, is first taken in by her grandmother and after her death becomes the ward of Dr. Leslie. We meet them both at the deathbed of Nan's mother—a crucial moment when their lives become intertwined. Almost as if by osmosis, Nan becomes enthralled by what she learns from and observes with her surrogate father and the depiction of Nan's growing love of medicine is the essence of the story.

Dr. Leslie's life and work are imbued with the belief that medicine is a "most delightful profession." In his conversation with an old classmate about illness, health, and the practice of medicine, they discuss the significance for doctors to understand the role of "the life power" in illness. In this we recognize current ideas of the importance of treating not only the disease but also caring for the person with the disease. This was Osler's message as well when he referred to physicians needing "a clear head and a kind heart" (2) in the face of "the misfortunes of our neighbors" (3). Nan learned from Dr. Leslie to see the humanity both in the physician and in the patient—the same perspective that Osler's students learned from him.

While Dr. Leslie is very attached to his books, he is well aware that practical wisdom and the ability to serve as the "soul's instrument" are necessary to be able to "balance the whole system, and aid nature to make the sick man well again." We easily imagine how Osler would have felt at home in Dr. Leslie's cozy study next to "his beloved library shelves," discussing the meaning of healing and the need to arrive at a broader understanding of illness and health. As he did in his own days, he would have been eager to share the insights about good doctoring generated in those discourses with physicians and trainees alike.

Today we lament what is said to be diminishing idealism and altruism among medical professionals and, with this, a shortage of role models for learners at the bedside. Sara Jewett shows an uncanny gift for prediction when she has Dr. Leslie reflect that "to excel in one's work becomes more and more a secondary motive; to do a great deal and be well paid for it ranks first." As an antidote, Osler would urge today's doctors and students to let them be inspired by the strength of Nan's convictions about the noble nature of the profession. Similarly, he would want readers of this book to learn from Nan's indomitable spirit when defending her choice of the profession in the face of rebuke by those around her. When confronted by comments like "nonsense," "a silly notion," and "unnatural" about her decision to enter a man's world, Nan remains steadfast, stating that she cannot "break faith with my duty." When refusing a lover's plea to marry him, she asserts "I don't know why God should have made me a doctor...but I see the blessedness of such a useful life...and am very thankful for such a trust."

Nan exemplifies the mental equilibrium and "cheerful equanimity" that Osler extolled as virtues for doctors to strive toward. While on an outing, she corrects a man's dislocated shoulder with "unwonted composure" and such confidence that her male friend "had not a word to say."

How can we not be moved by Nan's boldness and devotion and by her belief in having been given a gift by God to become a doctor? And while imbuing the profession with a religious dimension is apt not to resonate with most physicians today, Nan's idealistic spirit and high aims convincingly convey that:

> Nobody sees people as they are and finds the chance to help poor humanity as a doctor does. The decorations and deceptions of character must fall away before the great realities of pain and death. The secrets of many hearts and homes must be told to this confessor, and sadder ailments than the text-books name are brought to be healed by the beloved physicians. Teachers of truth and givers of the laws of life, priests and ministers—all these professions are joined in one with the gift of healing, and are each part of the charge that a good doctor holds in his keeping (4).

As teachers and mentors of students of medicine, it remains our duty to uphold Nan's visions depicted with so much sensitivity by Sarah Jewett and to share and emphasize the meaning of the "good doctor" with students in the classroom and at the bedside. Osler did no less in his days and would disseminate the book widely for this purpose today; not doing so would to him mean leaving students to "sail an uncharted sea..." (5).

An excerpt, about that country doctor:

> Dr. Leslie had somewhat unwillingly undertaken the country practice which had grown dearer to him with every year, but there were family reasons why he had decided to stay in Oldfields for a few months at least, and though it was not long before he was left alone, not only by the father and mother whose only child he was, but by his wife and child, he felt less and less inclination to break the old ties and transplant himself to some more prominent position of the medical world. The leisure he often had at certain seasons of the year was spent in the studies which always delighted him, and little by little he gained great repute among his professional brethren. He was a scholar and a thinker in other than medical philosophies, and most persons who knew anything of him thought it a pity that he should be burying himself alive, as they were pleased to term his devotion to his provincial life. His rare excursions to the cities gave more pleasure to other men than to himself, however, in these later years, and he laughingly proclaimed himself to be growing rusty and behind the times to Dr. Ferris, who smiled indulgently, and did not take the trouble to contradict so untrue and preposterous an assertion.

If one man had been a stayer at home; a vegetable nature, as Dr. Leslie had gone on to say, which has no power to change its locality or to better itself by choosing another and more adequate or stimulating soil; the other had developed the opposite extreme of character, being by nature a rover. From the medical school he had entered at once upon the duties of a naval appointment, and after he had become impatient of its routine of practice and its check upon his freedom, he had gone, always with some sufficient and useful object, to one far country after another. Lately he had spent an unusual number of consecutive months in Japan, which was still unfamiliar even to most professional travelers, and he had come back to America enthusiastic and full of plans for many enterprises which his shrewd, but not very persistent brain had conceived. The two old friends were delighted to see each other, but they took this long-deferred meeting as calmly as if they were always next-door neighbors. It was a most interesting thing that while they led such different lives and took such apparently antagonistic routes of progression, they were pretty sure to arrive at the same conclusion, though it might appear otherwise to a listener who knew them both slightly (4).

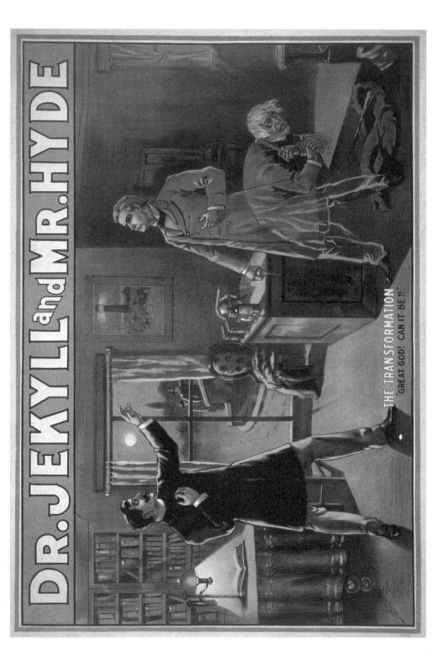

DR. JEKYLL and MR. HYDE

THE TRANSFORMATION.
"GREAT GOD! CAN IT BE !!"

Robert Louis Stevenson

The Body Snatchers and
The Strange Case of Dr. Jekyll and Mr. Hyde

MARTHA STODDARD HOLMES

Robert Louis Balfour Stevenson and William Osler present a fascinating contrast. Both were charismatic, idolized men, though one was a rebel against convention and bourgeois hypocrisy who spent most of his brief life in adventurous transit and the other was a model of moral and professional stability. Born one year apart, they never met, though their lives sometimes coincided in location and content: While Osler studied medicine in London in the 1870s, Stevenson skipped his law classes in Edinburgh; both visited leper colonies in the spring and summer of 1889. Stevenson's fiction might seem an ironic choice for Osler's library, given its gallery of fictional physicians gone terribly wrong: the medical student who ends up a grave-robber, his sociopathic supervisor, and, above all, the psychically split Henry Jekyll, who uses pharmacology to create a physical body for his repressed and murderous desires, seem anti-Oslers, extreme failures to follow his counsel on living simply, moderately, and with balance.

With all these portraits, however, Stevenson weaves a cautionary tale that complements Osler's advice and example to his students and colleagues by showing the perils of doing otherwise. Further, as a lifelong patient Stevenson wrote many of his works "in bed, in dreary 'health-resorts,' in the intervals of sharp attacks" of lung hemorrhage (1). Stevenson also generated several passionate nonfiction texts in Osler's library that capture the very best of the art of medicine, from the comfort the busy general practitioner brings to the bedside to the extreme self-sacrifice of the missionary who gives his life up to the care of the stigmatized sick.

The Body-Snatcher, first published as an extra Christmas number of *Pall Mall* in 1894, is based on the Burke and Hare grave-robbing case of 1827–1828 in Edinburgh, Stevenson's birthplace. While Osler comments that the tale is "unfairly told towards Knox, the great anatomist," Stevenson's emphasis is not on the surgeon-lecturer in charge (Mr. K—an obvious reference to Dr. Robert Knox) but on a morally flaccid medical student who gets caught in the middle of the traffic in corpses in the days before the Anatomy Act of 1832, a time when (as Osler notes) "the public compelled the schools to connive at the dirty work of the resurrectionists" (2). The narrative works retrospectively, beginning with Fettes, "an old drunken Scotchman" the locals nickname "The Doctor" because he "had been known, upon a pinch, to set a fracture or reduce a dislocation." When Macfarlane, a "great rich London doctor" visits the town, Fettes accosts him with their shared troubled past, the aftermath of which has been Macfarlane's success and his dissolution (3). Later, Fettes narrates how as a promising young medical student who had acquired favor with Mr. K—an anatomist then "at the top of his vogue" (4), he becomes second theater/lecture-room demonstrator and responsible for receiving cadavers for the dissecting-room. The surprisingly fresh-looking corpses he sees at a time when "the raw material of the anatomists kept perpetually running out" (5) does not trouble Fettes, because he is

> incapable of interest in the fate and fortunes of another, the slave of his own desires and low ambitions. Cold, light, and selfish in the last resort, he had that modicum of prudence, miscalled morality, which keeps a man from inconvenient drunkenness or punishable theft. He coveted, besides, a measure of consideration from his masters and his fellow-pupils, and he had no desire to fail conspicuously in the external parts of life. Thus he made it his pleasure to gain some distinction in his studies, and day after day rendered unimpeachable eye-service to his employer, Mr. K-. For his day of work he indemnified himself by nights of roaring, blackguardly enjoyment; and when that balance had been struck, the organ that he called his conscience declared itself content (6).

Fettes' comfortable hypocrisy is enabled by the philosophy of his teacher:

> It was the policy of Mr. K- to ask no questions in his dealings with the trade. "They bring the body, and we pay the price," he used to say, dwelling on the alliteration—"QUID PRO QUO." And, again, and somewhat profanely, "Ask no questions," he would tell his assistants, "for conscience' sake" (7).

When Fettes takes in a fresh corpse he recognizes as a young woman (possibly a prostitute) he had seen the day before in robust health, he is distressed enough to consult the first demonstrator, "Toddy" Wolfe Macfarlane, "a high favorite among all the reckless students, clever, dissipated, and unscrupulous to the last degree," who both confirms Fettes' suspicions and suggests that probably all their cadavers are murder victims (9). Macfarlane pushes his junior along a path of escalating ethical challenges by getting him to accept and pay for a cadaver Fettes recognizes as a man who had harassed Macfarlane the night before. Like so many of Stevenson's wrongdoers, Fettes has a moment of moral clarity that soon passes:

> A horrible sense of blackness and the treachery of fate seized hold upon the soul of the unhappy student. "My God!" he cried, "but what have I done? and when did I begin?" ... He saw, with inexpressible dismay, that there was no limit to his weakness, and that, from concession to concession, he had fallen from the arbiter of Macfarlane's destiny to his paid and helpless accomplice. He would have given the world to have been a little braver at the time, but it did not occur to him that he might still be brave (8).

Thus brilliantly, Stevenson anatomizes not only how we can through simple inattention or laziness become enmeshed in the most serious moral and legal crimes, and, even more so, how the work of rationalization and denial proceed (the idlers in "The Suicide Club," similarly, end up enmeshed in crimes of life and death by accident). Fettes does not suddenly change from any of these epiphanies; once he joins McFarlane in literally digging up a grave, it is only a supernatural event that ends his involvement, a moral growth resulting, ironically, in his dissolution into an alcoholic idler.

Osler writes that *The Body-Snatcher* is "a good story all the same," despite its implication of Knox. Indeed, it is a good story for physicians in particular. By making his Burke and Hare figures medical students, Stevenson dramatizes the psychological dilemma of the young professional, especially the one without a real sense of drive, focus, or purpose. Medical professionals in any era may be asked for complicity with morally shaky "scut work," whether through silence or action.

Along with *The Body-Snatcher*, the most memorable fictional physician in Stevenson's corpus is of course *The Strange Case of Dr. Jekyll and Mr. Hyde*, which dramatizes more extensively the problem of self-division and hypocrisy. As Dr. Henry Jekyll states the case:

> I saw that, of the two natures that contended in the field of my consciousness, even if I could rightly be said to be either, it was only because I was radically both; and from an early date, even before the course of

my scientific discoveries had begun to suggest the most naked possibility of such a miracle, I had learned to dwell with pleasure, as a beloved day-dream, on the thought of the separation of these elements. If each, I told myself, could but be housed in separate identities, life would be relieved of all that was unbearable; the unjust delivered from the aspirations might go his way, and remorse of his more upright twin; and the just could walk steadfastly and securely on his upward path, doing the good things in which he found his pleasure, and no longer exposed to disgrace and penitence by the hands of this extraneous evil (9).

While Jekyll and Hyde focuses on the separation of two limited concepts of "good" and "evil," the narrative nonetheless speaks to the situation of the white-coat wearer, all too likely to be taken for a god and thus all too likely to feel that there is no way to avow his or her private humanity. Surely Osler, the revered physician, experienced the strain of having thus demanding a public persona to perform. Jekyll's solution is a failure and a horror in ways that resonate for medical professionals: like *The Body-Snatcher*, *The Strange Case* dramatizes the difficulty of evolving and enacting an ethical self as a practitioner in an increasingly complex terrain of ethical challenges—and the grave dangers of trying to build such a self by compartmentalization or repression.

While these fictional physicians dramatize the worst professional behaviors, Stevenson's nonfiction presents numerous examples of physicians as "the flower...of our civilization," seen firsthand. He spent most of his life as an invalid, dealing with lung hemorrhages and eventually dying of a cerebral hemorrhage. Treated as consumptive, he may actually have had hereditary hemorrhagic telangiectasia (HHT, also called the Osler–Rendu–Weber Syndrome) (10). Chronic illness and a sense that life might be brief undoubtedly nurtured Stevenson's imagination and iconoclasm. While his parents expected that their only son would follow the family tradition by becoming a lighthouse engineer, he studied law, but did not practice, preferring to develop his writing through travel and adventure. The adventures were often medical, as when a trip to California to pursue his later-wife, a married, American woman, resulted in his near-death. *Underwoods*, a collection of poems published in 1887, commemorates his experiences of the best of the medical profession and anatomizing the physician as "the flower (such as it is) of our civilization":

Generosity he has, such as is possible to those who practise an art, never to those who drive a trade; discretion, tested by a hundred secrets; tact, tried in a thousand embarrassments; and what are more important, Heraclean cheerfulness and courage. So it is that he brings air and cheer into the sickroom, and often enough, though not so often as he wishes, brings healing (11).

Before dedicating the book to his physician in Bournemouth, Stevenson also singles out by name "a few out of many doctors who have brought me comfort and help" (12).

He takes a more passionate stance in defense of a caregiver whom he never met, Damien de Veuster ("Father Damien"), a Belgian Roman Catholic missionary priest who was ordained in Honolulu and was sent, by his own request, to the lepers' colony on Molokai Island, where he worked until he died of leprosy. A Presbyterian minister's text attacking the missionary's morals and suggesting his death was the fault of his vices spurred Stevenson's "An Open Letter to the Reverend Dr. Hyde," a fervent defense of Damien's style of caregiving and a scathing attack on Hyde, again with the theme of hypocrisy. The letter offers a portrait of Damien as a working class savior with a brusque style and a serious devotion to intelligent patient care. Stevenson, who went to Molokai to research his piece, writes movingly of the scenes Hyde has never himself witnessed:

> Had you visited the hospital and seen the butt-ends of human beings lying there almost unrecognisable, but still breathing, still thinking, still remembering; you would have understood that life in the lazaretto is an ordeal from which the nerves of a man's spirit shrink...It is not the fear of possible infection. That seems a little thing when compared with the pain, the pity, and the disgust of the visitor's surroundings, and the atmosphere of affliction, disease, and physical disgrace in which he breathes. I do not think I am a man more than usually timid; but I never recall the days and nights I spent upon that island promontory (eight days and seven nights), without heartfelt thankfulness that I am somewhere else. And observe: that which I saw and suffered from was a settlement purged, bettered, beautified; the new village built, the hospital and the Bishop-Home excellently arranged; the sisters, the doctor, and the missionaries, all indefatigable in their noble tasks. It was a different place when Damien came there and made this great renunciation, and slept that first night under a tree amidst his rotting brethren: alone with pestilence; and looking forward (with what courage, with what pitiful sinkings of dread, God only knows) to a lifetime of dressing sores and stumps" (13).

Stevenson also notes that while those who work in cancer hospitals can leave at the end of their workday, "Damien shut-to with his own hand the doors of his own sepulcher" (14). The letter is a powerful support of a style of health care that has become a beacon for today's situations of socially stigmatized illness, including HIV-AIDS. It would have resonated with Osler, however, because of his own memorable visit to a leper colony, as well as his work with smallpox patients. He visited a leper colony in Tracadie, New Brunswick, Canada in the summer of 1889, in the company of (among others) his future wife, Grace Revere Gross (2) and William Francis, who would eventually prepare the Bibliotheca Osleriana. One famous Osler story tells of his instant diagnosis of leprosy in a patient at Hopkins some months after this visit, and the lecture on leprosy and its noncontagiousness he delivered on the spot (2). More broadly, Osler's commitment to work with similarly stigmatized patients (and take on their stigma) is reflected in his work in the 1870s as a smallpox physician. As Bliss notes, "Being a smallpox doctor, a physician in the pesthouse, was to practice on the bottom rung of the medical ladder—not unlike a Christian missionary" (2)—a role Osler, the child of missionaries, would embrace. In this context, his enthusiasm for "Father Damien" makes complete sense.

In *Father Damien*, we again see the theme of the kind of hypocrisy Stevenson most loathes, that of the moralist who defines virtue and sin in strictly limited terms. His "A Christmas Sermon," similarly, discusses the uses and misuses of morality before death, focusing on the stocktaking that takes place at the end of the year as a window on the incrementally more momentous stocktaking at the end of a life—a particular link for Osler, whose teachings so often focused on scenes at the patient's bedside (and deathbed).

Osler the teacher, as well as Osler the humanist, surely found a lively commentary on the art of doctoring in the works of Robert Louis Stevenson. Reading the two men together, one regrets that they never met.

> Edmund Gosse's pen-picture of Robert Louis Stevenson equally applies to William Osler. Those who have written about him from later impressions than those of which I speak seem to me to give insufficient prominence to the gaiety of Stevenson. It was his cardinal quality in those early days. A childlike mirth leaped and danced in him; he seemed to skip the hills of life. He was simply bubbling with quips and jest; his inherent earnestness or passion about abstract things was incessantly relieved by jocosity; and when he had built one of his intellectual castles in the sand, a wave of humor was certain to sweep in and destroy it. I can not, for the life of me, recall any of his jokes; and written down in cold blood, they might not seem funny if I did. They were not wit

so much as humanity, the many-sided outlook upon life. I am anxious that his laughter-loving mood should not be forgotten, because later on it was partly quenched by ill health, responsibility and the advance of years. He was often, in the old days, excessively, delightfully silly— silly with the silliness of an inspired schoolboy; I am afraid our laughter sometimes sounded ill in the ears of age.

Cushing (15)

Boccaccio

Osler and *The Decameron*

ALLAN PETERKIN

The Toronto Globe and Mail recently named *The Decameron* by Boccaccio as one of the "Fifty Greatest Books" ever written. Describing the work as "energetic, fast-moving, bubbling over with life, this is a world where stupidity not sin is punished; where sexual pleasure, not chastity is the object of the game" (1).

Surmising as to why it became one of Sir William Osler's favorite books invites acts of biography, literary criticism, and speculative fiction. For me there was also an inevitable sense of personal identification with a man who was a Canadian physician of British descent, who lived and worked in Ontario and had ties to both McGill and the University of Toronto. I found myself laughing out loud as I moved through the 100 novellas it contains and can only imagine Osler doing the same and for probably the same reasons. Greed, lust, social climbing, and hypocrisy are clearly science- and technology-proof. The physician, like the priest and poet or storyteller, has a unique and privileged exposure to the foibles, suffering, and transcendent qualities of human nature. As we shall see, Osler was intimately familiar with all three of these storied roles and was a prankster to boot.

As he tells us in *The Student Life*, "Nothing will sustain you more potently than the power to recognize in your humdrum routine, as perhaps it may be thought, the true poetry of life—the poetry of the commonplace, of the ordinary man, of the plain, toil-worn woman, with their loves and their joys, their sorrows and their griefs. The comedy, too, of life will spread before you, and nobody laughs more than the doctor at the pranks Puck plays upon the Titanias and the Bottoms among his patients. The humorous side is really almost as frequently turned towards him as the tragic" (2).

The Decameron is a collection of 100 stories written between 1350 and 1353.

The Black Death, which had originated in China and spread along trade routes, struck Florence in 1348, ultimately killing 60–100 000 Florentines and half of the Italian population (including friends and family of Boccaccio). Here is Boccaccio's portrayal of his plague-infested city:

> In Florence, despite all that human wisdom and forethought could devise to avert it, as the cleansing of the city from many impurities by officials appointed for the purpose, the refusal of entrance to all sick folk, and the adoption of many precautions for the preservation of health; despite also humble supplications addressed to God, and often repeated both in public procession and otherwise, by the devout; towards the beginning of the spring of the said year the doleful effects of the pestilence began to be horribly apparent by symptoms that shewed as if miraculous.
>
> Not such were they as in the East, where an issue of blood from the nose was a manifest sign of inevitable death; but in men and women alike it first betrayed itself by the emergence of certain tumours in the groin or the armpits, some of which grew as large as a common apple, others as an egg, some more, some less, which the common folk called gavoccioli. From the two said parts of the body this deadly gavocciolo soon began to propagate and spread itself in all directions indifferently; after which the form of the malady began to change, black spots or livid making their appearance in many cases on the arm or the thigh or elsewhere, now few and large, now minute and numerous. And as the gavocciolo had been and still was an infallible token of approaching death, such also were these spots on whomsoever they shewed themselves. Which maladies seemed to set entirely at naught both the art of the physician and the virtues of physic; indeed, whether it was that the disorder was of a nature to defy such treatment, or that the physicians were at fault—besides the qualified there was now a multitude both of men and of women who practised without having received the slightest tincture of medical science—and, being in ignorance of its source, failed to apply the proper remedies; in either case, not merely were those that recovered few, but almost all within three days from the appearance of the said symptoms, sooner or later, died, and in most cases without any fever or other attendant malady.
>
> Moreover, the virulence of the pest was the greater by reason that intercourse was apt to convey it from the sick to the whole, just as fire devours things dry or greasy when they are brought close to it. Nay, the evil went yet further, for not merely by speech or association with the sick was the malady communicated to the healthy with consequent peril of common death; but any that touched the cloth of the sick or aught else that had been touched or used by them, seemed thereby to contract the disease (3).

It is within this tragic context that seven well-bred women and three men meet (by chance) in the Basilica di Santa Maria Novella. At the suggestion of the eldest lady, Pampinea, they decide to flee to a villa in the countryside at Fiesole, in order to distract themselves and preserve their health. A modern medical reader might find this act somewhat elitist and doomed to failure epidemiologically, but famous physicians of the time like Tommaso del Garbo, when not advising washing up with vinegar and rosewater, were suggesting good food, proper quarantine, and maintenance of a "gay, relaxed frame of mind" (4).

Each member of Boccaccio's storytelling *regatta* is named king or queen of the day and is charged with telling a story in the sumptuous garden of the villa they inhabit, an idealized setting which clearly invokes all of the trappings of courtly love. For all but two days, narrative themes are provided and are subscribed to by all except Dioneo, the bawdiest raconteur of the bunch and perhaps the storyteller most allied to Boccaccio himself.

Much has been made by scholars of the numerical and religious significance of the seven ladies representing the seven days it took for God to create the world and of the three virtues embodied by the three male storytellers (5). However, one of the reasons these tales endure is that Boccaccio is never preachy or heavy-handed around providing religious or moral instruction (as was expected of written tracts in his day). Instead he subverts, entertains, and reveals a near-secular, surprisingly nonjudgmental view of human nature. The tumultuous plague years produced a more powerful, assertive middle and merchant class and led to questioning of the role that the Catholic Church played in people's sexual and family lives.

Osler, the teller of yarns and much-loved teacher, must have found Boccaccio's craft as a storyteller to be astonishing. Although most of the stories in *The Decameron* are recycled from other sources (and then used again by the likes of Chaucer, Shakespeare, Swift, Molière, and Keats), he draws us in by his framing device, which has been likened to a collection of Chinese boxes or a hall of mirrors. We have stories within stories within stories. While we wonder what will happen to our ten, young storytellers and whether they will (in the heat of the moment), do more than joust verbally, sing, and play chess, they are busily furnishing us with characters we can never forget (and who sometimes tell tales of their own). The daily themes provide endless fodder for plot twists: misadventures that end well, things lost and regained, loves lost in disaster (or repaired post-disaster), disasters averted by verbal wit, wives who play tricks on their husbands (or tricks played on the opposite gender, an Oslerian activity), and finally, tales of munificence.

We begin on Day 1 with a false confession by a ruthless money lender, Ser Ciappelletto (who is practically sainted by the gullible monk who hears his last, confabulated confession) and end on Day 10 with poor Griselda, the low-born wife of a Marquis, who is put through hell by her husband, but passes the test through patience and nobility of spirit. Boccaccio tells us that his Decameron is dedicated to women, who, lacking the diversions of men (like hunting and fishing), must conceal their passions while sitting idly in their rooms. Seven of his storytellers are female. Women by far outnumber men in the novellas themselves and are often the primary agents in the pieces. They tie strings to their toes so that their lovers can tug at them below the bedroom window. They fool their husbands into getting inside a barrel and cleaning it so that it can be sold, while being "ridden," using that same barrel for support. They are lusty, enterprising, and usually more intelligent than the men. (Madonna Filippa even manages to get a statute on adultery changed by the court after being caught in the act herself. Gillette of Narbonne, in one of the rare portrayals of medical healing in the collection, cures the French king's fistula, which had been resistant to all forms of treatment.) His mother and sisters were beloved and he was deeply devoted to his wife. The earthiness of Boccaccio's female creatures can only have provided a titillating contrast to the culturally repressed, frail, passive, swooning, and corseted women of his time. And, lest we forget, Osler was a prankster himself (6, 7). He traveled (and sometimes wrote tongue-in-cheek letters) under a pseudonym— E. Y. Davis—that drove his wife to distraction (the use of this nom de plume suggests a "man of infinite jest" and conjures up a playful theme of disguise, another recurring Decameron trick).

Osler once added gravel from his driveway to his own urine (after passing a kidney stone) to befuddle the lab. On another occasion, he rolled a grapefruit behind a strict head-nurse, sending it down the ward corridor like a bowling ball.

Osler tells us, "Lift up one hand to heaven and thank your stars if they have given you the proper sense to enable you to appreciate the inconceivably droll situations in which we catch our fellow creatures" (2). He admired mirth and good-naturedness above all things and told his students to be compassionate whenever they encountered self-deception (an all too human frailty) in their patients. He even tells physicians not to scold their "best patients" when they find quack medicines in the sick room. "Deal gently with this deliciously credulous old human nature in which we work" (8).

Yet not all of the Decameron's stories are humorous or uplifting, some are macabre portrayals of human cruelty, loss, and the inscrutable vagaries of fate. Lisabetta's brothers slay her lover and he appears to her in a dream to reveal where he is buried. She takes the head from the corpse and plants it in a pot of basil over which she weeps each day. When her brothers take away the pot, she dies of heartbreak. A knight serves his lady the heart of her lover. When she learns what the delectable dish actually was, she flings herself from the window to her death. And lest we forget, all of the stories in *The Decameron* are told on the outskirts of plague-infested Florence, where huge cultural and economic upheaval is being unleashed.

Osler's deep Christian faith sustained him. He also loved both the simplicity and intricacies of nature. Boccaccio's utopian spring garden (away from the dangers of the city) provides beauty and structure and offers a creative space for reflection and the sharing of life-sustaining stories. This would not have been lost on Osler, the natural scientist. I can't help but think that the itinerant scholar would also have been attracted by Boccaccio's cosmopolitanism and humanism.

These 100 stories take place in Italy, Armenia, Spain, England, and Egypt and are peopled by Jews, Muslims, and Christians. There are millers and innkeepers, nuns and monks, merchants, physicians, and scholars alongside kings, queens, and knights (5). Fate is unpredictable, but in *The Decameron* it is not automatically construed to be divine punishment or retribution. Eros permeates that natural order and physical and emotional love is imperative, tantamount. People (men and women of all ages, from all classes and cultures, including the clergy!) are drawn to connect with one another despite unforeseen dangers. Authority is meant to be challenged. They somehow survive through instinct, action, ingenuity, resilience and wit, all manifested alongside very real expressions of vengeance, deception, and greed.

Examples of the capacity to survive in the face of adversity abound in *The Decameron*. Because of fate, the beautiful daughter of the Sultan of Babylon is passed around among nine men "in varied places," but she can eventually return to her country of origin, fully intact (even "virginal") and make a suitable marriage to a king. Andreuccio da Perugia goes to Naples on a horse-buying expedition but is tricked by a woman pretending to be his long-lost sister. He falls, newly penniless into the feces-filled hole below her house but wins the day when he manages to enter the crypt of a bishop, steals a ruby ring from the corpse in the tomb, and is richly resurrected! (9).

We know that Osler turned to his beloved books (as revealed in this collection of essays) to find distraction, comfort, and inspiration....He prioritized humor throughout his life and career, not as a form of escape, but as one of the "God-given" options to help human beings respond to suffering and loss. He was good at telling a tall tale. As a teacher and healer, he told countless stories in order to instruct, entertain, and to instill hope. Just as sharing stories brings the regatta together and lifts their spirits as their world is crumbling, Osler the writer, the minister's son and the medical raconteur knew that stories are powerful and that they are recreated in every telling, whether delivered from the pulpit, shared in the examining room, or stretched out over dinner in his club. Stories foster relationships and build community. Stories mean survival. Boccaccio ends his *Decameron* rather abruptly. Our chaste and merry 10 return to the basilica in Florence, whenceforth they carry on with their lives, for however long, in a ravaged city. Boccaccio then cheekily defends the style and content of his bawdy tales in his Author's Epilogue:

> Which stories, such as they are, may, like all things else, be baneful or profitable according to the quality of the hearer...Corrupt mind did never yet understand any word in a wholesome sense; and as such a mind has no profit of seemly words, so such as are scarce seemly may as little avail to contaminate a healthy mind as mud the radiance of the sun, or the deformities of earth the splendours of the heavens (10).

In short, his critics have dirty minds and his supporters know how to take a joke.

I'm certain that Osler chuckled at this final authorial prank, this last Boccaccian wink of the eye, each time he put the Decameron back on the shelf.

Pantagruel.

Les horribles et espouëta=
bles faietz ꝗ prouesses du tresrenõme
Pantagruel Roy des Dipsodes/
filz du grand geãt Gargan=
tua Cõposez nouuelle=
ment par maistre
Alcofrybas
Nasier.

❦ On les bend a Lyon en la maison
de Claude nourry/dict le Prince
pres nostre dame de Confort.

Rabelais

Rabelais:
Physician-Writer of Curative Purpose

TOBY GELFAND

There is no doubt that Osler delighted in an author whom he called "humanist, theologian, legist, traveler, physician, etc." In *The Evolution of Modern Medicine*, Osler quoted with evident pleasure the astrological forecasts Rabelais made "tongue-in-cheek" in his famous Pantagrueline Prognostication. The Bibliotheca Osleriana contains more than 60 entries for Rabelais, no fewer than 28 primary sources, beginning with the first dated collective edition of *Les Oeuvres* (1553) followed by eight successive French editions. Osler collected numerous publications—one is tempted to say virtually everything of medical interest—on Rabelais, as witnessed by items on Rabelais' knowledge of anatomy and physiology, "obstetrical science," on teeth, Rabelais at the Montpellier Faculty of Medicine, Rabelais at the Lyon Hôtel-Dieu hospital, to name just a few. Osler included in the Bibliotheca prima his copy of Rabelais 1543 edition of the Aphorisms of Hippocrates, a work of serious classical scholarship. Osler's library also reveals that he kept abreast of the latest research on Rabelais with a subscription to the *Revue des Etudes Rabelaisiennes* (10 vols. 1903–1912), volumes he characterized as "indispensable to all Rabelais students...illustrating the very best type of literary study, show what a group of trained men may do who know how to get at and use the sources." On the lighter side, Osler during the 1880s attended the "Rabelais Club," a dining (and presumably, drinking) club which nonetheless produced several volumes entitled *Recreations of the Rabelais Club*.

It would not be a stretch to say that Osler, in many respects, saw in Rabelais a model to be emulated, a physician who, unlike many authors with medical degrees, remained "actively engaged in professional [medical] work." Indeed Osler believed that his Renaissance predecessor's writings stood unique among masterpieces of world literature for the "curative purpose" with which they were composed and their "therapeutic value." He went on to say in a lengthy note in the Bibliotheca Litteraria: "For the sick gouty and the unfortunate in their sore discomfort Rabelais had composed the Books, as he could not possibly take under his personal care all who needed his services... the author in making public these joyous Books gives joyous pastime to many sick and languishing.... The careful physician has but one end in view—not to depress his patient in any way whatever." (see Book IV, Liminary epistle.)

Given Osler's sense of identification with Rabelais the physician, I have selected passages from the Books, especially the Prologues, with this genial therapeutic aspect in mind. These are, I think, the sections that especially captured the medical man's attention and to which he explicitly refers. Nonetheless Osler, himself known for a lively, often irreverent, sense of humor, would surely have appreciated and perhaps envied the ribald, earthy comedy permeating the Rabelaisian oeuvre as a whole, a wit that lived on for centuries in hospital interns and medical student's semi-clandestine celebrations down to and beyond Osler's own Victorian era. Rabelais, despite a life history of which relatively little is known beyond his writings, remained familiar in many ways to the sensibilities and erudition of Osler's colleagues. More so than the modern reader can easily apprehend, the Renaissance genius remained as in one title in Osler's library: *Notre sympathique Confrère*, François Rabelais.

SELECTIONS

Pantagrueline Prognostication (late 1532) Chapter 3. Of this Year's Maladies

So wanting to satisfy the curiosity of all good fellows, I unrolled all the records and rolls of the heavens, calculated the quarters of the moon, pried open all the thoughts, past and present, of all the Astrophiles, Hypernephelists, Anemophylakoi, Uranopetes, and Ombrophores, and conferred about everything with Empedocles....

This year the blind will not see much, the deaf will hear rather poorly, mutes will not talk much, the rich will be a little better off than the poor and the healthy will stay better than the sick. Many sheep, oxen, hogs, goslings, chickens, and ducks will die, and the mortality will not be so cruel among the monkeys and dromedaries. Old age will be incurable this year because of the past years. People who have pleurisy will have much pain in the side. Those who have diarrhea will go to the close-stool; catarrh will come down this year from the brain to the lower members; eye trouble will be inimical to sight; ears will be short and rare more than usual in Gascony. And there will reign over all the universe a most horrible and dreadful malady, malign, perverse, frightening, and unpleasant, which will leave everyone stunned, and many at their wits end, and quite often as in a dream composing syllogisms about the philosopher's stone and Midas's ears (1).

Book I, Author's Prologue

Most noble and illustrious drinkers, and you thrice precious pockified blades (for to you, and none else, do I dedicate my writings), [Rabelais warns readers not to make a superficial judgment of his books based upon their sometime flippant titles] *Now, opening this box you would have found within it a heavenly and inestimable drug, a more than human understanding, an admirable virtue,...For this cause interpret you all my deeds and sayings in the perfectest sense; reverence the cheese-like brain that feeds you with these fair billevezees and trifling jollities, and do what lies in you to keep me always merry.*

Be frolic now, my lads, cheer up your hearts, and joyfully read the rest, with all the ease of your body and profit of your reins. But hearken, joltheads, you viedazes, or dickens take ye, remember to drink a health to me for the like favour again, and I will pledge you instantly, Tout ares-metys (1).

Book II, Prologue of the Author

There are others in the world—these are no flimflam stories, nor tales of a tub—who, being much troubled with the toothache, after they had spent their goods upon physicians without receiving at all any ease of their pain, have found no more ready remedy than to put the said Chronicles betwixt two pieces of linen cloth made somewhat hot, and so apply them to the place that smarteth, sinapizing them with a little powder of projection, otherwise called doribus.

But what shall I say of those poor men that are plagued with the pox and the gout? O how often have we seen them, even immediately after they were anointed and thoroughly greased, till their faces did glister like the keyhole...their teeth dance like the jacks of a pair of little organs or virginals when they are played upon, and that they foamed from their very throats like a boar which the mongrel mastiff-hounds have driven in and overthrown amongst the toils,—what did they then? All their consolation was to have some page of the said jolly book read unto them....

And therefore, to make an end of this Prologue, even as I give myself to a hundred panniersful of fair devils, body and soul, tripes and guts, in case that I lie so much as one single word in this whole history; after the like manner, St. Anthony's fire burn you, Mahoom's disease whirl you, the squinance with a stitch in your side and the wolf in your stomach truss you, the bloody flux seize upon you, the cursed sharp inflammations of wild-fire, as slender and thin as cow's hair strengthened with quicksilver, enter into your fundament, and, like those of Sodom and Gomorrah, may you fall into sulphur, fire, and bottomless pits, in case you do not firmly believe all that I shall relate unto you in this present Chronicle... (1).

Book III, Chapter 7. How Panurge had a flea in his ear, and left off wearing his magnificent codpiece.

In what concerneth the breeches, my great-aunt Laurence did long ago tell me, that the breeches were only ordained for the use of the codpiece, and to no other end; which I, upon a no less forcible consequence, give credit to every whit, as well as to the saying of the fine fellow Galen, who in his ninth book, Of the Use and Employment of our Members, allegeth that the head was made for the eyes. For nature might have placed our heads in our knees or elbows, but having beforehand determined that the eyes should serve to discover things from afar.

And because I would gladly, for some short while, a year at least, take a little rest and breathing time from the toilsome labour of the military profession, that is to say, be married, I have desisted from wearing any more a codpiece, and consequently have laid aside my breeches. For the codpiece is the principal and most especial piece of armour that a warrior doth carry; and therefore do I maintain even to the fire (exclusively, understand you me), that no Turks can properly be said to be armed men, in regard that codpieces are by their law forbidden to be worn (1).

Book III, Chapter 8. How the codpiece is the first piece of harness among warriors.

By the whole rabble of the horned fiends of hell, the head being cut off, that single person only thereby dieth. But, if the ballocks be marred, the whole race of human kind would forthwith perish, and be lost for ever. This was the motive which incited the goodly writer Galen, Lib. 1. De Spermate, to aver with boldness that it were better, that is to say, a less evil, to have no heart at all than to be quite destitute of genitories; for there is laid up, conserved, and put in store, as in a secessive repository and sacred warehouse, the semence and original source of the whole offspring of mankind. Therefore would I be apt to believe, for less than a hundred francs, that those are the very same stones by means whereof Deucalion and Pyrrha restored the human race, in peopling with men and women the world, which a little before that had been drowned in the overflowing waves of a poetical deluge (1).

Book III, Chapter 31. How Rondibilis, the doctor advises Panurge.

"Therefore I beseech you, my good Master Rondibilis, should I marry or not?"

"By the raking pace of my mule, quoth Rondibilis, I know not what answer to make to this problem of yours. You say that you feel in you the pricking stings of sensuality, by which you are stirred up to venery. I find in our faculty of medicine, and we have founded our opinion therein upon the deliberate resolution and final decision of the ancient Platonics, that carnal concupiscence is cooled and quelled five several ways. First, By the means of wine."

"I shall easily believe that, quoth Friar John, for when I am well whittled with the juice of the grape I care for nothing else, so I may sleep."

"When I say," quoth Rondibilis, "that wine abateth lust, my meaning is, wine immoderately taken; for by intemperancy proceeding from the excessive drinking of strong liquor there is brought upon the body of such a swill-down boozer a chillness in the blood, a slackening in the sinews, a dissipation of the generative seed, a numbness and hebetation of the senses, with a perversive wryness and convulsion of the muscles—all which are great lets and impediments to the act of generation. Hence it is that Bacchus, the god of bibbers, tipplers, and drunkards, is most commonly painted beardless and clad in a woman's habit, as a person altogether effeminate, or like a libbed eunuch. Wine, nevertheless, taken moderately, worketh quite contrary effects, as is implied by the old proverb, which saith that Venus takes cold when not accompanied with Ceres and Bacchus. This opinion is of great antiquity, as appeareth by the testimony of Diodorus the Sicilian, and confirmed by Pausanias, and universally held amongst the Lampsacians, that Don Priapus was the son of Bacchus and Venus."

Secondly, The fervency of lust is abated by certain drugs, plants, herbs, and roots, which make the taker cold, maleficiated, unfit for, and unable to perform the act of generation; as hath been often experimented in the water-lily, heraclea, agnus castus, willow-twigs, hemp-stalks, woodbine, honeysuckle, tamarisk, chaste tree, mandrake, bennet, keckbugloss, the skin of a hippopotam, and many other such, which, by convenient doses proportioned to the peccant humour and constitution of the patient, being duly and seasonably received within the body—what by their elementary virtues on the one side and peculiar properties on the other—do either benumb, mortify, and beclumpse with cold the prolific semence, or scatter and disperse the spirits which ought to have gone along with and conducted the sperm to the places destined and appointed for its reception, or lastly, shut up, stop, and obstruct the ways, passages, and conduits through which the seed should have been expelled, evacuated, and ejected. We have nevertheless of those ingredients which, being of a contrary operation, heat the blood, bend the nerves, unite the spirits, quicken the senses, strengthen the muscles, and thereby rouse up, provoke, excite, and enable a man to the vigorous accomplishment of the feat of amorous dalliance.

"I have no need of those," quoth Panurge, "God be thanked, and you, my good master. Howsoever, I pray you, take no exception or offence at these my words; for what I have said was not out of any illwill I did bear to you, the Lord he knows."

Thirdly, The ardour of lechery is very much subdued and mated by frequent labour and continual toiling. For by painful exercises and laborious working so great a dissolution is brought upon the whole body, that the blood, which runneth alongst the channels of the veins thereof for the nourishment and alimentation of each of its members, hath neither time, leisure, nor power to afford the seminal resudation, or superfluity of the third concoction, which nature most carefully reserves for the conservation of the individual, whose preservation she more heedfully regardeth than the propagating of the species and the multiplication of humankind. Whence it is that Diana is said to be chaste, because she is never idle, but always busied about her hunting. For the same reason was a camp or leaguer of old called castrum, as if they would have said castum; because the soldiers, wrestlers, runners, throwers of the bar, and other such-like athletic champions as are usually seen in a military circumvallation, do incessantly travail and turmoil, and are in a perpetual stir and agitation.

To this purpose Hippocrates also writeth in his book, De Aere, Aqua et Locis, that in his time there were people in Scythia as impotent as eunuchs in the discharge of a venerean exploit, because that without any cessation, pause, or respite they were never from off horseback, or otherwise assiduously employed in some troublesome and molesting drudgery.

Fourthly, The tickling pricks of incontinency are blunted by an eager study; for from thence proceedeth an incredible resolution of the spirits, that oftentimes there do not remain so many behind as may suffice to push and thrust forwards the generative resudation to the places thereto appropriated, and therewithal inflate the cavernous nerve whose office is to ejaculate the moisture for the propagation of human progeny. Lest you should think it is not so, be pleased but to contemplate a little the form, fashion, and carriage of a man exceeding earnestly set upon some learned meditation, and deeply plunged therein, and you shall see how all the arteries of his brains are stretched forth and bent like the string of a crossbow, the more promptly, dexterously, and copiously to suppeditate, furnish, and supply him with store of spirits sufficient to replenish and fill up the ventricles, seats, tunnels, mansions, receptacles, and cellules of the common sense,—of the imagination, apprehension, and fancy,—of the ratiocination, arguing, and resolution,—as likewise of the memory, recordation, and remembrance; and with great alacrity, nimbleness, and agility to run, pass, and course from the one to the other, through those pipes, windings, and conduits which to skilful anatomists are perceivable at the end of the wonderful net where all the arteries close in a terminating point; which arteries, taking their rise and origin from the left capsule of the heart, bring through several circuits, ambages, and anfractuosities, the vital, to subtilize and refine them to the ethereal purity of animal spirits. Nay, in such a studiously musing person you may espy so extravagant raptures of one as it were out of himself, that all his natural faculties for that time will seem to be suspended from each their proper charge and office, and his exterior senses to be at a stand. In a word, you cannot otherwise choose than think that he is by an extraordinary ecstasy quite transported out of what he was, or should be; and that Socrates did not speak improperly when he said that philosophy was nothing else but a meditation upon death. This possibly is the reason why Democritus deprived himself of the sense of seeing, prizing at a much lower rate the loss of his sight than the diminution of his contemplations, which he frequently had found disturbed by the vagrant, flying-out strayings of his unsettled and roving eyes. Therefore is it that Pallas, the goddess of wisdom, tutoress and guardianess of such as are diligently studious and painfully industrious, is, and hath been still accounted a virgin. The Muses upon the same consideration are esteemed perpetual maids; and the Graces, for the like reason, have been held to continue in a sempiternal pudicity. I remember to have read that Cupid, on a time being asked of his mother Venus why he did not assault and set upon the Muses, his answer was that he found them so fair, so sweet, so fine, so neat, so wise, so learned, so modest, so discreet, so courteous, so virtuous, and so continually busied and employed,—one in the speculation of the stars,—another in the supputation of numbers,—the third in the dimension of geometrical quantities,—the fourth in the composition of heroic poems,—the fifth in the jovial interludes of a comic strain,—the sixth in the stately gravity of a tragic vein,—the seventh in the melodious disposition of musical airs,—the eighth in the completest manner of writing histories and books on all sorts of subjects,—and the ninth in the mysteries, secrets, and curiosities of all sciences, faculties, disciplines, and arts whatsoever, whether liberal or mechanic,—that approaching near unto them he unbended his bow, shut his quiver, and extinguished his torch, through mere shame and fear that by mischance he might do them some hurt *or prejudice. Which done, he thereafter put off the fillet wherewith his eyes were bound to look them in the face, and to hear their melody and poetic odes. There took he the greatest pleasure in the world, that many times he was transported with their beauty and pretty behaviour, and charmed asleep by the harmony; so far was he from assaulting them or interrupting their studies.*

Under this article may be comprised what Hippocrates wrote in the afore-cited treatise concerning the Scythians; as also that in a book of his entitled Of Breeding and Production, where he hath affirmed all suchmen to be unfit for generation as have their parotid arteries cut— whose situation is beside the ears—for the reason given already when I was speaking of the resolution of the spirits and of that spiritual blood whereof the arteries are the sole and proper receptacles, and that likewise he doth maintain a large portion of the parastatic liquor to issue and descend from the brains and backbone.

Fifthly, By the too frequent reiteration of the act of venery.

"There did I wait for you," quoth Panurge, "and shall willingly apply it to myself, whilst anyone that pleaseth may, for me, make use of any of the four preceding" (1).

Book IV Liminary Epistle (of January 28, 1552)

You know, most illustrious prince, how often I have been, and am daily pressed and required by great numbers of eminent persons, to proceed in the Pantagruelian fables; they tell me that many languishing, sick, and disconsolate persons, perusing them, have deceived their grief, passed their time merrily, and been inspired with new joy and comfort. I commonly answer that I aimed not at glory and applause when I diverted myself with writing, but only designed to give by my pen, to the absent who labour under affliction, that little help which at all times I willingly strive to give to the present that stand in need of my art and service. Sometimes I at large relate to them how Hippocrates in several places, and particularly in lib. 6. Epidem., describing the institution of the physician his disciple, and also Soranus of Ephesus, Oribasius, Galen, Hali Abbas, and other authors, have descended to particulars, in the prescription of his motions, deportment, looks, countenance, gracefulness, civility, cleanliness of face, clothes, beard, hair, hands, mouth, even his very nails; as if he were to play the part of a lover in some comedy, or enter the lists to fight some enemy. And indeed the practice of physic is properly enough compared by Hippocrates to a fight, and also to a farce acted between three persons, the patient, the physician, and the disease. Which passage has sometimes put me in mind of Julia's saying to Augustus her father. One day she came before him in a very gorgeous, loose, lascivious dress, which very much displeased him, though he did not much discover his discontent. The next day she put on another, and in a modest garb, such as the chaste Roman ladies wore, came into his presence. The kind father could not then forbear expressing the pleasure which he took to see her so much altered, and said to her: Oh! how much more this garb becomes and is commendable in the daughter of Augustus. But she, having her excuse ready, answered: This day, sir, I dressed myself to please my father's eye; yesterday, to gratify that of my husband. Thus disguised in looks and garb, nay even, as formerly was the fashion, with a rich and pleasant gown with four sleeves, which was called philonium according to Petrus Alexandrinus in 6. Epidem., a physician might answer to such as might find the metamorphosis indecent: Thus have I accoutred myself, not that I am proud of appearing in such a dress, but for the sake of my patient, whom alone I wholly design to please, and no wise offend or dissatisfy.

There is also a passage in our father Hippocrates, in the book I have named, which causes some to sweat, dispute, and labour; not indeed to know whether the physician's frowning, discontented, and morose Catonian look render the patient sad, and his joyful, serene, and pleasing countenance rejoice him; for experience teaches us that this is most certain; but whether such sensations of grief or pleasure are produced by the apprehension of the patient observing his motions and qualities in his physician, and drawing from thence conjectures of the end and catastrophe of his disease; as, by his pleasing look, joyful and desirable events, and by his sorrowful and unpleasing air, sad and dismal consequences; or whether those sensations be produced by a transfusion of the serene or gloomy, aerial or terrestrial, joyful or melancholic spirits of the physician into the person of the patient, as is the opinion of Plato, Averroes, and others. Above all things, the forecited authors have given particular directions to physicians about the words, discourse, and converse which they ought to have with their patients; everyone aiming at one point, that is, to rejoice them without offending God, and in no wise whatsoever to vex or displease them (1).

Book IV, Prologue of the Author

For my part, I am thereabouts, thanks to his blessed goodness; and by the means of a little Pantagruelism (which you know is a certain jollity of mind, pickled in the scorn of fortune), you see me now hale and cheery, as sound as a bell, and ready to drink, if you will. Would you know why I'm thus, good people? I will even give you a positive answer—Such is the Lord's will, which I obey and revere; it being said in his word, in great derision to the physician neglectful of his own health, Physician, heal thyself.

Galen had some knowledge of the Bible, and had conversed with the Christians of his time, as appears lib. 11. De Usu Partium; lib. 2. De Differentiis Pulsuum, cap. 3, and ibid. lib. 3. cap. 2. and lib. De Rerum Affectibus (if it be Galen's). Yet 'twas not for any such veneration of holy writ that he took care of his own health. No, it was for fear of being twitted with the saying so well known among physicians:

Iatros allon autos elkesi bruon.

He boasts of healing poor and rich,

Yet is himself all over itch.

This made him boldly say, that he did not desire to be esteemed a physician, if from his twenty-eighth year to his old age he had not lived in perfect health, except some ephemerous fevers, of which he soon rid himself; yet he was not naturally of the soundest temper, his stomach being evidently bad. Indeed, as he saith, lib. 5, De Sanitate tuenda, that physician will hardly be thought very careful of the health of others who neglects his own.

Asclepiades boasted yet more than this; for he said that he had articled with fortune not to be reputed a physician if he could be said to have been sick since he began to practise physic to his latter age, which he reached, lusty in all his members and victorious over fortune; till at last the old gentleman unluckily tumbled down from the top of a certain ill-propped and rotten staircase, and so there was an end of him.

If by some disaster health is fled from your worships to the right or to the left, above or below, before or behind, within or without, far or near, on this side or the other side, wheresoever it be, may you presently, with the help of the Lord, meet with it. Having found it, may you immediately claim it, seize it, and secure it. The law allows it; the king would have it so; nay, you have my advice for it. Neither more nor less than the law-makers of old did fully empower a master to claim and seize his runaway servant wherever he might be found. Odds-bodikins, is it not written and warranted by the ancient customs of this noble, so rich, so flourishing realm of France, that the dead seizes the quick? See what has been declared very lately in that point by that learned, wise, courteous, humane and just civilian, Andrew Tiraqueau, one of the judges in the most honourable court of Parliament at Paris.

Health is our life, as Ariphron the Sicyonian wisely has it; without health life is not life, it is not living life: abios bios, bios abiotos. Without health life is only a languishment and an image of death. Therefore, you that want your health, that is to say, that are dead, seize the quick; secure life to yourselves, that is to say, health (1).

Thinkers

Robert Burton

Robert Burton's *The Anatomy of Melancholy*

T. Jock Murray

We may not know the personal reasons why Sir William Osler recommended each volume on his list of bedside books for medical students, but we do know a great deal about why he loved *The Anatomy of Melancholy*. He called Robert Burton's book "the greatest medical treatise written by a layman" (1).

Soon after arriving at Oxford University as the new Regius Professor of Medicine, Osler set out on a search for the many editions of Burton's *The Anatomy of Melancholy* and the hundreds of volumes Burton referenced and quoted in this monumental work. Over the next few years, Osler lectured to groups about Burton, his great book, and his library. He even planned a new edition of Burton's *Anatomy*. We get a flavor of his love for the book from his talk at Yale University in 1913:

> No book of any language presents such a stage of moving pictures—kings and queens in their greatness and in their glory, in their madness and in their despair; generals and conquerors with their ambitions and their activities; philosophers of all ages, now rejoicing in the power of intellect, and again groveling before the idols of the tribe; the heroes of the race who have fought the battle of the oppressed in all lands; criminals small and great, from the petty thief to Nero with his unspeakable atrocities; the great navigators and explorers with whom Burton traveled so much in map and card, and whose stories were his delight; the martyrs and the virgins of all religions, the deluded and fanatics of all theologies; the possessed of devils and the possessed of God; the beauties, frail and faithful, the Lucretias and the Helens, all are there. The lovers, old and young; the fools who were accounted wise, and the wise who were really fools; the madmen of all history, to anatomize whom is the special object of this book; the world itself, against which he brings a railing

accusation—the motley procession of humanity sweeps before us on his stage, a fantastic but fascinating medley at which he does not know whether to weep or to laugh (2).

On entering his temporary rooms at Christ Church College, Oxford, Osler was struck by the experience of inhabiting the same rooms as Burton and Locke (3). As soon as he comfortably settled, he began searching the libraries at the Bodleian, Christ Church, and other Oxford institutions for all 17th-century editions of *The Anatomy of Melancholy* and the many books used by Burton. He located 580 volumes in the Bodleian and 429 in Christ Church, some with marginalia and notes by Burton. Because he felt the editions and the referenced works "should not be divorced," Osler brought together the volumes in a new bookcase at the Bodleian, and commissioned a copy of the Brasenose portrait of Burton to hang over the collection.

In the summer of 1907, he gave a lecture in the Extension Course at Oxford on *"An Introduction to the Study of Anatomy of Melancholy"* (4). He planned a series of three lectures on the man, his book, and the library. In November 1909, he spoke to the Biographical Society in Hanover Square, London, on *"The Library of Robert Burton"* relating his experience collecting the books (5). He abandoned his plan to bring out a new edition of Burton's work when he heard that W. Aldis Wright of Cambridge and Edward Bensley of Aberystwyth were already working on a new edition. (A copy of *The Anatomy of Melancholy* in the Osler Library has a letter from W. Aldis Wright tucked inside.)

Holbrook Jackson said, "Robert Burton was a bookman, first and last" (6). This would endear him to Osler, who was also a bookman. Osler also liked to sprinkle his writings with quotations from many sources in literature, medicine, and philosophy, but there is hardly anything in literature like Burton, who had over a 1000 references and quotations in his book, including many of Osler's favorites, such as Shakespeare, Montaigne, the Bible, Greek and Latin scholars, ancient philosophers, and many more. Burton quoted authors on every page and sometimes a dozen on a page. Osler said, "By profession a divine, by inclination Burton was a physician, and there is no English medical author of the seventeenth century whose writings have anything like the same encyclopedic character of a medical condition" (7).

Robert Burton (1577–1640) was born at Lindley in Leicestershire and educated at the free school of Sutton Coldfield and at Nuneaton Grammar School. He became a commoner at Brasenose College and a student at Christ Church, Oxford. When he took hold orders he became the Vicar of St. Thomas, Oxford, and was later appointed by his patron, Lord Berkeley, to be Rector of Seagrave, Leicestershire. We don't know much more about his life except as revealed in his great work. Antony A. Wood, historian at Oxford, made the puzzling comment that he held the 2 posts at St. Thomas and Seagrave "with much ado to his dying day."

In the book, he warns of the danger of solitariness for the melancholy, even though he was essentially a solitary person, content to be in his rooms surrounded by piles of books. He was not a recluse, however, and could be charming and entertaining company, cheerful and scintillating in his conversation, able to discuss a wide array of subjects and to versify on any topic. He never married and lived a life punctuated by long periods of melancholy, but was very self-aware of his emotional state and the influences upon it, and even stated that he had become "addicted" to the condition.

Although only identified with his one great book, Burton did write other things. A Latin play, "Philosophaster," was thought to be lost but a manuscript was found in 1862. There were also some smaller writings he had submitted to Oxford miscellanies.

To know Burton, however, one must read his great work, as he bares his experiences and his beliefs, his thoughts, and his hopes. And of course, we learn a great deal about his long experience with depression and his personal as well as academic interest in the problem.

Burton had prophesized to friends that he would die at age 63, and when he did it sparked rumors that he had entered Heaven by way of the noose. He was buried in the north aisle of Christ Church Cathedral and his older brother William Burton, author of a *History of Leicestershire*, provided a monument with his bust in color with the epitaph he wrote himself carved underneath:

> Paucis notus, paucioribus ignotus, hic jacet Democritus Junior, cui vitam dedit et mortem Melancholia
>> (Known by few, unknown by fewer, here lies Democritus the Younger, to whom melancholy gave life and death)

Osler not only brought together the editions of Burton's *Anatomy* but he also owned many copies. In the Osler Library at McGill University, there is a copy with the inscription "Alex Boswell/LB 1728," which probably was a copy owned by James Boswell's father. In the Library, there is also an unpublished paper by Osler, *"The Library of Robert Burton"* (B.O. 4637).

Burton had called his work a "patchwork," but Osler disagreed, saying it was "a great medical treatise (the greatest ever written by a layman) orderly in arrangement, intensely serious in purpose, and weighty beyond

belief with authorities...The centuries have made Burton's book a per-
manent possession of literature." He said that if the work had just been
a medical text it would have "since sunk in the ooze" like so many other
17th-century medical works, but it lives on because of the human sympathy
of his approach. On that point, Osler noted there were 86 medical texts in
the Burton library, "none of which are of great importance," and in medical
concepts Burton followed Galenical teachings with little attempt to keep up
with the changing views of the newer science of the day such as the work
of Harvey.

Burton's book was published in 1621, a plump quarto of 900 pages,
under the pseudonym of Democritus Junior. He admitted the book was
excessively long and needed further editing, but in each subsequent edition
he did little editing and kept adding more material.

Revised and enlarged several times before his death, the treatise originally set out to explore the causes and effects of melancholy, but eventually
covered many aspects of the human condition, with views from and about
science, history, politics, and social reform. The work is divided into three
main portions: the various kinds of melancholy; the various cures; and an
analysis of two specific forms—love melancholy and religious melancholy.
The text is rich in quotations and references, even in an age when heavy
referencing was common. Burton's prose style is informal, anecdotal, witty
but often rambling.

He adopted the pseudonym of Democritus Junior in his first edition
based on the story of Hippocrates visiting Abdera and finding Democritus
under a tree, a book on his knee, and surrounded by dissected animals as
he struggled to find the seat and cause of *astra bilis*, or melancholy. Burton
said he was writing the book that was on Democritus' knee.

Described as a "good humored pessimist" (8), he read hundreds of texts
about melancholy and developed, like Samuel Johnson, personal maneuvers to ward off "the black dog of melancholy" whenever he felt its looming presence. In fact, the writing of this monumental work was a form of
therapy. One might expect a work on melancholy by a melancholic man to
be particularly depressing reading but readers for centuries have found it an
interesting and often humorous work. Samuel Johnson said it was the only
book that caused him to arise from bed two hours earlier than he wished.

Burton writes a lot about medicine, physicians, and various remedies.
He said he got his love of medicine from his mother, a competent and wise
woman with "excellent skill in chirurgery, sore eyes, aches, &c., and such
experimental medicines, as all the country where she dwelt can witness,
to have done many famous and good cures upon diverse poor folks, that

were otherwise destitute of help" (9). Burton recognized he was meddling in physic but noted that many physicians were clerics and that melancholy was a "compound mixed malady," "a common infirmity of body and soul."

Burton's portrayal of melancholy and his own melancholy was "Philosophically, Medicinally, Historically opened & cut-up," he says in the subtitle of *Anatomy*. It is unlike any other text on the subject. Perhaps the works of Montaigne, also a favorite of Osler and on his bedside list of books for the student of medicine, could match Burton's introspective portrayal of the human condition. Osler also knew of an earlier book on melancholy, by physician-cleric Timothy Bright, *A Treatise on Melancholy*, which was undoubtedly used by Shakespeare as a basis for the psychology used in *Hamlet*. In the Osler Library at McGill are Osler's copies of Bright's thesis and six of his other works (B.O. 2128–2134).

Perhaps Burton's "addiction" to melancholy may explain some paradoxes in the work. He can be cheerful and witty when speaking of melancholy. He preaches a happy existence but does not practice it. He warns of solitariness but is a very solitary person. He writes of the importance and joys of travel but never traveled. His three-volume work has many apologies for being longwinded, and yet he expanded each edition. He worries that his discussion of love melancholy will go on too long, and continues for over 200 pages. He expounds on marriage and the importance of a good wife, and of love and a strong family relationship, yet never married. He is both superstitious and scientific, prudish and pornographic, cheerful and sad, morose and amusing.

Excerpts that would have interested Osler:

Osler would agree with the central recommendation in Burton's text—keep busy, do your work. Osler wrote an essay on the watchword of medicine, work, and Burton begins with this admonition, and repeats it even more strongly in the last paragraph of the book. Osler would also share his views on illness having aspects of mind as well as body, and on the need for physicians to have a priestly as well as a medical role. Osler, often called a therapeutic nihilist, would share Burton's critical acceptance of the physician's medicines. Both believed that tincture of time would heal many disorders.

> There is no greater cause of melancholy than idleness, "no better cure than business," as Rhasis holds (Vol. 1, p. 20) (10).
> It is a disease of the soul on which I am to treat, and as much appertaining to a divine as to a physician, and who knows not what an agreement there is betwixt these two professions? A good divine either is or ought to be a good physician, a spiritual physician at least,

as our Saviour calls himself, and was indeed, Mat. iv. 23; Luke, v. 18; Luke, vii. 8. They differ but in object, the one of the body, the other of the soul, and use divers medicines to cure; one amends animam per corpus, the other corpus per animam as [168] our Regius Professor of physic well informed us in a learned lecture of his not long since.... A divine in this compound mixed malady can do little alone, a physician in some kinds of melancholy much less, both make an absolute cure (Vol. 1, p. 37) (10).

If you require a more exact division of these ordinary diseases which are incident to men, I refer you to physicians; [889] they will tell you of acute and chronic, first and secondary, lethals, salutares, errant, fixed, simple, compound, connexed, or consequent, belonging to parts or the whole, in habit, or in disposition, &c. My division at this time (as most befitting my purpose) shall be into those of the body and mind (Vol. 1, p. 138) (10).

We must use our prayer and physic both together: and so no doubt but our prayers will be available, and our physic take effect (Vol. 2, p. 9) (10).

Physic itself in the last place is to be considered; "for the Lord hath created medicines of the earth, and he that is wise will not abhor them." Ecclus. xxxviii. 4. ver. 7.[0000] "of such doth the apothecary make a confection," &c. Of these medicines there be diverse and infinite kinds, plants, metals, animals, &c., and those of several natures, some good for one, hurtful to another: some noxious in themselves, corrected by art, very wholesome and good, simples, mixed, &c., and therefore left to be managed by discreet and skilful physicians, and thence applied to man's use. To this purpose they have invented method, and several rules of art, to put these remedies in order, for their particular ends (Vol. 2, p. 20) (10).

To that great inconvenience, which comes on the one side by immoderate and unseasonable exercise, too much solitariness and idleness on the other, must be opposed as an antidote, a moderate and seasonable use of it, and that both of body and mind, as a most material circumstance, much conducing to this cure, and to the general preservation of our health (Vol. 2, p. 69) (10).

Whosoever he is that shall hope to cure this malady in himself or any other, must first rectify these passions and perturbations of the mind: the chiefest cure consists in them. A quiet mind is that voluptas, or summum bonum of Epicurus, non dolere, curis vacare, animo tranquillo esse, not to grieve, but to want cares, and have a quiet soul, is the only pleasure of the world, as Seneca truly recites his opinion, not that of eating and drinking, which injurious Aristotle maliciously puts upon him, and for which he is still mistaken, male audit et vapulat, slandered without a cause, and lashed by all posterity. [3400] "Fear and sorrow, therefore, are especially to be avoided, and the mind to be mitigated with mirth, constancy, good hope; vain terror, bad objects are to be removed, and all such persons in whose companies they be not well pleased" (Vol. 2, p. 103) (10).

Mirth and merry company may not be separated from music, both concerning and necessarily required in this business. "Mirth," (saith [3495]Vives) "purgeth the blood, confirms health, causeth a fresh, pleasing, and fine colour," prorogues life, whets the wit, makes the body young, lively and fit for any manner of employment. The merrier the heart the longer the life; "A merry heart is the life of the flesh," Prov. xiv. 30. "Gladness prolongs his days," Ecclus. xxx. 22; and this is one of the three Salernitan doctors, Dr. Merryman, Dr. Diet, Dr. Quiet, [3496] which cure all diseases...(Vol. 2, p. 119) (10).

For, [3550] malus malum vult ut sit sui similis; one drunkard in a company, one thief, one whoremaster, will by his goodwill make all the rest as bad as himself, be of what complexion you will, inclination, love or hate, be it good or bad, if you come amongst them, you must do as they do; yea, [3552] though it be to the prejudice of your health, you must drink venenum pro vino. And so like grasshoppers, whilst they sing over their cups all summer, they starve in winter; and for a little vain merriment shall find a sorrowful reckoning in the end (Vol. 2, p. 126) (10).

Be not dismayed then, humanum est errare, we are all sinners, daily and hourly subject to temptations, the best of us is a hypocrite, a grievous offender in God's sight, Noah, Lot, David, Peter, &c., how many mortal sins do we commit? Shall I say, be penitent, ask forgiveness, and make amends by the sequel of thy life, for that foul offence thou hast committed? Recover thy credit by some noble exploit, as Themistocles did, for he was a most debauched and vicious youth, sed juventae maculas praeclaris factis delevit, but made the world amends by brave exploits; at last become a new man, and seek to be reformed (Vol. 2, p. 200) (10).

The country people use kitchen physic, and common experience tells us, that they live freest from all manner of infirmities, that make least use of apothecaries' physic. Many are overthrown by preposterous use of it, and thereby get their bane, that might otherwise have escaped: [4084] some think physicians kill as many as they save, and who can tell, [4085] Quot Themison aegros autumno occiderit uno? "How many murders they make in a year," quibus impune licet hominem occidere, "that may freely kill folks," and have a reward for it, and according to the Dutch proverb, a new physician must have a new churchyard; and who daily observes it not? Many that did ill under physicians' hands, have happily escaped, when they have been given over by them, left to God and nature, and themselves; 'twas Pliny's dilemma of old, [4086] "every disease is either curable or incurable, a man recovers of it or is killed by it; both ways physic is to be rejected. If it be deadly, it cannot be cured; if it may be helped, it requires no physician, nature will expel it of itself" (Vol. 2, p. 208) (10).

A faithful friend is better than gold.... (Vol. 3, p. 32) (10).

If they would care less for wealth, we should have much more content and quietness in a commonwealth (Vol. 3, p. 239) (10).

A wife is a young man's mistress, a middle age's companion, an old man's nurse: Particeps laetorum et tristium, a prop, a help, &c.

Man's best possession is a loving wife, She tempers anger and diverts all strife.

There is no joy, no comfort, no sweetness, no pleasure in the world like to that of a good wife....

Last of all: if the party affected shall certainly know this malady to have proceeded from too much fasting, meditation, precise life, contemplation of God's judgments (for the devil deceives many by such means), in that other extreme he circumvents melancholy itself, reading some books, treatises, hearing rigid preachers, &c. If he shall perceive that it hath begun first from some great loss, grievous accident, disaster, seeing others in like case, or any such terrible object, let him speedily remove the cause, which to the cure of this disease Navarras so much commends, [6815]avertat cogitationem a re scrupulosa, by all opposite means, art, and industry, let him laxare animum, by all honest recreations, "refresh and recreate his distressed soul;" let him direct his thoughts, by himself and other of his friends. Let him read no more such tracts or subjects, hear no more such fearful tones, avoid such companies, and by all means open himself, submit himself to the advice of good physicians and divines, which is contraventio scrupulorum, as [6816] he calls it, hear them speak to whom the Lord hath given the tongue of the learned, to be able to minister a word to him that is weary, [6817] whose words are as flagons of wine. Let him not be obstinate, headstrong, peevish, wilful, self-conceited (as in this malady they are), but give ear to good advice, be ruled and persuaded; and no doubt but such good counsel may prove as preposterous to his soul, as the angel was to Peter, that opened the iron gates, loosed his bands, brought him out of prison, and delivered him from bodily thraldom; they may ease his afflicted mind, relieve his wounded soul, and take him out of the jaws of hell itself. I can say no more, or give better advice to such as are any way distressed in this kind, than what I have given and said. Only take this for a corollary and conclusion, as thou tenderest thine own welfare in this, and all other melancholy, thy good health of body and mind, observe this short precept, give not way to solitariness and idleness. "Be not solitary, be not idle" (Vol. 3, pp. 431–432) (10).

After Osler's death in 1919, a book of essays was published on Burton (1926) and Osler's tripartite article on the man, his book and his library was "reconstructed" into a chapter with the assistance of Lady Osler, Dr. W.W. Francis, and Dr. Archibald Malloch. There is an additional chapter by Osler on Burton as a transmitter (9). Also included are two lists of the Burton's books and his will.

On the last page of Cushing's biography of Sir William Osler he commented that when Osler died his casket rested overnight in the chapel at Christ Church "with the quaint effigy of his beloved Robert Burton nearby." Although a copy of Thomas Browne's *Religio Medici* was placed on his casket, and was said to be his favorite book, no book occupied Osler's energy and his time more than Robert Burton's *The Anatomy of Melancholy*.

Ben Franklin

Life and Essays of Dr. Franklin

Arthur L. Caplan

When North Americans think of Ben Franklin, they think of Franklin the founder of a new nation, Franklin the scientist, and even Franklin the entrepreneur printer and newspaper magnate. Those especially well informed about the man may even think of Franklin the good citizen of Philadelphia creating fire departments and distributing lightning rods to protect homes and churches. Europeans may well think of Franklin as an extraordinary diplomat securing support from France for the American Revolution at a time when the French could not afford the cost. But, what does not come readily to mind is Franklin and medicine. So why does William Osler have Franklin's *Life and Essays* among his list of books?

True, Franklin did play a key role in the history of vaccination. Initially, he opposed inoculation for smallpox. A terrible personal tragedy, the death of his young son Francis, changed his thinking. Franklin wrote:

> In 1736 I lost one of my sons, a fine boy of four years old, by the smallpox taken in the common way. I long regretted bitterly and still regret that I had not given it to him by inoculation. This I mention for the sake of the parents who omit that operation, on the supposition that they should never forgive themselves if a child died under it; my example showing that the regret may be the same either way, and that, therefore, the safer should be chosen (1).

Franklin undertook a retrospective study of the efficacy of inoculation and quickly saw the clear benefit (2).

Still despite this contribution to pubic health, it is unlikely that Franklin made Osler's list for his application of the scientific method to the problem of whether the benefits outweighed the risks of smallpox inoculation. Osler's readings are dominated by texts that would teach an aspiring physician something about character and virtue. In that regard, the inclusion of Franklin makes perfect sense. Not only was Franklin's life a demonstration of the importance of character in dealing with others and in managing public affairs, but Franklin was also very much self-aware of his personal morality—its strengths and its weaknesses (3). Although this aspect of his thinking has faded over time Franklin thought of himself first and foremost as a moralist and Osler seems to have recognized precisely this fact.

Why is it so hard to recognize this aspect of this polymath's genius? Even people who don't really understand Franklin's work with electricity, his analysis of ocean currents, or his work with ovens and heating systems know that he made major contributions to science. Yet, despite the huge amount of time Franklin spent advancing his ethical views, he is not someone we think of when we think of famous moral philosophers or even famous American moral philosophers. Why?

I think there are a few reasons why Franklin's contributions to ethics are either ignored or undervalued. First, Franklin was cool toward religion and theology. He was as tolerant a person as has ever existed in America, but not someone who found moral certainty in the pronouncements of any of the dominant Christian denominations of his day. In fact, he was rather suspicious of the moral commitments of some of the more vociferous theologians of his time, arguing that they spent more time praying about the good then actually doing good.

> I had been religiously educated as a Presbyterian; and tho' some of the dogmas of that persuasion, such as the eternal decrees of God, election, reprobation, etc., appeared to me unintelligible, others doubtful, and I early absented myself from the public assemblies of the sect, Sunday being my studying day... (4).

In addition to his fierce secularism, Franklin oriented his ethical concerns to the here and now. He felt the purpose of ethics was trying to find ways to improve the lot of humanity, not to live according to a particular code of ethics simply to please a divine being. He argued that each person has an obligation to improve the overall well-being of his fellow man. He also argued that the road toward the good lay in cultivating those personality attributes that led to having moral character—an argument that must have greatly appealed to the virtue-oriented Osler.

A key problem confronting Franklin the ethicist that is much on his mind in the *Life and Essays* is his personal moral failings. Having a child out of wedlock, spending many years away from his wife, being seen by some as a huge flirt and womanizer, and eliciting some criticism from his fellow cofounders as something of a media hog—these are not flaws, failings, and misdeeds that are easily overcome if one wants to lay claim to the mantle of ethicist. It is not that one cannot contribute to morals without being beyond moral criticism, but rather that aspects of Franklin's life make that a difficult accomplishment.

Still, Franklin was usually honest and transparent about his personal flaws and failings. Sometimes, he features them in the *Life and Essays* as a way to let others learn from his slips and falls. The only exception was sex. He was circumspect about his sex life but no more so than any other politician or prominent citizen of his time—or today for that matter. One can almost hear Osler's admiring agreement about Franklin's deft touch both in teaching from his failings and being circumspect about the deeply intimate.

Ben Franklin was a believer in virtue ethics. He thought that the way to moral conduct was through moral character. To put it simply, he believed that good people will do the right thing and that good people, given the time to reflect and consider their choices and options, would come to value the common good over their own self-interest.

Today, moral theory is dominated by two schools of thought in the United States. In the first, consequentialism, it is the outcomes of acts and behavior that determine what is good or bad. The second is deontology, whereby if people adhere to the right rules or principles (the 10 commandments, the injunctions of the Koran, the principles discerned in the Bible, or secular versions of the same such as don't treat others as a means to an end, and always tell the truth), they are moral. Kantian principles are often invoked today. Americans tend to believe that it is either the bottom line that determines whether a person or an act or a policy is good—that is why so many worship at the church of economics! Or that by following a clear set of rules, and strictly sticking to them, you are doing right, and thus are good.

Not Franklin. He thought sticking to rules at best quaint and at worst a moral dodge since it put too much emphasis on the individual. Consequences counted, he would concede, but again, self-interest would tend to dominate individual calculation, tending to actions and policies not in the best interest of the community.

It was virtue, personal character, that was the key for Franklin. A person of character paying attention to the consequences would get things right more often than not, or at least provide the best chance at doing so. A person of character would be able to exercise prudent practical judgment—an Oslerian admonition if there ever were one.

Thus, we get Franklin in the *Life and Essays*, and for that matter in his *Autobiography* and his *Poor Richard's Almanack* brimming with injunctions to virtue. The young Franklin set out on an experiment to try to inculcate virtue in himself. When a young man he measured his day against a grid of virtues that included 1) temperance, 2) silence, 3) order, 4) resolution, 5) frugality, 6) industry, 7) sincerity, 8) justice, 9) moderation, 10) cleanliness, 11) tranquility, 12) chastity, and 13) humility. His glosses on each of these are in his inimitable style. For example, for temperance: "Eat not to dullness, drink not to elevation"; order: "Let all your things have their places, let each part of your business have its time"; moderation: "Avoid extremes, forbear resenting injuries, so much as you think they deserve"; tranquility: "Be not disturbed at trifles or at accidents common or unavoidable"; humility: "Imitate Jesus and Socrates" (4).

This elevation of the virtues and the project of teaching oneself to be virtuous strikes many today as corny at best and bourgeois at worst. But not for Franklin. His hero was Socrates with Jesus coming in a close second. Neither was particularly adept at advancing moral theories. Both did much better with the well-placed question, the parable, the story, or simply an exhortation. They questioned authority, remained humble, listened thoughtfully to the woes of others and counseled peace, duty, and consistency with one's values, even to the point of dying at the hands of those in societies that they had tried to aid.

> In truth, I found myself incorrigible with respect to Order; and now I am grown old, and my memory bad, I feel very sensibly the want of it. But, on the whole, tho' I never arrived at the perfection I had been so ambitious of obtaining, but fell far short of it, yet I was, by the endeavour, a better and a happier man than I otherwise should have been if I had not attempted it; as those who aim at perfect writing by imitating the engraved copies, tho' they never reach the wish'd-for excellence of those copies, their hand is mended by the endeavor, and is tolerable while it continues fair and legible (4).

There is a link between professionalism as it is being taught in medical schools today and Franklin's belief in a virtue ethics. Learn virtue by asking questions of authorities and experts. Adhere to the view that sustained inquiry is not inimical to forming good values but is the very key to building them. Those are Franklinesque values that are present in most courses on professionalism today.

Perhaps most appealing from an Oslerian point of view is Franklin's wit. Franklin wrote with bite. He could be funny and toss out a zinger with the best of them. His argument against slavery in the *Life and Essays* utilizing the defense of white slavery offered by the divan of Algiers, Sidi Mahomet Ibrahim, is as scathing a commentary as has ever been penned.

Have these Erika considered the Consequences of granting their Petition? If we cease our Cruises against the Christians, how shall we be furnished with the Commodities their Countries produce, and which are so necessary for us? If we forbear to make Slaves of their People, who in this hot Climate are to cultivate our Lands? Who are to perform the common Labours of our City, and in our Families? Must we not then be our own Slaves? And is there not more Compassion and more Favour due to us as Mussulmen, than to these Christian Dogs? We have now about 50,000 Slaves in and near Algiers. This Number, if not kept up by fresh Supplies, will soon diminish, and be gradually annihilated. If we then cease taking and plundering the Infidel Ships, and making Slaves of the Seamen and Passengers, our Lands will become of no Value for want of Cultivation; the Rents of Houses in the City will sink one half; and the Revenues of Government arising from its Share of Prizes be totally destroy'd! And for what? To gratify the whims of a whimsical Sect, who would have us, not only forbear making more Slaves, but even to manumit those we have (4).

And his argument, also in the *Life and Essays,* about the prospect of attaining immortality through the means of embalming human beings in a solution of good port wine is laugh-out-loud hilarious. Franklin was an adept handler of humor and did not lack an appreciation of the same in others. While joviality and Osler are not always closely associated, one has to think that something about Franklin's self-deprecating style and praiseworthy ability to stay in good humor in the most dismal of circumstances were key virtues that Osler felt might well fortify the physician and the patient in their clinical encounters.

Erasmus

The *Adages* of Erasmus

STEPHEN S. LEFRAK

Which of the multiple works by renaissance humanist Desiderius Erasmus would Osler recommend a contemporary physician place in his or her bed side library? The substantive question is "Why Erasmus and which text?" The methodological concern is that evidentiary justification for the textual choice should be found in Osler himself. Yet Osler rarely referenced Erasmus and with one exception, Erasmus did not comment at length on medicine. Osler, however, collected much of Erasmus' written work, several in multiple editions (1), and provides three criteria for accumulating books: "typographical considerations, the book's contents, and the life of its author" (2).

Desiderius Erasmus inhabited a Europe in intellectual and social ferment, for much of which he was arguably responsible. He was by all accounts a moderate and tolerant man. Although he never left the Roman Catholic Church, his work was characterized by the Catholic Counter Reformation as "laying the egg which Luther hatched" (3). He achieved considerable fame in his lifetime, which dissipated on the European continent as the church schism widened to a chasm and ensuing cataclysm. Nevertheless, he remained esteemed in England because of his academic work at Cambridge and service to Henry VIII as that monarch established the Church of England. Today, while Erasmus' name remains known by many, his intellectual achievements seem appreciated by few.

Osler's interest in the life and work of Erasmus might have arisen directly from his father who was an Anglican Minister in Canada and whose career path the young William Osler sought to emulate. Undoubtedly, Reverend Osler had some knowledge of Erasmus' role in the Reformation that he may have passed on to his family. Perhaps this would be sufficient reason for Dr. Osler to collect Erasmus' work. But regardless of "family history," Osler certainly aspired for his library to reflect the great minds that created the Western ethos that he so admired. Erasmus was one such intellect.

Erasmus was known as the "prince of humanists," and Sir William Osler was a physician celebrated for his humanism (4). However, as "humanism" echoes across the centuries, its implications are transformed. Erasmus' 16th-century "humanism" is better labeled "Christian Humanism." Erasmus dedicated his life and work to synthesizing the humanism of the ancient world with 16th-century Christianity. His methodology in part was textual criticism of the "New Testament" in its original Greek rather than the Latin as translated by the "church" fathers. Examining the lives and lessons of scripture in the original was more than a new technique; it was a new "theology" when compared to the Aristotelian scholasticism entrenched in the universities and cathedrals of the era. Erasmus understood his labors as a humanist to be grounded in his Christian faith. Never in doubt was the moral compass of "imitatio Christi."

Osler's "humanism" encompassed a broad scope of human interests and a pointed focus on the patient. He was one of the great observers of the patient and Osler's "humanism" required studying the patient, their words, and their embodiment as the original and critical text of medicine. Osler led medical education out of the lecture hall to the bedside. His was a new "medicine," dependent on clinical observation and laboratory science. As Erasmus led the way from Scholasticism to the Reformation by textual criticism, so Osler led the way from "scholastic" medicine to the patient as text, to be critically read and cared for. This analogous vocation might be sufficient justification for the revered clinician to advise reading the theologian.

Which text of Erasmus would Sir William suggest for a physician's bedside? Osler might well choose Erasmus' *Adages* (5), not only because Osler himself frequently used adages in his lectures, books, and bedside teaching, but also because

> A library represents the mind of its collector...who wishes to know the books and lives of the men who wrote them (6).

The *Adages* was Erasmus' first book published in 1500, but they were a constant occupation throughout his life and he published three editions. The number of proverbs grew from the original 818 to 4251 proverbs with commentary published just three years before his death. They reflect accurately both his "life and his work," thus satisfying Osler's criteria.

Erasmus' collection of *Adages* conceivably made him the first best-selling author in the print era. In *Adages*, Erasmus presents proverbs in use in his epoch, discusses their meaning, and elucidates their classical sources. Erasmus defines proverb as "a saying in popular use remarkable

for some shrewd and novel turn" (7). With this book, Erasmus successfully built a bridge and a synthesis between his contemporary Christian
society and the ancient pagan world. This was his mission of Christian
Humanism.

Osler would tell the physician reader to place Erasmus' *Adages* within
easy reach for reading before sleep as he or she would find it relaxing,
interesting, and educational. It makes for bedside reading that would bring
a smile to anyone's face, including tired physicians, as well as providing a
unique look at Western language and thought. It is astonishing how many
of these proverbs remain in popular use today.

Our physician-reader pondering the conflicting opinions of various con-
sultants about his or her patient might find Erasmus' discussion of "So
many men, so many opinions" literally enlightening. Erasmus writes:

> Nothing is more widely known even today than this saying of
> Terrence…in "Phormio"…when he says of three advisers "the first says
> yes, the second says no, and the third says let's think about it" (7).

Does not every physician face this opinion glut in this multi consultant era
of medicine? But Erasmus adds:

> St Paul the Apostle seems to have made a reference to this when he
> says that for the putting aside of strife, we should allow every man to
> have his own convictions. If the general run of theologian had listened
> to this advice there would not now be such fierce contention about
> little questions of no moment at all; for there certainly are some things
> of which one may remain in ignorance without any lack of piety (8).

In elucidating a modest statement in common use, Erasmus brilliantly
expresses his concern for the great themes that unite us, and his disdain for
the petty arguments that are so divisive in his time and ours.

One could browse these thousands of aphorism and read many that are
familiar, such as "Better luck next time" of which Erasmus points out:

> Among the Greek proverbs we find this. Better the second time. This
> is applied to affairs which have had little success on the first try, but
> sometimes turn out more favorably the second time; a mistake in the
> first plan is corrected in the later one (8).

Which physician does not wish for that on more days than we would like to
admit? Its source is attributed by Erasmus to Plato.

> Plato in the fourth book of the Laws seems to refer to it as throwing
> knuckle bones or some similar game, because it often happens that

when a player finds the game going against him, he asks to begin it again from the outset, hoping that he will have more luck. Plato says "So once again, as players are used to say, let us see whether a second try has a better result" (8).

Erasmus finishes his comments with Euripides:

> At home if something goes not well
> With later thoughts we set it right,
> But life is not the same (9).

Which physician who cares for the ill would not share those thoughts? "I should have done it differently but it's too late?" Would physicians sleep more soundly knowing these thoughts were universal and ancient?

Physicians may reassure the "worried well" in our disease-obsessed culture by alluding to their concerns as "and what if the sky should fall?" Erasmus tells us this is

> Aristotle who in his fifth book of Metaphysics explains that early primitive men were convinced that the sky which they saw overhead was held up on the shoulders of Atlas. If he were to withdraw from under it the result would be that it would fall from its height on to the earth (10).

Erasmus abhorred war and spoke out against it in a number of venues. His discussion of the proverb "war is sweet for those who have not experienced it" would hold special meaning for Osler who loathed war (11) and not only because he lost his only child in Flanders during the carnage of World War I. Sir William would want all of us to absorb the words of Erasmus:

> This is one of the choicest of proverbs.... From Pindar we have "War is sweet for those who have not tried it, but anyone who knows what it is, is horrified beyond measure if he meets it in his heart." You can have no idea of the dangers and evils of some aspects of human affairs until you have tried them... (12).

Erasmus continues:

> If there is any activity which should be approached with caution, or rather which should be avoided by all possible means, resisted and shunned, that activity is war, for there is nothing more wicked, more disastrous, more widely destructive, more persistently ingrained, more hateful more unworthy in every respect of man... yet it is remarkable how widely these days how rashly, for what trivial reasons war is begun, how cruelly and barbarously it is waged, not only by pagans but by Christians... (12).

This commentary matured into a book by Erasmus forewarning of the appalling bloodbath of the religious wars that were to come to Europe after the schism in Christianity that Erasmus so greatly feared.

But Erasmus explores the meaning beyond armed conflict that physicians should ponder:

> The adage could be applied in the same way to any affair carrying great risk and attended by suffering such as no one would face unless he were young and inexperienced... (13).

While this applies broadly, it is especially pertinent to medical interventions. Which physician has not accompanied a patient's heroic but doomed journey through intensive treatment of terminal disease; and as with a recurrent nightmare, lived the journey again and again as inexperienced patients choose to suffer similar routes? How do physicians meaningfully but humanely inform their patient's choice by sharing their previously gained familiarity with the suffering to come?

Erasmus' *Adages* demonstrates that our contemporary language and intellectual framework are firmly embedded in ancient Greece and Rome. The *Adages* is superb reading anywhere, anytime. In bed, one can browse the volumes or proceed proverb by proverb and find adages that are in common use but whose 2500-year-old roots are concealed. Erasmus' revelations of the antiquarian sources of "to have one foot in the grave," "to being in the same boat" or "to put the cart before the horse" will forever change how the reader hears conversation, and what more of bedside reading could one ask?

Of course, I may be "talking to the wall" (14).

Maimonides

Prescient Thinker:
Maimonides and Medical Ethics

M. Sara Rosenthal

Considered one of the most influential contributors to philosophy and Jewish law, Moses Maimonides (1138–1204) was a prominent physician to both Jews and Muslims. Known as Rabbi Moses (Moshe) ben Maimon, and nicknamed "Rambam," his Arabic name was Abu Imran Musa ibn Maymun ibn Ubayd Allah. Born in Cordoba, Spain, he relocated to Fez to avoid religious persecution, and did his medical training there. He moved to Cairo, Egypt, in 1166, where he started to practice and teach medicine. He was a physician to Qadi al-Fadil, counselor and secretary to the ruler, Saladin. He later became a court physician to Malikal-Afdal in 1199. Maimonides described his general patient population as comprising "Jews and Gentiles, nobles and common people, judges and policemen, friends and foes—a mixed multitude" (1). In a letter to a student dated 1199, he discusses his schedule, which obliged him to attend to his patients at court daily, and then he returned to town in the afternoon: "I dismount from my animal, wash my hands, go forth to my patients, and entreat them to bear with me while I partake of . . . the only meal I eat in 24 hours. Then I go forth to attend to my patients, and write prescriptions and directions for their various ailments . . . until two hours or more into the night . . . " (1).

Maimonides composed 10 works in medicine that are considered authentic. A table in the appendix of this volume outlines Maimonides' medical writings and contributions, which cannot be given their scholarly due in this brief chapter. I have selected passages that will reveal his interests, scholarly accomplishments, professional ethics, and unique patient population. Maimonides refers to his patients in many of the works as his "Master" and self-identifies as "the servant" (2).

Oath of Maimonides is essentially an ethics and professionalism oath for physicians translated by Harry Friedenwald. This oath is notable stressing core competencies, standards of awareness and proficiency, empathy, veracity, and hints at disclosure of medical error.

> The eternal providence has appointed me to watch over the life and health of Thy creatures. May the love for my art actuate me at all time; may neither avarice nor miserliness, nor thirst for glory or for a great reputation engage my mind; for the enemies of truth and philanthropy could easily deceive me and make me forgetful of my lofty aim of doing good to Thy children.
>
> May I never see in the patient anything but a fellow creature in pain.
>
> Grant me the strength, time and opportunity always to correct what I have acquired, always to extend its domain; for knowledge is immense and the spirit of man can extend indefinitely to enrich itself daily with new requirements.
>
> Today he can discover his errors of yesterday and tomorrow he can obtain a new light on what he thinks himself sure of today. Oh, God, Thou has appointed me to watch over the life and death of Thy creatures; here am I ready for my vocation and now I turn unto my calling (3).

In his *Medical Letter*, Maimonides addresses the nephew of Saladin, who apparently suffered from manic-depressive disorder (4). Maimonides is advising alcohol for his Muslim patient, while acknowledging the cultural conflict between what the patient's religion forbids, and what he as a physician prescribes. The advice he is giving is no doubt unpopular, and he risks this to uphold his physician duties. Noteworthy are the concepts of beneficence, autonomy, informed decision making, and cultural ethics.

> His servant is well aware that our Master, which his broad intelligence and profound understanding will be able to conduct himself in the proper manner, in accordance with the previous treatise and these chapters....
>
> However, his poor constitution and the weakness of his natural faculties—already in his youth, and how much more so in his old age—constitute a barrier between him and many pleasures. I do not mean pleasures, rather good deeds, the most important and elevated of which is to serve our Master in actual practice....
>
> Our Master should not criticize his humble servant for having mentioned in this treatise that use of wine and songs, both of which are abhorred by the religion. For this servant did not command acting in this manner; he merely stated that which is dictated by this profession.

Indeed, the religious legislators know, as do the physicians, that wine has benefits for man.

A physician is bound... to present with a beneficial regimen, whether it is forbidden or permitted; the patient is endowed with the freedom to choose whether to follow or not. If [the physician] fails to mention everything that may be helpful, be it forbidden or permitted, he is guilty of acting dishonestly, for he did not offer trustworthy advice.

It is well known that religious law commands what is beneficial and prohibits what is harmful with respect to the world-to-come. The physician, on the other hand, instructs what will benefit the body and warns about what will harm it in this world.

The difference between religious commandments and medical counsel is that religion commands and coerces a person to do what will benefit him in the future, and prohibits what will harm him in the future, and punishes for it. The physician, on the other hand, counsels [a person] about what will benefit him, and wants him about what will cause him harm. He does not use coercion, nor does he punish; he merely presents the information to the patient in the manner of advice. And it is his [the patient's] choice [whether to follow that advice].

The reason for this is obvious. The harm and benefit from a medical perspective are immediate and clearly evident. Thus, there is no need for coercion or punishment. As for religious commandments, however, the harm and benefit that they bring are not evident in this world. The fool might, therefore, imagine to himself that everything that is said to be harmful is not harmful, and everything that is said to be beneficial is not beneficial, because these things are not clearly evident to him. For this reason, religious law compels one to practice good and punishes for doing evil, for the good and evil will only become apparent in the world-to-come. All this is benevolence toward us, a favor to us in light our foolishness, mercy upon us owing to the weakness of our understanding... (4).

The *Treatise on Asthma* was written at the request of an anonymous, high-ranking patient. It is not a health treatise about asthma per se, but a treatise tailored to his patient. In some ways, this functions as a medical history and medical opinion; in other ways, as a public health text. Of particular note is advice dispensed on diet and lifestyle. This first excerpt is from the Introduction, in which Maimonides explains the purpose of the work:

My honorable, esteemed, beloved and successful master... has informed me about this chronic disease from which he suffers which is called asthma. He has ordered me to write for him something about the foods that he should avoid and those that he should take and about the kind of regimen that is best for this disease, according to the explanations of the esteemed physicians. It is well known among the physicians that this disease can have many causes and that the regulation of the healing of diseases differs according to the different causes. And it is well known among the physicians that one cannot treat a disease in a proper way unless one has first examined the temperament of the patient in general and the temperament of every organ in particular. . . . Then one should examine the fatness or leanness of the body of the patient. . . . And then one should examine his age, the condition of his town, his habit, the time of the year, and the temperament of the weather at that moment. If my intention in the composition of this treatise were to be all-embracing—namely, [to impart] knowledge about the treatment of this disease for every individual case, place, time [of year] and cause—it would become very lengthy and it would be necessary to examine all the aforementioned issues in detail. But this is not the purpose of this treatise. . . . Rather, the purpose of this treatise is specific: namely, to deal with the requirement brought forward by my exalted Master. . . .

I also know that you are middle-aged and that your body is intermediate between leanness and heaviness and that your general temperament is very close to the balanced type, though it tends somewhat toward heat, and that the temperament of your brain is hotter than it should be. I inferred this from the fact that you are harmed—as you told me—by the odors of hot ingredients, that you cannot stand their smell, that your hair feels very heavy for you, that you find relief [only] by shaving it very frequently, and that you are [made] very uncomfortable by covering your head with a large turban. . .

You told me. . .that the air of Alexandria is very harmful for you and that you go to Cairo whenever you expect the onset of an attack. . .because the air of Cairo is lighter and calmer so that it is easier for you to bear that attack. You also told me. . .that a number of physicians have treated you as they thought necessary but that has not eliminated the disease (5).

This next excerpt is from chapter 1, "On the best regimen in general." This presents what today would be considered a holistic or integrative medical approach. Note that "khudha" refers to "chronic headache."

Everyone who looks into this treatise should know that all chronic diseases which occur in cycles—such as gout, arthritis, stones [in kidneys and gallbladder], asthma, migraine and the headache called khudha in Arabic, and other similar diseases—are impossible or difficult to heal.

In the case of each of these diseases, if one adheres to a good regimen and abstains from everything from which one should abstain and relies on that on which one should rely, one necessarily prolongs the interval between the cycles, diminishes the occurrences [of attacks] in a cycle, alleviates the suffering and pain which they cause, and makes it easier to bear them. But when one adheres to a bad regimen and gives in to one's lusts and habits without abstaining [from anything], it necessarily reduces the time between the cycles and increases the occurrence and severity [of the attacks] during the cycle...It is well known that the regimen of healthy and sick people in general has been summarized by the physicians in...categories...[(1)] the air that surrounds us;[(2)] the food and drink;[(3)] physical exercise and rest, which is opposite to it;[(4)] movements of the soul; [(5)] sleeping and waking; and [(6)] excretion and retention...(5).

The next two excerpts are, respectively, from chapter 2 "On the provision of rules concerning the foods to be eaten or avoided in relation to this disease" and from chapter 3 "On the [different] kinds of foods which should be avoided or consumed, [selected] from those foods that are readily available and common among us."

Note the dietary advice in light of current knowledge about carbohydrates and saturated fats; dietary influences on blood glucose and lipids; low glycemic index eating and gluten allergies; and cholesterol. Chapter 3 refers to Tannur, which is a circular oven; while furn is a regular oven. The reference to Quataif means "flaky pastries." What does not appear below is further advice on consuming fresh water fish over meat.

Every...food which produces thick or sticky humors should be avoided, and similarly everything that is very nutritious, even if it is good. Every...food which is rich in superfluities should be avoided, but one should take that kind of food which is moderate or somewhat less in its quantity [of superfluities] and which is neither sticky nor thick in quality, but is somewhat fine. The reason for this is clearly—namely that, when foods are digested in the organs and when the superfluity from the third digestion is minimal and is not sticky or thick, they are dissolved in a concealed way and leave [the body] through evaporation and perspiration...(5).

...every kind of food prepared from wheat flour that has been thoroughly sifted is thick and sticky and digests slowly, but...is very nutritious. Its harm is only eliminated when flour is used that is not sifted as much, when the leaven is...recognizable in the bread, [when] the bread is well salted and the dough well kneaded, when it is baked in a tannur, and when it is well done. Any bread [prepared] in this way is better than that prepared from [whole] grains. After bread baked in a tannur comes breads baked in a furn and next in excellence after flour which is not sifted as much comes flour prepared from wheat which has been neither soaked in water nor peeled. Instead, the flour is sifted lightly so that not all the bran is removed, and it should be well ground. For, when this flour is kneaded and made into bread, as have mentioned, it is good regular food, easy to digest, with a moderate nutritional effect. Anything made from wheat [prepared] in a different way is bad and harmful for people in general and for my honorable Master in particular, such as that [food] prepared from wheat itself....Neither should it be [prepared] from flour which is boiled...Nor should it be that which is prepared from the dough, such as noodles...Nor should [food] be made from that [flour] which is mixed with oil or fried...Qataif are also very bad because they are unleavened and sticky and are a poor [quality] bread. If, in addition, they are covered with sugar or eaten with honey...is a serious cause of diseases developing in healthy people— and even more so in sick people, whose humors we want to thin and the stickiness of whose humors we want to remove. Since all these different kinds of bread are thick food [that is, food producing thick humors], oil increases their stickiness, as we mentioned. When one adds honey or sugar to them, they cause great harm to the liver, because the liver favors this kind of food and is so susceptible to it that it penetrates to the ends of the liver until the veins are obstructed [by sticky humors]....One should also avoid all the...kinds of thick meat, such as that of cattle, goats, and grown sheep...one should choose the meat of fowl which is not fat...(5).

This next excerpt is from chapter 5, entitled "On the quantity of food." Again note that Maimonides is writing to a selected patient population surrounded by affluence, in which limiting quantity was likely unusual advice, given that food access was more of a problem for the masses. What is not excerpted here is a reiteration of drinking wine after eating, as well as references to the timing of eating and sleeping in other chapters (for example, sleeping three to four hours after eating is recommended but not immediately after).

Therefore, every human individual should calculate the amount which he should eat when he is healthy and know the amount which, if he consumes it in the springtime, can be easily tolerated and well and easily digested. That amount should be taken as one's basic portion; one should reduce it gradually as the heat increases and increase it gradually as the cold increases. The main principle in this entire matter is to avoid harmful satiation and distension of the stomach, because when any organ is distended, its functions are necessarily impaired. When the stomach distends more than is natural for it, all its functions weaken, and it can no longer contain the food, which then becomes a burden to it, and so loathsome that it requires water—although there is no thirst— so that the food can be discharged from it and its burden...relieved as [the food] is dissolved in water. This [explains the reason for the urge to] drink large amounts of water after satiation (5).

The Treatise on Hemorrhoids is a personalized health book intended for a particular affluent patient. This treatise emphasizes, again, moderation in eating. This excerpt is from chapter 1 entitled "General essay on good (or normal) digestion":

> For good foods, even of the finest quality, will be poorly digested if the stomach becomes engorged with them. It is important to follow (the rule) that a person should not satiate his appetite but should rather terminate his meal whiles some residue of this appetite remains. He should also remove his attention away from the stomach so that it not distend to the point of protruding like a swollen tumor. For there are some people whose appetite is very strong, to the point that the stomach distends to this proportion, and in spite of all this, they strongly lust (for more food) (6).

The *Medical Aphorisms* does not illustrate Maimonides' authorship, but scholarship, since he is selecting aphorisms, and reorganizing them for colleagues and future generations of medical students or scholars. This work comprises 25 treatises of approximately 1500 aphorisms, drawn mostly from Galen. Each treatise deals with a subspecialty in medicine. This work quotes, paraphrases, or summarizes Galen. In treatise 25, Maimonides offers a criticism of Galen, but the rest of the treatises are actually Galen's words, selected by Maimonides (2). The most informative excerpt is the Author's Introduction, which tells us in Maimonides own words, the purpose of this work, as well as his teaching philosophy.

> People have often composed works in the form of aphorisms on [different] kinds of sciences. The science most in need of this is the science of medicine, because it has branches of knowledge that are difficult to conceptualize, like most of the exact sciences, and [because] it has branches of knowledge that are difficult only with respect to remembering what has been written down about them....However, aspiring [to master] this science is difficult in most cases because it requires retaining a very large amount of memorized material, not merely of general principles but also [of] particulars, which can almost be compared to the individual details that cannot be encompassed by the knowledge

of one individual scholar...I have made these preliminary remarks merely as a justification for those aphorisms that I have included in my book. And I do not claim to have authored these aphorisms that I have set down in writing. I would rather say that I have selected them—that is, I have selected them from Galen's words from all his books, both from his original works and from his commentaries to the books of Hippocrates...most of the aphorisms that I have selected are in the very words of Galen, or his words and the words of Hippocrates, because the words of both are mixed in Galen's commentaries to Hippocrates' books; [in the case of] others, the sense [expressed] in the aphorism is partly in Galen's words and partly in my own; [in the case of] yet other aphorisms, my own words express the idea that Galen mentioned....I have gathered the sum of the idea of that aphorism and have articulated it in a concise expression. Since I know that there are more people who blindly follow the opinion of someone else than people who investigate for themselves....I considered it appropriate to refer, at the end of every aphorism I cite, to that section in Galen's exposition in which he has explained that aphorism....To refer to all the places is superfluous and has no use at all....But I preferred [to quote] his expression of an idea that is often repeated in his exposition in [only] one of its places and have recorded it [in that way].

I have selected these aphorisms for myself only, so that I would have a ready record of them. Similarly, anyone who is like me or who is less knowledgeable than I am can benefit from them....Similarly, what I consider to be of peculiar interest may not be of peculiar interest for someone else, and what I consider to be mostly unknown may be well known to someone else...(7).

Many of Maimonides' recommendations seem to parallel accepted standards in health and lifestyle advice supported by evidence-based medicine, as well as post-Belmont Report principles in medical ethics. Given that his recommendations were informed by his own clinical observations and intellect, his writings are remarkably prescient of current understanding of medicine and medical ethics.

Pascal

Osler and Pascal:
Meditations on Being Human

JEREMIAH CONWAY

Books can be recommended casually, and they can be recommended with a certain look in the eye that says to another—you *have* to read this. Recommendations of the latter sort presuppose a great deal: knowledge of the work, insight into the other person, and strong suspicions about why book and reader need to find each other. What, then, did Sir William Osler find in Blaise Pascal's *Pensées* that would lead him to recommend this famous, but (let's be honest) largely unread masterpiece of 17th-century French literature to physicians and medical students?

Part of the answer may lie in the fact that Pascal (1623–1662) embodied such complex interests. He was, for example, an accomplished scientist and mathematician. Entirely home-schooled, Pascal had invented, before his 20th birthday, the first mechanical adding machine and completed a treatise on conic sections. He went on to formulate a mathematical theory of probability, invented the first syringe, developed the hydraulic press, and conducted pioneering experiments on mercury columns in barometers. He helped design and implement the first public transportation system in Paris, half the profits of which were dedicated to the poor.

Pascal, however, regarded these accomplishments as secondary to his pursuit of religious issues, which form the basis of the *Pensées* (1). Blessed with a fine, scientific intellect, he pushed relentlessly against its boundaries, recognizing (in words remarkably similar to Osler's own) that "the human heart has a hidden want which science cannot supply" (2). Pascal wrestled with questions whether it was possible to acquire or sustain religious faith through the use of reason, whether the magnificent complexity of the natural world provides proof of God's existence, and, if not (as Pascal concluded on both questions), whether other sources of spiritual persuasion are available? It is hard to overestimate the intensity of his search. Several times as an adult, he underwent extraordinary moments of spiritual rapture that marked him deeply. One of these experiences (an ecstatic meditation on the life of Jesus) on 23 November 1654 left such an impression that Pascal sewed his remembrance of the event into his coat and carried it with him until the day he died.

While Osler was a knowledgeable student of the Bible and, as a young man, had considered entering the ministry, my suspicion is that he did not recommend Pascal to medical students as a religious thinker. Osler thought it wise to keep one's medical practice and one's religious convictions separate from one another. Instead, I suspect that what Osler found riveting in *Pensées* are its trenchant analyses of human motivation and behavior. Pascal had a keen eye for the dilemmas, the contradictions, the heartrending frailties, and foibles of the human condition. His was a powerful intellect insistently aware of reason's limitations, someone who struggled to restrain an ambitious intelligence from overshadowing the claims of the heart. Pascal used the meditations of the *Pensées* as a means to puncture the pride and arrogance of those, starting with himself, who would try to disguise a paltriness of spirit with intellectual cleverness.

It is a sobering thought that Pascal's range of accomplishments—scientific, mathematical, literary, and religious—were achieved despite harrowing illness (throughout most of his adult life, he could take only liquid nourishment, administered drop by drop) and an early death at the age of 39. I suspect that Osler appreciated this complexity of scientific insight, psychological acumen, the search for larger meaning, and proximity to human pain. Osler sought to educate physicians who, like Pascal, struggle with the demands of both scientific expertise and the responsibilities of being a confidant of human suffering.

Pensées is an odd book in many ways. It remains unclear whether Pascal wanted to have it published, why he left it unfinished, and what organization it would have had, if it had been published during his lifetime. The text, as we have it, is a collection of notes—some polished reflections, others little more than cryptic jottings—compiled into loose bundles. After Pascal's death, this jumble of notes was gathered, edited, arranged, and published by family and friends in 1670 under the less-than-snappy title, *Pensées de M. Pascal sur la religion, et sur quelques autres sujets* (*Thoughts of Monsieur Pascal about religion and other subjects*).

Pascal recognized the difficulty of his theme, commenting that many people despise religion and have good cause for doing so. As is the case today, Pascal lived in a world where religion was often a bastion of blustering certainty and the violence that finds justification there. Pascal's religiosity issued from a very different source, one that forces a reconsideration of the word itself. "Religion" comes from two roots: "*re*," which means to do again or go back, and "*legare*," which means to bind. Understood in this light, religion is the attempt to bind again or bind back; it is the process of seeking connection to the deepest sources of our being. As such, religion is anything but the province of the terminally sure. Quite the contrary, the search to rebind or reconnect makes no sense without a profound sense of being lost. Dante had it right: It is only after one finds oneself in a deep, dark wood that one undertakes the journey out. Religion is not for those who think they possess answers but for those who recognize the need to search. Consistent with this sense of religion, Pascal thought that religion should never be imposed or enforced:

> The conduct of God, who disposes all things kindly, is to put religion into the mind by reason, and into the heart by grace. But to will to put it into the mind and heart by force and threats is not to put religion there, but terror,—terorrem potius quam religionem (3).

In contrast to a long line of philosophers (for example, Descartes or Malebranche in France) who thought they could demonstrate the existence of God through rational argument or through the observation of nature, Pascal remained unconvinced:

> The metaphysical proofs of God are so remote from the reasoning of men, and so complicated, that they make little impression; and if they should be of service to some, it would be only during the moment that they see such demonstration; but an hour afterwards they fear they have been mistaken. Quod curiositate cognoverunt superbia amiserunt [200] (3).
>
> The visible world provides neither argument that God is absent from his Creation, nor that He is manifestly present therein; it argues the presence of a hidden God. All things are marked by that presence (3).

Pascal sharpened this sense of existential dilemma throughout his notes. Human beings, he found, exist in the midst of two infinities: as specks within the inconceivable vastness of the universe (as the technology of the telescope was increasingly revealing) and as observers of the infinitesimally small (opened by the microscope):

> For in fact what is man in nature? A Nothing in comparison with the Infinite, an All in comparison with the Nothing, a mean between nothing and everything. Since he is infinitely removed from comprehending the extremes, the end of things and their beginning are hopelessly hidden from him in an impenetrable secret, he is equally incapable

of seeing the Nothing from which he was made, and the Infinite in which he is swallowed up.... This is our true state; this is what makes us incapable of certain knowledge and of absolute ignorance. We sail within a vast sphere, ever drifting in uncertainty, driven from end to end.... Nothing stays for us. This is our natural condition, and yet most contrary to our inclination; we burn with desire to find solid ground and an ultimate sure foundation whereon to build a tower reaching to the Infinite. But our whole groundwork cracks, and the earth opens to abysses. Let us therefore not look for certainty and stability. Our reason is always deceived by fickle shadows; nothing can fix the finite between the two Infinites, which both enclose and fly from it (3).

Surrounded by infinities, great and small, Pascal concluded that human reason must recognize its limitations: "The last proceeding of reason is to recognize that there is an infinity of things which are beyond it. It is but feeble if it does not see so far as to know this. But if natural things are beyond it, what will be said of supernatural?" (3).

While certainty is a pipe dream, a measure of self-knowledge is possible, and this is as important to gain as it is painful to face. Pascal's investigations paint a stark, unflattering portrait of the human condition, rivaled, perhaps, only by the Hebrew scriptures (a parallel that is not accidental, given his careful study of the Old Testament). According to Pascal, we are vain, inconstant, restless creatures, perpetually engaged in distractions so that we do not have to face the tedium of life without them:

Distraction: When I have occasionally set myself to consider the different distractions of men, the pains and perils to which they expose themselves at court or in war, whence arise so many quarrels, passions, bold and often bad ventures, etc., I have discovered that all the unhappiness of men arises from one single fact, that they cannot stay quietly in their own chamber.... As men who naturally understand their own condition avoid nothing so much as rest, so there is nothing they leave undone in seeking turmoil. They have another secret instinct, a remnant of the greatness of our original nature, which teaches them that happiness in reality consists only in rest, and not in stir... vanity, the pleasure of showing off.... So we are wrong in blaming them. Their error does not lie in seeking excitement, if they seek it only as a diversion; the evil is that they seek it as if the possession of the objects of their quest would make them really happy (3).

Wretchedness: The only thing which consoles us for our miseries is diversion, and yet this it the greatest of our miseries. For it is this which principally hinders us from reflecting upon ourselves, and which makes us insensibly ruin ourselves. Without this we should be in a state of weariness, and this weariness would spur us to seek a more solid means of escaping from it (3).

Diversion: As men are not able to fight against death, misery, ignorance, they have taken it into their heads, in order to be happy, not to think of them at all (3).

The aim of such meditations is provocation about our way of being human. Their aim is to jolt and shock by casting an unblinking eye on human wretchedness (much like Buddhists focus on the overwhelming extent of unnecessary suffering in life):

I spent a long time in the study of the abstract sciences, and was disheartened by the small number of fellow-students in them. When I commenced the study of man, I saw that these abstract sciences are not suited to man, and that I was wandering farther from my own state in examining them, than others in not knowing them. I pardoned their little knowledge; but I thought at least to find many companions in the study of man, and that it was the true study which is suited to him. I have been deceived; still fewer study it than geometry. It is only from the want of knowing how to study this that we seek the other studies. But is it not that even here is not the knowledge which man should have, and that for the purpose of happiness it is better for him not to know himself? (3).

The thinking reed: Man is but a reed, the most feeble thing in nature; but he is a thinking reed. The entire universe need not arm itself to crush him. A vapour, a drop of water suffices to kill him. But, if the universe were to crush him, man would still be more noble than that which killed him, because he knows that he dies and the advantage which the universe has over him; the universe knows nothing of this (3).

The greatness of man is great in that he knows himself to be miserable. A tree does not know itself to be miserable. It is then being miserable to know oneself to be miserable; but it is also being great to know that one is miserable (3).

These reflections are also provocative in the sense that they seek to call forth a hunger for a different way of being human—the model of which Pascal found in Jesus. By detailing the vain thoughtlessness that is so often the substance of our lives, Pascal hoped to awaken the need for change in our way of living, from self-absorbed pleasure-seeking (which, he considered, a lost, fruitless battle) to the cultivation of a more loving heart. While there is, according to Pascal, no rational proof of any religious faith, and therefore none for his struggle to model his life on that of Jesus, he was convinced that "the heart has its reasons, which the reason knows not" (3). He staked his life on the emotional insight that the human heart finds lasting satisfaction only in generating and receiving love.

I think Osler recommended Pascal's meditations on being human because he knew that physicians must be more than medical technologists, that to care for suffering in a *humane* manner more is required than medical expertise. The physician, Hiram Bender, once described his career as a physician in words that echo Pascal:

> Medicine is concerned with the problem of keeping you alive; but serious illness asks the question for you, What is life for?
>
> Sometimes I hate what I do, but most of the time I accept it as a way of life that has made me, given me a special vision of our shared humanity. Not always ennobling; often downright negative. But frequently enough as inspiring in a poetical way as anything I have read or heard of. I don't know what will happen to this side of medicine as we make medical practice so highly technical and so dominated by cost accounting, bureaucratic rules, and an adversarial relationship with patients. Perhaps we are killing what is best in this ancient profession, like so much else in modern living. We replace intuition and emotion and moral passion with ever more minute rationality and turn questions about ends—the big ends: death, disability, suffering—into tinkering with technology (4).

C'est à ce prix que vous mangez du sucre
en Europe.

Candide Chapitre 19.

J. M. Moreau le J.ʳᵉ inv.   1787   Baquoy filius Sculp.

Voltaire

Osler and Voltaire:
Men of the Enlightenment

LAWRENCE J. SCHNEIDERMAN

When might the hybrid Canadian-American-Englishman William Osler have discovered the works of a Frenchman who lived almost a century and a half before him, and what might have caught his attention? Perhaps it was the rave review by a German, Goethe—in today's publishing world it would be a coveted book blurb: "Depth, genius, imagination, taste, reason, sensibility, philosophy, elevation, originality, nature, intellect, fancy, rectitude, facility, flexibility, precision, art, abundance, variety, fertility, warmth, magic, charm, grace, force, and eagle's sweep of vision, vast understanding, rich instruction, excellent tone, urbanity, vivacity, delicacy, correctness, purity, clearness, elegance, harmony, brilliancy, rapidity, gaiety, pathos, sublimity, universality, perfection, indeed—behold Voltaire."

More likely the humanist physician did not need this hyperbolical description to come upon the leading celebrity of the 18th century. What he may not have fully appreciated is how many similarities they shared. Voltaire was not an original philosopher and Osler made no great new medical discoveries. But both men, through the power of their personalities, popularized a valuable source of knowledge and empiricism, Osler to his medical colleagues, Voltaire to the intellectual world at large. Both, though unprepossessing in physique, were charismatic in presence, beloved, and admired by their contemporaries. Indeed, it is possible that over the course of Osler's own life most if not all Goethe's fervent encomiums were used by colleagues and friends to describe him—this, despite the two men's frequently breaking ranks with social conventions in their behavior and their writings. The youthful Osler was a prankster who brought his nascent divinity career at Trinity College School to an abrupt end when an outraged proctor declared: "Sir, you are persistently and essentially bad—you are a disgrace to yourself, to your family, to your college, to your church—and—and—you may go now sir!" Osler did go—to study medicine. He then proceeded to remove the top hat of a physician he disliked with a snowball, which led to "a formal charge of assault, appearance before a magistrate, a fine, and much laughter" (1).

Voltaire's punishments for his own misbehavior (satirical verses from childhood on and in his later years ferocious and deadly mockery of the Church, the king, and entrenched aristocracy) were more substantial, and included prolonged exile from the court and repeated imprisonment in the Bastille.

Both were readers. Depending on his biographer, Osler spent one half hour (1) or one hour (2) each night devoted to bedtime reading of "non-medical classics." This heavy dose of erudition undoubtedly contributed to his public speaking style, larded with classical quotations, pompous by today's standards.

As for writing, both were extraordinarily prolific. In addition to plays and essays and satirical verses, along with historical and scientific works, Voltaire, during his 84 years, composed over 20 000 letters and over 2000 books and pamphlets (3). Osler, by the time of his death at age 70, had published a legendary textbook of medicine, countless letters, and 730 articles, a smaller number, but astronomical in comparison with his peers, contemporary and future (2).

Though separated in time, both were men of the Enlightenment, rationalists and skeptical empiricists constantly at odds with prevailing dogmas, superstition, and flagrant charlatanism; seekers of truth and justice even while recognizing human failings.

Here is Voltaire in *The Philosophical Dictionary*:

> He who has heard the thing told by twelve thousand eyewitnesses, has only twelve thousand probabilities, equal to one strong probability, which is not equal to certainty (4).

And Osler in *Aequanimitas*:

> In seeking absolute truth we aim at the unattainable, and must be content with finding broken portions (5).

Here are the two men on justice, Voltaire in *The Philosophical Dictionary*:

> It is said of Marcus Brutus that, before killing himself, he uttered these words: "O virtue! I thought you were something; but you are only an empty phantom!"....I am very virtuous says this excrement of theology, for I have the four cardinal virtues, and the three divine. An honest man asks him—"What is the cardinal virtue?" The other

answers—"Strength, prudence, temperance and justice." [The honest man replies:] "If you are just, you have said everything; your strength, your prudence, your temperance, are useful qualities. If you have them, so much the better for you; but if you are just, so much the better for the others. But it is not enough to be just, you must do good; that is what is really cardinal. And your divine virtues, which are they?" (4).

And Osler in *Aequanimitas*:

> ...there is a struggle with defeat which some of you will have to bear, and it may be well for you in that day to have cultivated a cheerful equanimity....Even with disaster ahead and ruin imminent, it is better to face them with a smile, and with the head erect, than to crouch at their approach. And, if the fight is for principle and justice, even when failure seems certain, where many have failed before, cling to your ideal, and, like Childe Roland before the dark tower, set slug-horn to you lips, bow the challenge, and calmly await the conflict (5).

Here is Voltaire on human failings in *The Philosophical Dictionary*:

> People say sometimes—"Common sense is very rare." What does this phrase signify? That in many men reason set in operation is stopped in its progress by prejudices, that such and such man who judges very sanely in one matter, will always be vastly deceived in another. This Arab, who will be a good calculator, a learned chemist, an exact astronomer, will believe nevertheless that Mohammed put half the moon in his sleeve (4).

And Osler in *Aequanimitas*:

> One of the first essentials in securing a good-natured equanimity is not to expect too much of the people amongst whom you dwell...and in matters medical the ordinary citizen of today has not one whit more sense than the old Romans, whom Lucian scourged for a credulity which made them fall easy victims to the quacks of the time...(5).

Both had little patience with the extremes of formal religion, Osler benignly so, Voltaire furiously so. The latter coined the famous motto, *Ecrase l'infâme!* (Crush the infamous!), aimed principally at religious fanaticism, which Voltaire equated with stupidity, as in this brief swipe at "an Archmagus named Yebor, the most stupid of the Chaldeans and, consequently, the most fanatic." And at greater length in his novel, *Zadig*:

> There had reigned in Babylon, for the space of fifteen hundred years, a violent contest that had divided the empire into two sects. The one pretended that they ought to enter the temple of Mitra with the left

foot foremost; the other held this custom in detestation and always entered with the right foot first. The people waited with great impatience for the day on which the solemn feast of the sacred fire was to be celebrated, to see which sect Zadig would favor. All the world had their eyes fixed on his two feet, and the whole city was in the utmost suspense and perturbation. Zadig jumped into the temple with his feet joined together... (4).

And at even greater length in the *Philosophical Dictionary*:

Wretched human beings, whether you wear green robes, turbans, black robes or surplices, cloaks and neckbands, never seek to use authority where there is question only of reason, or consent to be scoffed at throughout the centuries as the most impertinent of all men, and to suffer public hatred as the most unjust.

A hundred times has one spoken to you of the insolent absurdity with which you condemned Galileo, and I speak to you for the hundred and first, and I hope you will keep the anniversary of it for ever; I desire that there be graved on the door of your Holy Office: "Here seven cardinals, assisted by minor brethren, had the master of thought in Italy thrown into prison at the age of seventy; made him fast on bread and water because he instructed the human race, and because they were ignorant" (4).

Here is Osler in his historical treatise *The Evolution of Modern Medicine*:

What Socrates did for philosophy Hippocrates may be said to have done for medicine. As Socrates devoted himself to ethics, and the application of right thinking to good conduct, so Hippocrates insisted upon the practical nature of the art, and in placing its highest good in the benefit of the patient. Empiricism, experience, the collection of facts, the evidence of the senses, the avoidance of philosophical speculations, were the distinguishing features of Hippocratic medicine. One of the most striking contributions of Hippocrates is the recognition that diseases are only part of the processes of nature, that there is nothing divine or sacred about them. With reference to epilepsy, which was regarded as a sacred disease, he says, "It appears to me to be no wise more divine nor more sacred than other diseases, but has a natural cause from which it originates like other affections; men regard its nature and cause as divine from ignorance" (6).

In a style he could have absorbed from the Frenchman, Osler derided inflated claims and unproven treatments. For example, on learning of the fad to employ rectal injections of gas as treatment for tuberculosis, Osler dismissed with Voltairian ridicule:

> As the enemy has not yielded to the attack *a fronte*, the tactics have changed, and we are asked to assault him *a tergo* (7).

And upon learning that an elderly surgeon had opined that if everyone's appendix could be removed soon after birth, eventually people would be born without them, Osler deftly observed that a like practice had been in universal use among a prominent people, but young Hebrews continued to be born with a prepuce as surely as young Gentiles.

There was, however, one enormous difference between the two men—their attitudes toward women. Osler was almost certainly celibate throughout his bachelorhood and declared in his textbook of medicine, "There are other altars than those of Venus upon which a young man may light fires....Idleness is the mother of lechery." Voltaire was an unabashed libertine. Yet, for all Osler's high-minded preaching, Voltaire almost certainly would win more women's votes today. The revered physician adamantly opposed—even insulted—women who sought to enter medicine. Again and again he made it clear to their faces that they had no business in the profession and belonged at home, serving as dutiful physician's wives. (Remarkably, though, the women physicians adored and worshipped Osler as much as the men did.) As for the lecherous Voltaire, he lit many fires on the altars of Venus with strong and independent women. His mistresses included the legendary Madame du Chatelet, a brilliant and outspoken polymath, who included famous scientists among her admirers and lovers. Yet, despite their incontestably different attitudes toward carnality they demonstrated a remarkably similar expression of uninhibited physical affection in their correspondence. For example, note the amazing intensity in their communications—fervent and intimate (Voltaire, very fervent, very intimate)—to their female cousins.

Here's Osler to his niece, Bea:

> ...I send you 50 kisses & Gwendolyn 50 kisses. May two punches, Grant a small slap, Gwyn a little poke with your left thumb, Jack a kick with your little toe, Willie a butterfly kiss with your left eye, Joshua a kiss on the right ear, Mammy one on the forehead, Auntie a prick with one of Lizzle's needles, and Mr. Bath—what shall we give him—tickle his toes for me in the morning (1).

Here's Voltaire to his niece, Countess Bentinck:

> I cover your sweet ass, your adorable body with kisses...If my miserable condition permits, I will throw myself at your knees and kiss all your delicacies. In the meantime I press a thousand kisses on your round breasts, and on your ravishing bottom....and on all your person which has so often given me erections and plunged me in a flood of delight (4).

(One can only wonder: was it the celibate William or the married Sir William who came across those words while in bed—and then what...?)

But above all, what unites Osler and Voltaire can be found in the Method of Zadig, the very exemplar of empiricism. Even before Sherlock Holmes (and Arthur Conan Doyle's model, Joseph Bell) were making famous their remarkable skills at detection through close observation of seemingly trivial details, Voltaire had created the wise, yet hapless Zadig. Here is a key excerpt from this work, whose melancholy moral must have appealed to Osler:

> One day, as he was taking a solitary Walk by the Side of a Thicket, he espy'd one of the Queen's Eunuchs, with several of his Attendants, coming towards him, hunting about, in deep Concern, both here and there, like Persons almost in Despair, and seeking, with Impatience, for something lost of the utmost Importance.
>
> "Young Man," said the Queen's chief Eunuch, "have not you seen, pray, her Majesty's Dog?"
>
> Zadig very cooly replied, "You mean her Bitch, I presume."
>
> "You say very right Sir," said the Eunuch.
>
> "'tis a Spaniel-Bitch indeed.—And very small" said Zadig. "She has had Puppies too lately; she's a little lame with her left Fore-foot, and has long Ears."
>
> "By your exact Description, Sir, you must doubtless have seen her," said the Eunuch, almost out of Breath.
>
> "But I have not Sir, notwithstanding, neither did I know, but by you, that the Queen ever had such a favourite Bitch."
>
> Just at this critical Juncture, so various are the Turns of Fortune's Wheel! The best Palfrey in all the King's Stable had broke loose from the Groom, and got upon the Plains of Babylon. The Head Huntsman with all his inferior Officers, were in Pursuit after him, with as much Concern, as the Eunuch about the Bitch. The Head Huntsman address'd himself to Zadig, and ask'd him, whether he hadn't seen the King's Palfrey run by him.
>
> "No Horse," said Zadig, "ever gallop'd smoother; he is about five Foot high, his Hoofs are very small; his Tail is about three Foot six Inches long; the studs of his Bit are of pure Gold, about 23 Carats; and his Shoes are of Silver, about Eleven penny Weight a-piece."
>
> "What Course did he take, pray, Sir? Whereabouts is he," said the Huntsman?
>
> "I never sat Eyes on him," reply'd Zadig, "not I, neither did I ever hear before now, that his Majesty had such a Palfrey."

The Head Huntsman, as well as the Head Eunuch, upon his answering their Interrogatories so very exactly, not doubting in the least, but that Zadig had clandestinely convey'd both the Bitch and the Horse away, secur'd him, and carried him before the grand Desterham, who condemn'd him to the Knout, and to be confin'd for Life in some remote and lonely Part of Siberia. No sooner had the Sentence been pronounc'd, but the Horse and Bitch were both found. The Judges were in some Perplexity in this odd Affair, and yet thought it absolutely necessary, as the Man was innocent, to recal their Decree. However, they laid a Fine upon him of Four Hundred Ounces of Gold, for his false Declaration of his not having seen, what doubtless he did: And the Fine was order'd to be deposited in Court accordingly: On the Payment whereof, he was permitted to bring his Cause on to a Hearing before the grand Desterham.

"Ye bright Stars of Justice, ye profound Abyss of universal Knowledge, ye Mirrors of Equity, who have in you the Solidity of Lead, the Hardness of Steel, the Lustre of a Diamond, and the Resemblance of the purest Gold! Since ye have condescended so far, as to admit of my Address to this August Assembly, I here, in the most solemn Manner, swear to you by Orosmades, that I never saw the Queen's illustrious Bitch, nor the sacred Palfrey of the King of Kings. I'll be ingenuous, however, and declare the Truth, and nothing but the Truth. As I was walking by the Thicket's Side, where I met with her Majesty's most venerable chief Eunuch, and the King's most illustrious chief Huntsman, I perceiv'd upon the Sand the Footsteps of an Animal, and I easily inferr'd that it must be a little one. The several small, tho' long Ridges of Land between the Footsteps of the Creature, gave me just Grounds to imagine it was a Bitch whose Teats hung down; and for that Reason, I concluded she had but lately pupp'd. As I observ'd likewise some other Traces, in some Degree different, which seem'd to have graz'd all the Way upon the Surface of the Sand, on the Side of the fore-Feet, I knew well enough she must have had long Ears. And forasmuch as I discern'd; with some Degree of Curiosity, that the Sand was every where less hollow'd by one Foot in particular, than by the other three, I conceiv'd that the Bitch of our most august Queen was somewhat lamish, if I may presume to say so.

As to the Palfrey of the King of Kings, give me leave to inform you, that as I was walking down the Lane by the Thicket-side, I took particular Notice of the Prints made upon the Sand by a Horse's Shoes; and found that their Distances were in exact Proportion; from that Observation, I concluded the Palfrey gallop'd well. In the next Place, the Dust of some Trees in a narrow Lane, which was but seven Foot broad, was here and there swept off, both on the Right and on the Left, about three Feet and six Inches from the Middle of the Road. For which Reason I pronounc'd the Tail of the Palfrey to be three Foot and a half long, with which he had whisk'd off the Dust on both Sides as he ran along. Again, I perceiv'd under the Trees, which form'd a Kind of Bower of five Feet high, some Leaves that had been lately fallen on the Ground, and I was sensible the Horse must have shook them off; from whence I conjectur'd he was five Foot high. As to the Bits of his Bridle, I knew they must be of Gold, and of the Value I mention'd; for he had rubb'd the Studs upon a certain Stone, which I knew to be a Touch-stone, by an Experiment that I had made of it. To conclude, by the Prints which his Shoes had left of some Flint-Stones of another Nature, I concluded his Shoes were Silver, and of eleven penny Weight Fineness, as I before mention'd."

The whole Bench of Judges stood astonish'd at the Profundity of Zadig's nice Discernment. The News was soon carried to the King and the Queen. Zadig was not only the whole Subject of the Court's Conversation; but his Name was mention'd with the utmost Veneration in the King's Chambers, and his Privy-Council. And notwithstanding several of their Magi declar'd he ought to be burnt for a Sorcerer; yet the King thought proper, that the Fine he had deposited in Court, should be peremptorily restor'd. The Clerk of the Court, the Tipstaffs, and other petty Officers, waited on him in their proper Habit, in order to refund the four Hundred Ounces of Gold, pursuant to the King's express Order; modestly reserving only three Hundred and ninety Ounces, part thereof, to defray the Fees of the Court. And the Domesticks swarm'd about him likewise, in Hopes of some small Consideration.

Zadig, upon winding up of the Bottom, was fully convinc'd, that it was very dangerous to be over-wise; and was determin'd to set a Watch before the Door of his Lips for the future. An Opportunity soon offer'd for the Trial of his Resolution. A Prisoner of State had just made his Escape, and pass'd under the Window of Zadig's House. Zadig was examin'd thereupon, but was absolutely dumb. However, as it was plainly prov'd upon him, that he did look out of the Window at the same Time, he was sentenc'd to pay five Hundred Ounces of Gold for that Misdemeanor; and moreover, was oblig'd to thank the Court for their Indulgence; a Compliment which the Magistrates of Babylon expect to be paid them.

"Good God!" Said he, to himself, "have I not substantial Reason to complain, that my impropitious Stars should direct me to walk by a

Wood's-Side, where the Queen's Bitch and the King's Palfrey should happen to pass by? How dangerous is it to pop one's Head out of one's Window? And, in a Word, how difficult is it for a Man to be happy on this Side the Grave?" (4).

How happy this bedtime story must have made Dr. Osler before he extinguished his bed lamp and went to sleep.

Dramatists

Henrik Ibsen

Henrik Ibsen: *An Enemy of the People*

JOEL D. HOWELL

Why was Henrik Ibsen's *An Enemy of the People* a play with which William Osler felt a particular affinity? To answer this question, we need to consider how Osler and others of his age would have understood the play. Like any great work of art, this play can be appreciated on many levels, not all of which are completely consistent with one another. Any answer about the basis for Osler's selection must, of course, be largely speculative. However, if we understand something about Osler's life and times, such speculation can help inform our appreciation for why he thought this work of art was especially worthy of note.

Perhaps, one reason why Osler included this work in his library is that the play, like Osler himself, stood at a great divide in our understanding of the nature of disease. *An Enemy of the People* was written in 1882, the very year that Robert Koch, a German physician, discovered the microorganism that causes tuberculosis. But more than simply describing a finding relevant for tuberculosis, Koch showed how to use cultures and stains as part of a method for demonstrating the "cause" of a specific disease. In so doing, he opened the floodgates to the discovery of the causes of a wide range of infectious diseases. These new ideas also raised the possibility—indeed, the likelihood—that much of human disease was caused by organisms invisible to the naked eye and undetectable by ordinary means. This leap of faith was as hard for some of Koch's contemporaries, as it was for some of the characters in *An Enemy of the People*.

One reason for that difficulty was that the germ theory called into question the notion that immorality was the root cause of human suffering. Florence Nightingale had a hard time accepting the germ theory of disease for precisely this reason. If disease came from filth, and one chose to keep a filthy household or live an unclean life, then one could be seen as deserving of illness. On the other hand, if disease could come from a single microscopic organism, invisible to the naked eye, then any clean-living, upstanding citizen could be afflicted the same way as one who was less deserving. This just didn't seem right. The germ theory would thus seem to challenge deeply held notions about dirt, disease, and morality. In the play, Ibsen seems to invoke both unseen objects and immorality as the root cause of disease. The new germ theory raised yet another set of issues having to do with commerce. As the medical historian Erwin Ackerknecht famously argued, adopting the ideas that certain diseases were contagious could lead to economic losses (1). This theme, too, is to be found in Ibsen's play.

Osler's own life spanned the great divide before and after the germ theory. As a young man, Osler was fascinated by the unseen world revealed though the microscope. His very first publication, at age 19, was *Christmas and the Microscope*, on microscopic life in a winter stream. At Trinity College, Osler saw the parasite *Trichinella spiralis* in what was his first piece of research. But although Osler was clearly comfortable with microscopes, he trained well before the germ theory was to transform medical science. In some early work, Osler wondered if platelets were formed from or turned into bacteria. He finished his MD at McGill in 1872 (2).

A decade later, Osler doubtless was excited to hear of Koch's discovery of the tubercule bacillus. He traveled to Berlin in 1884, where he heard of the discovery of the organism that causes cholera as well as heard rumors of still more discoveries in the air (which turned out to be accurate). Osler had worked with parasites, so he was at ease with the notion of invisible objects causing disease. Still, he was cautious about the claims that bacteria caused disease. Osler wrote "One is startled by the rapid diffusion of knowledge of these matters among the laity. The properties of various bacilli form subjects for table talk and, naturally, the amount of nonsense and pseudoscience which prevails is what might be expected" (2). While certainly aware of the published literature, Osler was himself never fully comfortable with newer tools of bacteriology, such as staining and culturing.

Later in his life, Osler became active in public health movements, par-ticularly the need for better sewage systems and for pure water to clean the streets, especially in Baltimore. Both of these initiatives would doubt-less improve health, but both had been well accepted long before the germ theory rose to prominence (and neither needed the germ theory to serve as central rationale). Osler's interests in sanitary systems reflect the fact that the boundaries between physician and public health advocate were not so far apart in Osler's day as they have since become (3, 4).

(excerpts from the play)

ACT I

The play opens in the sitting room of Dr. Thomas Stockman's home. Stockman is the Medical Officer for the Municipal Baths in a small coastal Norwegian village. We learn from the Mayor (Stockman's brother) that the entire village is united around a "common interest," the opening of the "fine new, handsome baths." The baths are already bringing the village economic prosperity, and new baths are expected to draw even more tourists and to bring even more money to the town.

Dr. Thomas Stockman arrives, noting that "It is a splendid time to live in." He had previously lived in a much smaller town—to him, the new ideas and new people with whom he comes in contact have the same effect as if he were "transported into the middle of a crowded city." There is friction between the Stockman and the Mayor. For one, both would like to be seen as the prime originator of the idea for the baths. Also, the Mayor is troubled by what he sees as Stockman's contrarian tendencies. "You have an ingrained tendency to take your own way, at all events; and, that is almost equally inadmissible in a well ordered community. The individual ought undoubtedly to acquiesce in subordinating himself to the community—or, to speak more accurately, to the authorities who have the care of the community's welfare."

Stockman is visited by two editors of the local paper. Interestingly, they use anatomic, biologic metaphors to describe the role of the town baths: the "main artery of the town's life blood," the "nerve center of our town," and "the town's pulsating heart."

But Stockman has been concerned about Molledal, the tannery that lies upstream from the baths, and his suspicions have recently been confirmed:

. . . .

DR. STOCKMAN. The whole place is a pest-house! . . . . The whole Bath establishment is a whited, poisoned sepulcher. I tell you—the gravest possible danger to the public health! All the nastiness up at Molledal, all that stinking filth, is infecting the water in the conduit-pipes leading to the reservoir; and the same cursed, filthy poison oozes out onto the shore too— . . . I have investigated the matter most conscientiously. For a long time past I have suspected something of the kind. Last year we had some very strange cases of illness among the visitors—typhoid cases, and cases of gastric fever . . . At the time, we supposed the visitors had been infected before they came; but later on, in the winter, I began to have a different opinion; and so I set myself to examine the water, as well as I could....I had none of the necessary scientific apparatus; so I sent samples, both of the drinking-water and of the sea water, up to the University, to have an accurate analysis made by a chemist...It proves the presence of decomposing organic matter in the water—it is full of infusioria. The water is absolutely dangerous to use, either internally or externally.

. . . .

Stockman's reference to "decomposing organic matter" is completely consistent with both pre-germ theory ideas about disease and obvious empirical evidence. It was believed that diseases can change from one to another, and that even a small amount of putrefying matter could contaminate a large quantity of water.

Stockman feels quite good about having discovered this danger; he and others, initially, believe that the town will be pleased that he has identified the problem, that "such an important truth as been brought to light." What's more, he has also identified a solution—one only needs to move some of the intake pipes, and all will be well. The act ends on an up-beat note as Stockman feels wonderful that he has been able to do a "service to his native town and to his fellow-citizens" (5).

ACT II

But the major problem is simply this—the doctor is asking the town to take his assertion on faith, on faith in his expertise and the expertise of the university chemists. Stockman was already convinced—he had drafted his report even before the university chemists' letter appeared. But who could know for sure what is in the water? For, as his father-in-law Kiil is the first to point out, the danger is invisible.

. . . .

MORTEN KIIL. This tale about the water supply, is it true?

DR. STOCKMANN. Certainly it is true...

MORTEN KIIL. Oh well, it is better never to trust anybody; you may find you have been made a fool of before you know where you are. But it is really true, all the same?

DR. STOCKMANN. You can depend upon it that it is true. Won't you sit down? (Settles him on the couch.) Isn't it a real bit of luck for the town—

MORTEN KIIL (suppressing his laughter). A bit of luck for the town?

DR. STOCKMANN. Yes, that I made the discovery in good time.

MORTEN KIIL (as before). Yes, yes, Yes!—But I should never have thought you the sort of man to pull your own brother's leg like this!

DR. STOCKMANN. Pull his leg!

MRS. STOCKMAN. Really, father dear—

MORTEN KIIL (resting his hands and his chin on the handle of his stick and winking slyly at the doctor). Let me see, what was the story? Some kind of beast that had got into the water-pipes, wasn't it?

DR. STOCKMANN. Infusoria—yes.

MORTEN KIIL. And a lot of these beasts had got in...—a tremendous lot.

DR. STOCKMANN. Certainly; hundreds of thousands of them, probably.

MORTEN KIIL. But no one can see them—isn't that so?

DR. STOCKMANN. Yes; you can't see them,

MORTEN KIIL (with a quiet chuckle). Damn—it's the finest story I have ever heard!

DR. STOCKMANN. What do you mean?

MORTEN KIIL. But you will never get the Mayor to believe a thing like that.

DR. STOCKMANN. We shall see.

MORTEN KIIL. Do you think he will be fool enough to—?

DR. STOCKMANN. I hope the whole town will be fools enough.

. . . .

Kiil's refusal to accept invisible agents of disease is far from irrational, though we may now believe him to be wrong. The physician Ignaz Semmelweis had previously argued for hand-washing as a means of preventing the spread of disease from the autopsy suite to laboring women in the Vienna General Hospital. His detractors argued, not without some logic, that it was hard to imagine that something under the fingernails, something so small that one could not see it, would be sufficient to kill a person. Here, Stockman is claiming that "hundreds of thousands" of invisible organisms can cause enough sickness to close the baths.

The Mayor comes by. He has learned that the proposed solution would be extremely expensive, and would take at least two years to build. He insists that Stockmann back down from his position that the bath's are poisoned, and threatens to fire him from his job if he does not. The two argue (5).

ACT III

Stockmann is now convinced that the issue is broader than he had previously realized. Rather than a technical problem, it has become a moral one. In a discussion with the paper's editors:

. . . .

> DR. STOCKMANN. *Because it is not merely a question of water-supply and drains now, you know. No—it is the whole of our social life that we have got to purify and disinfect.*
>
> DR. STOCKMANN. *Who the devil cares whether there is any risk or not! What I am doing, I am doing in the name of truth and for the sake of my conscience.*

The Mayor comes by to discuss the paper's role in the controversy. He emphasizes the economic hardship that publicity would cause the townspeople, all based, as the paper's printer says, on "merely imagination." The Mayor convinces the paper not to back Dr. Stockmann or to publish his report (5).

ACT IV

The townspeople gather to hear Stockmann speak.

> DR. STOCKMANN. *I have already told you that what I want to speak about is the great discovery I have made lately—the discovery that all the sources of our moral life are poisoned and that the whole fabric of our civic community is founded on the pestiferous soil of falsehood.*

Stockmann here uses the same language about the moral failings of people as he used earlier about the dangers in the baths.

> DR. STOCKMANN. *Very well, gentlemen, I will say no more about our leading men. And if anyone imagines, from what I have just said, that my object is to attack these people this evening, he is wrong—absolutely wide of the mark. For I cherish the comforting conviction that these parasites—all these venerable relics of a dying school of thought—are most admirably paving the way for their own extinction; they need no doctor's help to hasten their end. Nor is it folk of that kind who constitute the most pressing danger to the community. It is not they who are most instrumental in poisoning the sources of our moral life and infecting the ground on which we stand. It is not they who are the most dangerous enemies of truth and freedom amongst us.*

Dr. Stockman next speaks against the idea that the majority must not only rule but also be correct. (Two editors of the local paper speak first.)

HOVSTAD. The majority always has right on its side.

BILLING. And truth too, by God!

DR. STOCKMANN. The majority never has right on its side. Never, I say! That is one of these social lies against which an independent, intelligent man must wage war. Who is it that constitute the majority of the population in a country? Is it the clever folk, or the stupid? I don't imagine you will dispute the fact that at present the stupid people are in an absolutely overwhelming majority all the world over. But, good Lord!—you can never pretend that it is right that the stupid folk should govern the clever ones...

Stockman goes on to attack his opposition as being, basically, backward. He uses language that evokes a sort of genetic superiority, manifest by superior physical characteristics.

DR. STOCKMANN. I have already said that I don't intend to waste a word on the puny, narrow-chested, short-winded crew whom we are leaving astern.

He is basing his voice on new, progressive ideas.

DR. STOCKMANN. Yes, believe me or not, as you like; but truths are by no means as long-lived as Methuselah—as some folk imagine. A normally constituted truth lives, let us say, as a rule seventeen or eighteen, or at most twenty years—seldom longer. But truths as aged as that are always worn frightfully thin, and nevertheless it is only then that the majority recognizes them and recommends them to the community as wholesome moral nourishment. There is no great nutritive value in that sort of fare, I can assure you; and, as a doctor, I ought to know. These "majority truths" are like last year's cured meat—like rancid, tainted ham; and they are the origin of the moral scurvy that is rampant in our communities.

His language comes closer and closer to the idea of eugenics, the idea that better humans are to be produced by better breeding, just as animals.

DR. STOCKMANN (reflecting) The common people are nothing more than the raw material of which a People is made. (Groans, laughter and uproar.) Well, isn't that the case? Isn't there an enormous difference between a well-bred and an ill-bred strain of animals? Take, for instance, a common barn-door hen. What sort of eating do you get from a shriveled up old scrag of a fowl like that? Not much, do you! And what sort of eggs does it lay? A fairly good crow or a raven can lay pretty nearly as good an egg. But take a well-bred Spanish or Japanese hen, or a good pheasant or a turkey—then you will see the difference. Or take the case of dogs, with whom we humans are on such intimate terms. Think first of an ordinary common cur—I mean one of the horrible, coarse-haired, low-bred curs that do nothing but run about the streets and befoul the walls of the houses. Compare one of these curs with a poodle whose sires for many generations have been bred in a gentleman's house, where they have had the best of food and had the opportunity of hearing soft voices and music. Do you not think that the poodle's brain is developed to quite a different degree from that of the cur? Of course it is. It is puppies of well-bred poodles like that, that showmen train to do incredibly clever tricks—things that a common cur could never learn to do even if it stood on its head. (Uproar and mocking cries.)

A CITIZEN (calls out). Are you going to make out we are dogs, now?

ANOTHER CITIZEN. We are not animals, Doctor!

DR. STOCKMANN. Yes but, bless my soul, we are, my friend! It is true we are the finest animals anyone could wish for; but, even among us, exceptionally fine animals are rare. There is a tremendous difference between poodle-men and cur-men.

The crowd is unconvinced by his arguments and declares Stockman to be "An enemy of the People" (5).

ACT V

Stockman comes home to discover that he has lost his job, his daughter has lost her job, his friend has lost his job, Stockman has lost his house, his family has lost their inheritance, and their home has been vandalized. But he finally declares that "The strongest man in the world is he who stands most alone."

So at the end, we have one brave man standing against the world to speak the truth (although he's actually not exactly alone, as he is there with his wife, sons, daughter, and a friend) He has been ostracized by the town he is trying to help. Disaster seems to lie in store for the town, and probably Stockmann as well (5).

As a member of the medical elite, Osler would have resonated to the notion that Stockmann possessed special expertise lacked by most community members. As someone who himself worked to improve public health, Osler would have appreciated Stockmann's attempt to serve as a physician for the population. And, as someone who lived long enough to see old friends become enemies in World War I (which took his son), Osler may have appreciated the play's warnings against tyranny.

Molière

Osler and Molière:
The Physician in Spite of Himself

BERNADETTE HÖFER

Until the middle of the 19th century, medicine was far from being the enlight-ened profession it is today. Lack of medical education, training, and knowledge about ailments often led to a brutal confrontation between physician and patient, manifest in aggressive bleedings and purging that were believed to remove the corrupted humor within the patient's body. In fact, these treatments often did more harm than good. It was a common notion up to the end of the 17th century that disease resulted from an excess or corruption of the four humors (bile, yellow bile, phlegm, and blood). The French playwright and satirist Molière challenges the irrational authority of physicians, ridicules medical jargon, and mockingly conveys the full force and flavor of the medical principles and practices of his time. In his comedy, *The Physician in Spite of Himself* (1666), he adopts a humorous perspective in order to expose the lack of medical education of many physicians and the hazardous method of camouflaging ignorance behind incomprehensible terminology and imposing dress (1). William Osler would have read *The Physician in Spite of Himself* both as a comedy and as a didactic play. On the one hand, Molière's farcical play (2) makes us laugh, as it depicts a drunken woodcutter, Sganarelle, whom his wife—moved by revenge for having been beaten by her husband— unwillingly transforms into a physician (3). However, the woodcutter becomes more and more convinced of his excellence in that new profession. On the other hand, Osler would have wanted to read the play as a warning against choosing the profession for the wrong reasons: Not because of one's conviction and desire to provide optimal treatment based on a bond of trust between the physician and his patient, but because of the authority and remuneration attached to that career.

Molière's comedy touches in a lighthearted way upon the abuse of medical authority. The main character Sganarelle is taken to Géronte's home to cure his daughter Lucinde who seems to be struck dumb but who, in order to get rid of a husband favored by her father, has feigned her illness. Her parents do not hesitate to find the best physician who could cure her from her malady. While it puts conventional physicians at loss for effective remedies, Sganarelle reveals an astonishing insouciance and masquerades behind impressive dress and medical jargon. While he initially wears "a ruff, and a yellow and green coat," he then changes into "a physician's gown with a very pointed cap" (4). He thinks that appearance and mode of dress can turn anyone into a physician and even comes to believe that his outward appearance has produced a *real* professional with the skills necessary to cure. Osler would have been amused at a character who hides his ignorance beneath ill-equipped scientific endeavors and a false authority:

> *Sgan. Do not make yourself uneasy. But tell me, does this pain oppress her much?*
>
> *Gér.: Yes, Sir.*
>
> *Sgan. So much the better. Is the suffering very acute?*
>
> *Gér. Very acute.*
>
> *Sgan. That is right. Does she go to . . . you know where?*
>
> *Gér. Yes.*
>
> *Sgan. Freely?*
>
> *Gér. That I know nothing about.*
>
> *Sgan. Is the matter healthy?*
>
> *Gér. I do not understand these things.*
>
> *Sgan. [Turning to the patient] Give me your hand. [To Géronte] The pulse tells me that your daughter is dumb.*
>
> *Gér. Sir, that is what is the matter with her; ah! Yes, you have found it out at the first touch.*
>
> *Sgan. Of course!*
>
> *Jącq. See how he has guessed her complaint!*
>
> *Sgan. We great physicians, we know matters at once. An ignoramus would have been nonplussed, and would have told you: it is, that, or the other; but I hit the nail on the head from the very first, and I tell you that your daughter is dumb.*
>
> *Gér. Yes; but I should like you to tell me whence it arises.*
>
> *Sgan. Nothing is easier; it arises from loss of speech.*
>
> *Gér. Very good. But the reason of her having lost her speech, pray?*

Sgan. Our best authorities will tell you that it is because there is an impediment in the action of her tongue.

Gér. But, once more, your opinion upon this impediment in the action of her tongue.

Sgan. Aristotle on this subject says...a great many clever things.

Gér. I dare say.

Sgan. Ah! He was a great man!

Gér. No doubt.

Sgan. Yes, a very great man [Holding out his arms, and putting a finger of the other hand in the bend]. A man who was, by this, much greater than I. But to come back to our argument: I am of opinion that this impediment in the action of her tongue is caused by certain humours, which among us learned men, we call peccant humours; peccant—that is to say...peccant humours; inasmuch as the vapours formed by the exhalations of the influences which rise in the very region of diseases, coming...as we may say to...Do you understand Latin?

Gér. Not in the least.

Sgan. [Suddenly rising] You do not understand Latin?

Gér. No.

Sgan. [Assuming various comic attitudes] Cabricias arci thuram, catalamus, singulariter, nominativo, haec musa, the muse, bonus, bona, bonum. Deus sanctus, est-ne oratio Latinas? Etiam, Yes. Quare? Why? Quia substantivo et adjectivum, concordat in generi, numerum, et casus (5).

It is chiefly pompous pedantry, incomprehensible anatomical jargon, and daunting medical ignorance that Molière brings to light through his buffoon. Sganarelle's pretense of medical exactitude is clearly exposed as faulty by the layman Géronte:

Sgan. Thus these vapors which I speak of, passing from the left side, where the liver is, to the right side, where we find the heart, it so happens that the lungs, which in Latin we call armyan, having communication with the brain, which in Greek we style nasmus, by means of the vena cava, which in Hebrew, is termed cubile, meet in their course the said vapours, which fill the ventricles of the omoplata; and because the said vapours...now understand well this argument, pray...and because these said vapours are endowed with a certain malignity... listen well to this, I beseech you.

Gér. Yes.

Sgan. Are endowed with a certain malignity which is caused...pay attention here, if you please.

Gér. I do.

Sgan. Which is caused by the acridity of these humours engendered in the concavity of the diaphragm, it happens that these vapours... Ossabandus, nequeis, nequer, potarinum, quipsa milus. That is exactly the reason that your daughter is dumb.

Jacq. Ah! How well this gentleman explains all this.

Luc. Why does not my tongue wag as well as his?

Gér. It is undoubtedly impossible to argue better. There is but one thing that I cannot make out: that is the whereabouts of the liver and the heart. It appears to me that you place them differently from what they are; that the heart is on the left side, and the liver on the right.

Sgan. Yes; this was so formerly; but we have changed all that, and we now-a-days practice the medical art on an entirely new system.

Gér. I did not know that, and I pray you pardon my ignorance.

Sgan. There is no harm done; and you are not obliged to be so clever as we are (6).

We laugh at the learned ignorance of this 17th-century would-be physician whose knowledge of anatomy is clearly limited. All this suggests that Molière lashes out at the contemporary medical community, which hides lack of skills and education behind verbal maneuvers, overheard and misquoted Latin, Greek, and Hebrew words and builds its practice on fantasy, rather than fact. Osler's humorous nature was well known among his contemporaries, and he liked Molière's pithy style and the compelling satire on the comic character who tries to pass as a figure of authority.

The playwright, however, also criticizes how physicians of his time engaged in the medical practice solely for monetary reasons. Sganarelle concludes in the third act that medicine is truly lucrative:

Sgan. It is the best trade of all; for, whether we manage well or ill, we are paid just the same. Bad workmanship never recoils upon us; and we cut the material we have to work with pretty much as we like. A shoemaker, in making a pair of shoes, cannot spoil a scrap of leather without having to bear the loss; but in our business, we may spoil a man without it costing us a farthing. The blunders are never put down to us, and it is always the fault of the fellow who dies. The best of this profession is, that there is the greatest honesty and discretion among the dead; for you never find them complaining of the physician who has killed them (7).

There could be no clearer contrast between Sganarelle's motivation to practice for money and the careful study of medicine for passion and desire to cure that started around Molière's time with enlightened physicians, among them the Englishman Thomas Sydenham (1624–1689) and the Dutch physician Hermann Boerhaave (1668–1738). It is thus not the profession in itself that is ridiculed in Molière's comedy but only a medical community that exploits people's belief in them to fill their pockets for ineffective treatments, which are more likely to kill their patients than to cure them.

Death is mentioned throughout this satire, thus pointing to the noxious consequences that reprehensible treatments could potentially produce. For example, Sganarelle informs Géronte that his daughter "must not die without a prescription of the physician," and the servant Thibaut fears "that those big physicians kill, I do not know how many, with that new-fangled notion" (8). Molière alludes to the blurring of the distinction between life and death in the pseudomedical treatments of his times. The farce adopts a more serious undertone, as comedy could quickly turn into tragedy when there is little faith in the medical profession and when physicians become associated with killing gullible patients (9). When incompetence reigns, suffering and agony can be increased up to the point that the victim may even die under the physician's order. With this in mind, it is impossible not to be aware of Molière's genuine critique of the damaging consequences that lack of knowledge combined with unsuitable treatments could produce.

In suggesting *The Doctor in Spite Himself* to other physicians, Osler would have insisted on the question of what makes a good physician. Molière, after all, identifies an important problem of his time: How to make sure that the interest of future physicians in medicine is earnest and how to determine the qualities of a good physician. This theme is woven throughout Sganarelle's attempts to pose as a physician and his success to "cure" Lucinde through the right treatment. Humbleness is a central theme of the play. While the servant Valère wrongly admires Sganarelle for "keep[ing] buried his great talents" (10), Molière—much as Osler—highlights the idea that the physician needs to be aware of the mysteries of disease and of his own limitations in order to practice with virtue, knowledge, and care. Amiability and genuineness are other qualities, in addition to competence. Sganarelle observes: "It is the best sign in the world when a physician makes the patient laugh" (11). Osler, much as the French playwright, stressed during his lifetime that humane qualities and psychological insight define a good physician as much as technical skills. Physicians must be attentive to their patients and offer comfort through humor and care. Molière's more reasonable characters understand that Lucinde's illness is caused by love sickness. According to her secret lover Léandre, "love is the real cause" (12) of her feigned dumbness while the nurse Jacqueline argues that, "the best medicine to give to...[Cléonte's] daughter would...be a handsome strapping husband, for whom she could have some love" (13).

> *Léan. You must know then, Sir, that this disease which you wish to cure is a feigned complaint. The physicians have argued about it, as they ought to do, and they have not failed to give it as their opinion,—this one, that it arose from the brain; that one, from the intestines; another, from the spleen; another, again, from the liver; but the fact is that love is its real cause, and that Lucinde has only invented this illness in order to free herself from a marriage with which she has been harassed....*
>
> *Sgan. Come along, then, Sir. You have inspired me with an inconceivable interest in your love; and if all my medical science does not fail me, the patient shall either die or be yours* (14).

While medicine indisputably has its uses, physicians also need to be able to "read" their patients' emotions and to learn how to listen to their untold stories. And it is exactly that position that William Osler defended throughout his medical career. Consider the identification with which he must have read Molière's idea that physicians are more than performing physicians but that they need to combine intellectual activity with humanistic and social involvement.

One of the pleasures in reading *The Physician in Spite of Himself* lies in Molière's idea to reform through laughter. "If the mission of comedy is to correct men's vices" (15) in good faith and through the exposition of exaggerated follies, we can say that the French playwright excels at observing and correcting the practices and principles of the early modern medical community. Osler conceded that Molière deserved praise, as he believed in comedy's potential to correct bad behavior. The buoyant tone that this humanistic reform adopts is once more reflected in the lighthearted ending of the play, in which Sganarelle reveals to his wife: "I forgive you the blows on account of the dignity to which you have elevated me; but prepare yourself henceforth to behave with great respect towards a man of my consequence; and consider that the anger of a physician is more to be dreaded than people imagine" (16).

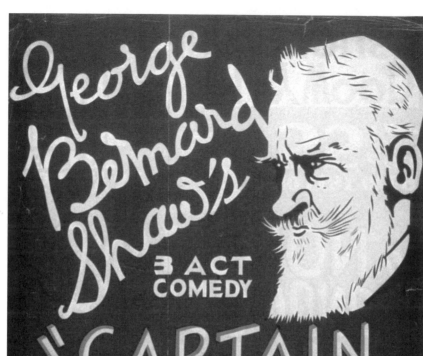

George Bernard Shaw's

3 ACT COMEDY

"CAPTAIN BRASSBOUND'S CONVERSION"

NIGHTLY 8:30 EXCEPT MON. & TUES.

FEDERAL THEATRE PROJECT USA WORK PROGRAM W.P.A.

NO SEAT OVER 55¢ TAX INC.

SEPT. 23 THRU OCT. 17

HOLLYWOOD PLAYHOUSE

VINE ST. NEAR HOLLYWOOD BLVD

George Bernard Shaw

Osler and George Bernard Shaw

JOHN K. CRELLIN

The entry for George Bernard Shaw's three plays, *The Doctor's Dilemma*, *Getting Married*, and *The Shewing-up of Blanco Posnet* (1911) in the catalog of Osler's library is annotated by the compilers: "With a cynical 'Preface on Doctors'" (1). They were referring to Shaw's preface to *The Doctor's Dilemma* (first performed in 1906).

Did Osler share the opinion? Did he see Shaw as just one of many writers (Molière, for instance, who featured prominently in Osler's library) to create theater by lampooning physicians? Perhaps, but Osler also recognized that Shaw touched on some of the same concerns he himself had raised over the years when exhorting medical students and physicians to fulfill the role of a "good" physician and to maintain an honorable profession. Both Shaw and Osler saw that physicians had the same potential human failings as anyone else, for instance, egoism, greed, and jealousy. Although Osler—once called a "professional optimist"—did not generally dwell on negativity, in 1911 he wrote:

> What happens in the grate [where a fire has died down] illustrates very
> often the condition of the [medical] profession in a town or county;
> single or in cliques the men have fallen apart, and, as in the dead and
> dying embers, there is neither light nor warmth; or the coals may be
> there alive and bright, but covered with the ashes of discord, jealousy,
> and faction (2).

Shaw, in subtitling *The Doctor's Dilemma* "a Tragedy," focused on ethical issues many of which he linked to the cut and thrust of private medical practice. A key issue, the "dilemma" discussed by the many physicians in the play was deciding on the worth of a patient to society when scarce medical resources had to be allocated. Shaw's illustrative example—it also dealt with how physician self-interests could shape decision making—was

{ 325 }

the apparently life-saving choice between two patients: One, a genius artist who was a "blackguard" scoffing at everyday morality, and the other, a self-sacrificing general practitioner who, in working unceasingly among the poor, jeopardized his own health.

The play's key decision maker was the newly knighted Sir Colenso Ridgeon, modeled on the London bacteriologist Almroth Wright (himself knighted in 1906). Ridgeon, à la Wright, discovered opsonins—substances in the blood that "prepared" bacteria to be ingested by white blood cells. Subsequent to his discovery, Wright established a laboratory at St. Mary's Hospital to measure opsonin levels in patients to guide his serum treatments for microbial infections. Wright's facilities, however, were limited—the genesis of the ethical conundrum raised in the play.

Various reasons contributed to Osler taking special interest in Shaw's critiques of medicine, many of which, if overstated, were informed. Osler himself had taken particular notice of Wright's vigorous promotion of science at a time when medicine was commonly viewed as becoming increasingly "scientific." In calling Wright the "Celtic Siren," Osler publicly chastised Wright's view that the clinician of the future would be a laboratory worker. Osler retorted: "The old art cannot possibly be replaced by, but must be absorbed in, the new science." This was generally in line with Shaw's opinion that "Doctoring is an art, not a science." Although Osler could not agree with many of Shaw's critiques of medical science—for example, his antivivisection and antivaccination views—he recognized that physicians had to be aware of them in order to respond effectively.

Clearly, many reasons existed for Osler not only to have the preface and play ready to dip into as bedside reading—though it was hardly soporific—but also to recommend it for prompting reflection on the changing face of medicine and how Shaw stereotyped physicians. Moreover, were Osler with us today, he would surely agree with the many physicians, who, in recent years, have argued that the preface and play continue to have relevance. As one wrote in 2003: "No student, nor any teacher can be regarded as properly educated who had not read and internally argued with Shaw's preface" (3).

Commentaries on Shaw's views of physicians invariably stress their harshness (sometimes in terms of Shaw's "hatred" of physicians, "intemperate" language, and so on); however, Shaw, who was a keen observer of medicine, did appreciate that physicians were human, and subject to systemic problems, many of which he linked to private medicine. His close attention to health care issues, interpreted through his Fabian socialist ideas and interest in such health "reforms" as vegetarianism, is reflected in the many diverse topics covered in his preface to *The Doctor's Dilemma*; for example his subheadings included: Doubtful Character borne by the Medical Profession; Doctors' Consciences; Recoil of the Dogma of Medical Infallibility on the Doctor; Why Doctors do not Differ; The Craze for Operations; Medical Poverty; The Psychology of Self-Respect in Surgeons; Are Doctors Men of Science?; Bacteriology as a Superstition; Economic Difficulties of Immunization; Trade Unionism and Science; Doctors and Vivisection; Limitations of the Right to Knowledge; The Vaccination Craze; Statistical Illusions; The Doctor's Hardships; The Public Doctor, and The Latest Theories.

Selecting from the wealth of topics those passages especially appealing to Osler can only be guesswork. However, he likely took particular notice of Shaw's views on the character of the physician (excerpt A), which need to be read in the context of Shaw's appreciation of systemic difficulties that faced physicians (excerpt B). Shaw, too, was very conscious of poor communication between physician/scientist and patient as illustrated in excerpt C, which spotlights the public's failure to understand "statistics"—a matter that continues to resonate. In closing his preface, Shaw perhaps had his tongue in cheek (he was a great provocateur) with some of the list of summary issues (excerpt D); nevertheless they continue to prompt reflection. While such passages are to be read in the context of their times, certain "messages" are clearly provocative today, even in the absence of financial poverty among physicians.

Over the years, physicians have paid more attention to Shaw's preface than to his play. Yet, as Osler surely appreciated, the play is "fun" reading if only for satirizing physicians. Excerpt E reprints an exchange between a surgeon and an impoverished general practitioner. Shaw described the surgeon Cutler Walpole as "a clever operator.... He seems never at a loss, never in doubt: one feels that if he made a mistake he would make it thoroughly and firmly." Dr. Blenkinsop, on the other hand, "is a very different case from the other [physicians]. He is clearly not a prosperous man. He is flabby and shabby, cheaply fed and cheaply clothed."

A. *"Doubtful Character borne by the Medical Profession"*

"I do not know a single thoughtful and well-informed person who does not feel that the tragedy of illness at present is that it delivers you helplessly into the hands of a profession which you deeply mistrust.... The character the medical profession has got just now [may] be deserved or it may not: there it is at all events; and the doctors who have not realized this are living in a fool's paradise. As to the honor and conscience

of doctors, they have as much as any other class of men, no more and no less. And what other men dare pretend to be impartial where they have a strong pecuniary interest on one side? Nobody supposes that doctors are less virtuous than judges; but a judge whose salary and reputation depended on whether the verdict was for plaintiff or defendant, prosecutor or prisoner, would be as little trusted as a general in the pay of the enemy. To offer me a doctor as my judge, and then weight his decision with a bribe of a large sum of money and a virtual guarantee that if he makes a mistake it can never be proved against him, is to go wildly beyond the ascertained strain which human nature will bear. It is simply unscientific to allege or believe that doctors do not under existing circumstances perform unnecessary operations and manufacture and prolong lucrative illnesses. The only ones who can claim to be above suspicion are those who are so much sought after that their cured patients are immediately replaced by fresh ones. And there is this curious psychological fact to be remembered: a serious illness or a death advertizes the doctor exactly as a hanging advertizes the barrister who defended the person hanged" (4).

B. "The Doctor's Hardships"

"A review of the counts in the indictment I have brought against private medical practice will show that they arise out of the doctor's position as a competitive private tradesman: that is, out of his poverty and dependence. And it should be borne in mind that doctors are expected to treat other people specially well whilst themselves submitting to specially inconsiderate treatment. The butcher and baker are not expected to feed the hungry unless the hungry can pay; but a doctor who allows a fellow-creature to suffer or perish without aid is regarded as a monster. Even if we must dismiss hospital service as really venal, the fact remains that most doctors do a good deal of gratuitous work in private practice all through their careers. And in his paid work the doctor is on a different footing to the tradesman. Although the articles he sells, advice and treatment, are the same for all classes, his fees have to be graduated like the income tax. The successful fashionable doctor may weed his poorer patients out from time to time, and finally use the College of Physicians to place it out of his own power to accept low fees; but the ordinary general practitioner never makes out his bills without considering the taxable capacity of his patients (4).

Then there is the disregard of his own health and comfort which results from the fact that he is, by the nature of his work, an emergency man. We are polite and considerate to the doctor when there is nothing the matter, and we meet him as a friend or entertain him as a guest; but *when the baby is suffering from croup, or its mother has a temperature of 104 degrees, or its grandfather has broken his leg, nobody thinks of the doctor except as a healer and saviour. He may be hungry, weary, sleepy, run down by several successive nights disturbed by that instrument of torture, the night bell; but who ever thinks of this in the face of sudden sickness or accident? We think no more of the condition of a doctor attending a case than of the condition of a fireman at a fire. In other occupations night-work is specially recognized and provided for. The worker sleeps all day; has his breakfast in the evening; his lunch or dinner at midnight; his dinner or supper before going to bed in the morning; and he changes to day-work if he cannot stand night-work. But a doctor is expected to work day and night"* (4).

C. *"Statistical Illusions"*

"Public ignorance of the laws of evidence and of statistics can hardly be exaggerated. There may be a doctor here and there who in dealing with the statistics of disease has taken at least the first step towards sanity by grasping the fact that as an attack of even the commonest disease is an exceptional event, apparently over-whelming statistical evidence in favor of any prophylactic can be produced by persuading the public that everybody caught the disease formerly. Thus if a disease is one which normally attacks fifteen per cent of the population, and if the effect of a prophylactic is actually to increase the proportion to twenty per cent, the publication of this figure of twenty per cent will convince the public that the prophylactic has reduced the percentage by eighty per cent instead of increasing it by five, because the public, left to itself and to the old gentlemen who are always ready to remember, on every possible subject, that things used to be much worse than they are now (such old gentlemen greatly outnumber the laudatores tempori acti), will assume that the former percentage was about 100. The vogue of the Pasteur treatment of hydrophobia, for instance, was due to the assumption by the public that every person bitten by a rabid dog necessarily got hydrophobia. I myself heard hydrophobia discussed in my youth by doctors in Dublin before a Pasteur Institute existed, the subject having been brought forward there by the skepticism of an eminent surgeon as to whether hydrophobia is really a specific disease or only ordinary tetanus induced (as tetanus was then supposed to be induced) by a lacerated wound. There were no statistics available as to the proportion of dog bites that ended in hydrophobia; but nobody ever guessed that the cases could be more than two or three per cent of the bites. On me, therefore, the results published by the Pasteur Institute produced no such effect as they did on the ordinary man who thinks that the bite of a mad dog means certain hydrophobia" (4).

D. "The Latest Theories"

[Let] me sum up my conclusions as dryly as is consistent with accurate thought and live conviction.

1. Nothing is more dangerous than a poor doctor: not even a poor employer or a poor landlord.

2. Of all the anti-social vested interests the worst is the vested interest in ill-health.

3. Remember that an illness is a misdemeanor; and treat the doctor as an accessory unless he notifies every case to the Public Health authority.

4. Treat every death as a possible and under our present system a probable murder, by making it the subject of a reasonably conducted inquest; and execute the doctor, if necessary, as a doctor, by striking him off the register.

5. Make up your mind how many doctors the community needs to keep it well. Do not register more or less than this number; and let registration constitute the doctor a civil servant with a dignified living wage paid out of public funds.

6. Municipalize Harley Street.

7. Treat the private operator exactly as you would treat a private executioner.

8. Treat persons who profess to be able to cure disease as you treat fortune tellers.

9. Keep the public carefully informed, by special statistics and announcements of individual cases, of all illnesses of doctors or in their families.

10. Make it compulsory for a doctor using a brass plate to have inscribed on it, in addition to the letters indicating his qualifications, the words "Remember that I too am mortal."

11. In legislation and social organization, proceed on the principle that invalids, meaning persons who cannot keep themselves alive by their own activities, cannot, beyond reason, expect to be kept alive by the activity of others. There is a point at which the most energetic policeman or doctor, when called upon to deal with an apparently drowned person, gives up artificial respiration, although it is never possible to declare with certainty, at any point short of decomposition, that another five minutes of the exercise would not effect resuscitation. The theory that every individual alive is of infinite value is legislatively impracticable. No doubt the higher the life we secure to the individual by wise social organization, the greater his value is to the community, and the more pains we shall take to pull him through any temporary danger or disablement. But the man who costs more than he is worth is doomed by sound hygiene as inexorably as by sound economics.

12. Do not try to live for ever. You will not succeed.

13. Use your health, even to the point of wearing it out. That is what it is for. Spend all you have before you die; and do not outlive yourself.
14. Take the utmost care to get well born and well brought up. This means that your mother must have a good doctor. Be careful to go to a school where there is what they call a school clinic, where your nutrition and teeth and eyesight and other matters of importance to you will be attended to. Be particularly careful to have all this done at the expense of the nation, as otherwise it will not be done at all, the chances being about forty to one against your being able to pay for it directly yourself, even if you know how to set about it. Otherwise you will be what most people are at present: an unsound citizen of an unsound nation, without sense enough to be ashamed or unhappy about it (4).

E. Excerpt from Act I

WALPOLE. It amuses me to hear you physicians and general practitioners talking about clinical experience. What do you see at the bedside but the outside of the patient? Well: it isn't his outside that's wrong, except perhaps in skin cases. What you want is a daily familiarity with people's insides; and that you can only get at the operating table. I know what I'm talking about: I've been a surgeon and a consultant for twenty years; and I've never known a general practitioner right in his diagnosis yet. Bring them a perfectly simple case; and they diagnose cancer, and arthritis, and appendicitis, and every other itis, when any really experienced surgeon can see that it's a plain case of blood-poisoning.

BLENKINSOP. Ah, it's easy for you gentlemen to talk; but what would you say if you had my practice? Except for the workmen's clubs, my patients are all clerks and shopmen. They daren't be ill: they can't afford it. And when they break down, what can I do for them? You can send your people to St Moritz or to Egypt, or recommend horse exercise or motoring or champagne jelly or complete change and rest for six months. I might as well order my people a slice of the moon. And the worst of it is, I'm too poor to keep well myself on the cooking I have to put up with. I've such a wretched digestion; and I look it. How am I to inspire confidence? [He sits disconsolately on the couch].

RIDGEON [restlessly] Don't, Blenkinsop: it's too painful. The most tragic thing in the world is a sick doctor.

WALPOLE. Yes, by George: it's like a bald-headed man trying to sell a hair restorer. Thank God I'm a surgeon! (4).

An Unforgettable Journal

Daniel Defoe

Daniel Defoe: *A Journal of the Plague Year*

CHARLES M. ANDERSON

> A Plague is a formidable Enemy, and is arm'd with Terrors that every
> Man is not sufficiently fortified to resist, or prepar'd to stand the shock
> Against... (1).
>
> Daniel Defoe
A Journal of the Plague Year

Even a cursory perusal of Sir William Osler's writing reveals his enormous reading background both in medicine and beyond. His propensity
for literary allusion and his recognition that reading broadly and deeply
in both the literature of the field and literature in general are qualities that
make a physician an exceptional physician. Most importantly, Osler had
a commitment to a higher education in which libraries and books were
central:

> For each one of us to-day, as in Plato's time, there is a higher as
> well as a lower education... This higher education so much needed
> to-day is not given in the school, is not to be bought in the market
> place, but it has to be wrought out in each one of us for himself;
> it is the silent influence of character on character and in no way
> more potently than in the contemplation of the lives of the great and
> good of the past, in no way more than in "the touch divine of noble
> natures gone" (2).

In *An Alabama Student*, Osler shows us precisely how reading enables the
physician to practice a deeply humane medicine, even in the face of sacrifice, and how it fortifies and moves one common physician, who could be
any physician, into that place in which character influences character and
generates action for the good of the many:

> In the spring of 1833 we were visited by the scarlet fever in its most
> malignant form; during the prevalence of this epidemic more than

fifty infants perished in Huntsville...I treated nine bad cases, and four terminated fatally; I lost nearly half in almost every instance. An older practitioner was called in, but I am not certain that in their own proper practice they were more fortunate. In more than one instance there lay more than one dead child in the same house at the same time. I feel certain that this was a most malignant disease; but I do not feel certain that in every case our best physicians remembered the united counsel of Hippocrates and Ovid, that "nothing does good but what may also hurt," and which should never be lost sight of by the man of medicine (3).

Reading Defoe's *A Journal of the Plague Year* must have connected Osler to many, many outbreaks of disease in his own time that, despite remarkable advances in medical treatment, proved as frustratingly unresponsive to traditional as well as experimental procedures as Dr. Bassett's treatments of scarlet fever. The book must have reminded him that pandemics as formidable as the plague lurked just beyond the visible horizon, as they always had. I like to imagine Osler recognizing that the reading of fictions, such as Defoe's *Journal*, might go beyond the acquisition of medical knowledge and beyond the gathering of useful allusions to the creation of virtual realities in which the power of imagination, mobilized by image, metaphor, and story, might engage medical readers in the "higher education" essential to the character of physicians prepared to meet conditions far beyond their own experience and bedside education.

I think this recognition would have served Osler well near the end of his life, when pandemic rose above the horizon in an endless stream of wounded and broken soldiers returning from the brutal trenches of World War I and an equally overwhelming stream of Spanish Influenza casualties closer to home. Defoe's compelling, virtual world would have given Osler a familiarity with the field on which he found himself in 1918, an understanding of the emotional, spiritual, and medical realities he faced. Michael Bliss, in his *William Osler: A Life in Medicine*, cites a letter written to Harvey Cushing by Mrs. William McDugal in 1923 that captures an image of Osler from this period, which connects directly to the section of Defoe's *Journal* that I offer readers below, an image not of the horrors of plague, but of the possibility of love and compassion, even in the face of death:

> He usually entered the sick room as a little goblin...and instantly turned the sickroom into fairyland—talking fairy language with us about the dolls, flowers, birds & the behavior of the weather....The most exquisite moment came one cold raw November morning— when he brought out from inside his coat a beautiful red rose carefully

wrapped up in paper & told little Janet how he had watched this last rose of summer growing in his garden & how the rose had called out to him as he passed by to take her along with him to see his little lassie. . . . That morning we all had a fairy tea party. . . . Sir William talking to the rose, his little lassie & her Mother—in a most exquisite way & presently he slipped out of the room, just as mysteriously as he entered it, all crouched down on his heels (4).

As literature opens rich, virtual worlds to its readers, so did Osler open a livable and loving space for Janet McDougal in the midst of their encounter with a "formidable enemy" as terrible as Defoe's plague, an enemy that carried her off only days later.

Defoe's 1722 *Journal* is a harrowing, obsessive, and frightening recreation of London during the 1665 plague. It is an intense journey, and medical readers would be well served to read every word. They will find both food for thought and an invitation to enter a place beyond everyday experience, a place only the metaphoric literary imagination can, as Aristotle puts it in Book III of *The Rhetoric*, "bring before the eyes" (5). They will see the cost of ignorance and charlatanism; hear arguments for and against confinement, flight, heat, and cold; witness the spectacle of dead carts unceremoniously dumping thousands upon thousands into mass graves; and wonder at the humanity and courage of physicians, clergy, government officials, and others who risked their lives to protect and provide for the sick and for the well alike. They may have nightmares.

For the purposes of this volume, I offer a softer side of the *Journal*, one small story that captures something of the compassion Osler exhibited in his own plague year. It occurs almost in the center of Defoe's book, and may be seen as a central exemplar of care for those one loves as well as compassion for those one merely encounters when the "formidable enemy" has most fully deployed its most terrible forces.

From A *Journal of the Plague Year* (1).

. . . I saw a poor Man walking on the Bank, or Sea-wall, as they call it, by himself, I walked a while also about, seeing the Houses all shut up; as last I fell into some Talk, at a Distance, with this poor Man; first I asked him, how People did thereabouts? Alas, sir! says he, almost all desolate; all dead or sick: Here are very few Families in this Part, or in that Village, pointing at Poplar, where half of them are not dead already, and the rest sick. Then he pointing to one House, There they are all dead, said he, and the House stands open; no Body dares go into it. A poor Thief, says he, ventured in to steal something, but he paid dear for his Theft; for he was carried to the ChurchYard too, last Night. Then he pointed to several

other Houses. There, says he, they are all dead; the Man and his Wife, and five Children. There, says he, they are shut up, you see a Watchman at the Door; and so of other Houses. Why, says I, What do you here all alone? Why, says he, I am a poor desolate Man; it has pleased God I am not yet visited, tho' my family is, and one of my Children dead. How do you mean then, said I, that you are not visited. Why, says he, that's my House, pointing to a very little low boarded house, and there my poor Wife and two Children live, said he, if they may be said to live; for my Wife and one of the Children are visited, but I do not come at them. And with that Word I saw the Tears run very plentifully down his Face; and so they did down mine too, I assure you.

But said I, Why do you not come at them? How can you abandon your own Flesh, and Blood? Oh, Sir! says he, the Lord forbid; I do not abandon them; I work for them as much as I am able; and blessed be the Lord, I keep them from Want; and with that I observ'd, he lifted up his Eyes to Heaven, with a Countenance that presently told me, I had happened on a Man that was no Hypocrite, but a serious, religious good Man, and his Ejaculation was an Expression of Thankfulness, that in such a Condition as he was in, he should be able to say his Family did not want. Well, says I, honest Man, that is a great Mercy as things go now with the Poor: But how do you live then, and how are you kept from the dreadful Calamity that is now upon us all? Why, Sir, says he, I am a Waterman, and there's my Boat, says he, and that Boat serves me for a House; I work in it in the Day, and I sleep in it in the Night; and what I get, I lay down upon that Stone, says he, shewing me a broad Stone on the other Side of the Street, a good way from his House, and then, says he, I halloo, and call to them till I make them hear; and they come and fetch it.

Well, Friend, says I, but how can you get any Money as a Waterman? Does any Body go by Water these Times? Yes, Sir, says he, in the Way I am employ'd there does. Do you see there, says he, five Ships lie at Anchor, pointing down the river, a good way below the Town, and do you see, says he, eight or ten Ships lie at the Chain, there, and at Anchor yonder, pointing above the Town. All those Ships have Families on board, of their Merchants and Owners, and such like, who have lock'd themselves up, and live on board, close shut in, for fear of the Infection; and I tend on them to fetch Things for them, carry Letters, and do what is absolutely necessary, that they may not be obliged to come on Shore; and every Night I fasten my Boat on board one of the Ship's Boats, and there I sleep by my self, and, blessed be God, I am preserv'd hitherto.

Well, said I, Friend, but will they let you come on board, after you have been on Shore here, when this is such a terrible Place, and so infected as it is?

Why, as to that, said he, I very seldom go up the Ship Side, but deliver what I bring to their Boat, or lie by the Side, and they hoist it on board; if I did, I think they are in no Danger from me, for I never go into any House on Shore, or touch any Body, no, not of my own Family; But I fetch Provisions for them.

Nay, says I, but that may be worse, for you must have those Provisions of some Body or other; and since all this Part of the Town is so infected, it is dangerous so much as to speak with any Body; for this Village, said I, is as it were, the Beginning of London, tho' it be at some Distance from it.

That is true, added he, but you do not understand me Right, I do not buy provisions for them here; I row up to Greenwich and buy fresh Meat there, and sometimes I row down the River to Woolwich and buy there; then I go to single Farm Houses on the Kentish Side, where I am known, and buy Fowls and Eggs, and Butter, and bring to the Ships, as they direct me, sometimes one, sometimes the other; I seldom come on Shore here; and I come now only to call to my Wife, and hear how my little Family do, and give them a little Money, which I receiv'd last Night.

Poor Man! said I, and how much hast thou gotten for them?

I have gotten four Shillings, said he, which is a great Sum, as things go now with poor Men; but they have given me a Bag of Bread too, and a Salt Fish and some Flesh; so all helps out.

Well, said I, and have you given it them yet?

No, said he, but I have called, and my Wife has answered, that she cannot come out yet, but in Half an Hour she hopes to come, and I am waiting for her: Poor Woman! says he, she is brought sadly down; she has a Swelling, and it is broke, and I hope she will recover; but I fear the Child will die; but it is the Lord!—Here he stopt, and wept very much.

Well, honest Friend, said I, thou hast a sure Comforter, if thou hast brought thy self to be resign'd to the will of God, he is dealing with us all in Judgment.

Oh, Sir, says he, it is infinite Mercy, if any of us are spar'd; and who am I to repine!

Sayest thou so, said I, and how much less is my Faith than thine? And here my Heart smote me, suggesting how much better this Poor Man's Foundation was, on which he staid in the Danger, than mine; that he had no where to fly; that he had a Family to bind him to Attendance, which I had not; and mine was meer Presumption, his a true Dependance, and a Courage resting on God: and yet, that he used all possible Caution for his Safety.

I turn'd a little way from the Man, while these Thoughts engaged me, for indeed, I could no more refrain from Tears than he.

At length, after some further Talk, the poor Woman opened the Door, and call'd, Robert, Robert; he answered and bid her stay a few Moments, and he would come; so he ran down the common Stairs to his Boat, and fetch'd up a Sack in which was the Provisions he had brought from the Ships; and when he returned, he hallooed again; then he went to the great Stone which he shewed me, and emptied the Sack, and laid all out, every Thing by themselves, and then retired; and his Wife came with a little Boy to fetch them away; and he called, and said, such a Captain had sent such a Thing, and such a Captain such a Thing, and at the End adds, God has sent it all, give Thanks to him. When the Poor Woman had taken up all, she was so weak, she could not carry it at once in, tho' the Weight was not much neither; so she left the Biscuit which was in a little Bag, and left a little Boy to watch it till she came again.

Well, but says I to him, did you leave her the four Shillings too, which you said was your Week's Pay?

YES, YES, says he, you shall hear her own it. So he calls again, Rachel, Rachel, which it seems was her Name, did you take up the Money? YES, said she. How much was it, said he? Four Shillings and a Groat, said she. Well, well, says he, the Lord keep you all; and so he turned to go away.

As I could not refrain contributing Tears to this Man's Story, so neither could I refrain my Charity for his Assistance; so I call'd him, Hark thee Friend, said I, come hither; for I believe thou art in Health, that I may venture thee; so I pull'd out my Hand, which was in my Pocket before, here, says I, go and call thy Rachel once more, and give her a little more Comfort from me. God will never forsake a Family that trust in him as thou dost; so I gave him four other Shillings, and bade him go lay them on the Stone and call his Wife.

I have not Words to express the poor Man's thankfulness, neither could he express it himself; but by Tears running down his Face; he call'd his Wife, and told her God had mov'd the Heart of a Stranger upon hearing their Condition, to give them all that Money; and a great deal more such as that, he said to her. The Woman too, made Signs of the like Thankfulness, as well to Heaven, as to me, and joyfully pick'd it up; and I parted with no Money all that Year, that I thought better bestow'd (1).

The Shoulders upon Which We Stand

Avicenna

Avicenna: The Osler of the Middle Ages

OMID ZARGARI

SABA HODA

Abu-'Ali al-Husayn ibn-Sina (AD 980–1037) is the most famous scientist of Islam and one of the most famous of all races, places, and times (1). Those of you in the West might know him as Avicenna, if indeed he is known to you at all. Born in Bukhara in what is now Uzbekistan, Avicenna ultimately settled in Hamadan, central Persia, and is Iran's greatest gift to medicine.

Avicenna's earliest education was in Bukhara under the direction of his father who was the governor of a village. Since his father's house was a meeting place for learned men, from his earliest childhood Avicenna was able to profit from the company of the outstanding individuals of his day. A precocious child, gifted with an exceptional memory that he retained throughout his life, he is reputed to have memorized the Quran and much of Arabic poetry by the age of 10 (2).

AVICENNA THE PHYSICIAN

Regarding the learning of medicine, Avicenna says:

> Then I desired to study medicine, and took to reading the books written on this subject. Medicine is not one of the difficult sciences, so naturally I became proficient in it in the short time. Soon, the excellent scholars of medicine began to study under me. I began to treat patients, and through my experience I acquired an amazing practical knowledge and ability in methods of treatment (3).

Before he was 16 years old, he had mastered what was to be learned of Greek, Latin, physics, mathematics, logic, and metaphysics. At the same age, he began the study and practice of medicine; and before he had completed his 21 years, he wrote *The Canon of Medicine,* his most important medical work. It was translated into Latin toward the end of 12th century AD by Gerard of Cremona, Dominicus Gundissalinus, and John Avendeath. *The Canon of Medicine* became a reference source and the principal authority for medical studies in the universities of Europe and Asia from the 12th until the end of the 17th century (1). Between 1500 and 1674, some 60 editions of part or the whole of *The Canon of Medicine* were published in Europe, mostly intended for use in university medical training. Avicenna enjoyed an undisputed place of honor equaled only by the early Greek physicians Hippocrates and Galen.

Sarton further states:

> The Canon is an immense encyclopedia of medicine. It contains some of the most illuminating thoughts pertaining to distinction of medias- tinitis from pleurisy; the contagious nature of phthisis; the distribution of diseases by water and soil; the careful description of skin troubles; and the explication of sexual diseases and perversions and nervous ailments (1).

Osler, one Western physician who certainly knew him, described Avicenna as the "author of the most famous medical textbook ever written." He noted that the Canon remained "a medical bible for a longer time than any other work" (4).

Avicenna begins *The Canon* with a definition of the science of medicine:

> Medicine is the science by which we learn the various states of the human body in health and when not in health, and the means by which health is likely to be lost, and when lost, is likely to be restored (5).

Avicenna believed that the human body cannot be restored to health unless the causes of both health and disease are determined. His view of medicine was based on the synthesis of Aristotelian natural philosophy with Galenic humoral physiology. At the same time, it drew on clinical experience in the Hippocratic tradition and comparative assessment of observational experiments (6). *The Canon of Medicine* was the final codification of Greco-Islamic medicine. Like another Persian alchemist–physician–philosopher, Mohammad Zakariyya Razi or Rhazes (AD 865–925), Avicenna challenged the thoughts and writings of Socrates, Aristotle, and Galen regarding the dichotomy of the mind and body and espoused the concept of mental health and self-esteem as being essential to a patient's welfare. He noted the close relationship between emotions and the physical condition and felt that music had a definite physical and psychological effect on patients. Furthermore, he stated that the etiology of disease must be understood, for only then is it possible to begin treatment.

AVICENNA THE PHILOSOPHER

After he became a physician, Avicenna embarked on the study of philosophy. He wrote in his autobiography that he had read Aristotle's *Metaphysics* 40 times until he had all of it in his memory, but still could not understand it until he found Farabi's book about *Metaphysics* and then suddenly he found the answer to all of his questions (3).

In Iran today, Avicenna is most famous for his dominance in philosophy and has been described by many as "the leader of Islamic philosophy." But, it should be borne in mind that at the time of Avicenna natural philosophy and medicine, although distinct, had great overlaps. This overlap was at the center of much debate among followers of Galen as a physician and those of Aristotle as a philosopher.

Galen, as a dominant physician, was in disaccord with Aristotle on many issues, the most central of which was whether the powers that control animal life have one single source (the heart, as Aristotle believed) or three distinct sources (the brain, heart, and liver, as Galen argued). He also challenged Aristotle's views on the male and female roles in sexual generation. In the work of Avicenna, the traditions of Galen and Aristotle intersect. He composed the *Kitab al-Shifa* (Book of Healing), a vast philosophical and scientific encyclopedia. Avicenna gained a perspective of Galenic medicine through his knowledge of the medicine and philosophy of India and China and his own clinical experience.

Of Avicenna's 450 works, around 240 have survived. One hundred and fifty of these deal with philosophy and 40 with medicine. He wrote extensively on psychology, geology, mathematics, logic, and astronomy. His writings on geometry encompass mechanics, kinematics, hydrostatics, optics, and geodesy. His books on mathematics included musical theory and includes as well his proofs of the first four of Euclid's Five Postulates. (The fifth has yet to be proved.) His work in astronomy was astounding for his time: He devised an instrument for measuring the coordinates of stars, a precursor to the alt-azimuth instrument, viewed the transit of Venus with the naked eye and correctly concluded that celestial body lay between the earth and the sun and correctly stated that the velocity of light was finite.

It has been said that Avicenna had the mind of Goethe and the genius of Leonardo da Vinci (7). He remains, with Osler, one of the most brilliant stars in the sky of medicine.

> *Up from Earth's Centre through the Seventh Gate,*
> *I rose, and on the Throne of Saturn sate,*
> *And many Knots unravel'd by the Road,*
> *But not the Master-Knot of Human Fate* (8).

In his autobiography, Abu-'Ali al-Husayn ibn-Sina left this thought for us:

> ...it is important to gain knowledge. Grasp of the intelligibles deter-mines the fate of the rational soul in the hereafter, and therefore is crucial to human activity (7).

To answer the charges of Avicenna and Osler, a bedside library is a fine beginning.

Contributors' Biographical Sketches

Charles M. Anderson, PhD, is a professor of rhetoric and writing at the University of Arkansas at Little Rock. He teaches literature and medicine at the University of Arkansas for Medical Sciences. He is Executive Editor of *Literature and Medicine*. He is author of *Richard Selzer and the Rhetoric of Surgery* and coeditor of *Writing and Healing: Toward an Informed Practice*.

Louise Aronson, MD, MFA, is an associate professor in the Division of Geriatrics at the University of California at San Francisco where she codirects the Medical Humanities Initiative and has developed innovative curricula in reflective learning, public writing, and advocacy journalism. She is also a fiction writer whose stories appear in medical and literary journals.

Pamela Brett-MacLean, PhD, is codirector of the Arts & Humanities in Health & Medicine Program at the University of Alberta. She edits two humanities columns in the University's *Health Sciences Journal*, and is a founding cochair of the Canadian Association for Medical Education's "Arts, Humanities and Social Sciences in Medicine" Interest Group.

Arthur L. Caplan, PhD, is currently the Emmanuel and Robert Hart Professor of Bioethics and the director of the Center for Bioethics at the University of Pennsylvania. He is the author or editor of 29 books and over 500 papers in refereed journals. His most recent books are *Smart Mice Not So Smart People* (Rowman Littlefield, 2006) and the *Penn Guide to Bioethics* (Springer 2009).

Albert Howard Carter, III, PhD, is an adjunct professor of social medicine, School of Medicine, University of North Carolina, Chapel Hill, and a part-time massage therapist at the N.C. Cancer Hospital. He is author of *First Cut: A Season in the Human Anatomy Lab* and *Our Human Hearts: A Medical and Cultural Journey*.

Rita Charon, MD, PhD, is a professor of clinical medicine and the founder and director of the Program in Narrative Medicine at Columbia University, where she supervises the Master of Science in Narrative Medicine program. She is the author of *Narrative Medicine: Honoring the Stories of Illness* and the coeditor of *Psychoanalysis and Narrative Medicine* and *Stories Matter*.

Jeremiah Conway, PhD, is an associate professor of philosophy at the University of Southern Maine and a former director of the University Honors Program. One of his regular courses is on "The Nature of Compassion," combining work in philosophy, literature, and spiritual traditions. In 2005, he received the University Award for Teaching Excellence.

Jack Coulehan, physician and poet, is Professor Emeritus of Medicine and Senior Fellow of the Center for Medical Humanities, Compassionate Care, and Bioethics at Stony Brook University. Among his books are *Medicine Stone, Chekhov's Doctors*, and *The Medical Interview: Mastering Skills for Clinical Practice*.

John K. Crellin, MD, PhD, holds British qualifications in medicine and in pharmacy and an MSc and PhD in the history of science. His career spans three countries, at the Wellcome Institute for the History of Medicine in the UK, at Southern Illinois and Duke in the US, and at Memorial University of Newfoundland, where he was Professor of Medical History.

Thomas P. Duffy is Professor of Medicine and Director of the Program for Humanities in Medicine at Yale. He is a member of the Bioethics Consortium at Yale and has examined the mentoring relationship between Osler and Harvey Cushing. He is an active member of the Sherlock Holmes Society and the Baker Street Irregulars.

David J. Elpern, MD, has had a medical career on Kauai, and in rural Williamstown, MA. Osler reminds him daily that "the practice of medicine is an art, not a trade, a calling not a business." He edits the weblog, Cell2Soul, which brings patients, their families, and caregivers together to consider nontechnical aspects of health, disease, and healing.

Lynn C. Epstein, MD, is Clinical Professor of Psychiatry at the Tufts University Medical School, and Clinical Professor Emerita at Brown University. At Brown, she taught "The Doctor: Subject and Author," and started the Sheridan Literature & Medicine Lectureship. She is a member of the American Osler Society.

Toby Gelfand, PhD, is Jason A. Hannah Professor of History of Medicine at the University of Ottawa. His publications include *Professionalizing Modern Medicine*; *Paris Surgeons and Medical Science and Institutions in the 18th Century*; and *Charcot: Constructing Neurology*. He has lectured on Rabelaisian humor among French hospital interns.

Marin Gillis, LPh, PhD, is the first director of the Division of Medical Humanities and Ethics at the University of Nevada School of Medicine. She holds two graduate degrees in philosophy, from Belgium and Canada, and academic appointments in psychiatry and behavioral sciences, philosophy, and women's studies.

Dr. Saba Hoda began his medical study in Tehran University of Medical Sciences and is a pathologist in Rasht, Iran. His other areas of interest include traditional and alternative medicine, yoga, mythology, and history of medicine.

Bernadette Höfer, PhD, is Assistant Professor of French at the Ohio State University. From 2005 to 2008, she was a junior fellow at Harvard University. Her forthcoming book *Psychosomatic Disorders in Seventeenth-Century French Literature*, examines the mind/body question and she has written on Descartes, Lafayette, Molière, Spinoza, Surin, and Michel de Certeau.

Martha Stoddard Holmes is Associate Professor of Literature and Writing Studies at California State University, San Marcos. She is the author of *Fictions of Affliction* and the coeditor of *The Teacher's Body: Embodiment, Authority, and Identity in the Classroom*. Her current work is *Queering the Marriage Plot: Disability and Desire in the Victorian Novel*.

Claire Hooker, PhD, is the coordinator of medical humanities at the University of Sydney. Her research interests are in risk, public health ethics, medical education, infectious disease control, and the history of radio astronomy. Her books include *Irresistible Forces* (a historical study of women scientists) and *Contagion: Historical and Cultural Studies*.

Joel D. Howell, MD, PhD, is the Victor Vaughan Professor of History of Medicine at the University of Michigan, where he is a professor in the Departments of Internal Medicine, History, and Health Services. He writes on the history of medical technology, including *Technology in the Hospital: Transforming Patient Care in the Early Twentieth Century*.

Brian Hurwitz, MD, is the D'Oyly Carte Chair of Medicine and the Arts at King's College London, UK. Based in the Department of English, he is the director of the Centre for the Humanities and Health. His books include *Narrative-Based Medicine: Dialogue and Discourse in Clinical Practice*; *Narrative Research in Health and Illness*; and *Health Care Errors and Patient Safety*.

Liva H. Jacoby, PhD, MPH, directs the four-year medical ethics course at Albany Medical College. She has incorporated more humanities into the course to strengthen the concept of the "art of medicine." She collaborates with the Albany Institute for History and Art where medical students work with senior citizens in a visual arts and medicine program.

Lyuba Konopasek, MD, is Associate Professor of Pediatrics (Education). She is the director of the first-year doctoring course and the pediatrics clerkship at Weill Cornell. She has co-led *The Art of Observation*, a collaborative program between the Frick Collection and Weill Cornell to enhance students' observational skills.

Michael A. LaCombe, MD, is a practicing cardiologist. This is his 12th book, five of which, on medical humanities topics, have been published by ACP Press. His book of stories, *Bedside: The Art of Medicine*, was published by University of Maine Press in the summer of 2009. His chief accomplishments, however, are a wonderful wife, five great kids, and three grandchildren.

Dr. Stephen S. Lefrak is Professor of Medicine at Washington University School of Medicine. He directs the Program on Humanities in Medicine and has taught medical ethics and has served as a chairman of the Barnes Jewish Hospital Ethics Committee. In addition to speaking nationally and internationally, he has authored more than 100 medical articles.

Paul S. Mueller, MD, MPH, is Associate Professor of Medicine at the Mayo Clinic. He is the codirector of the Mayo Clinic Program in Professionalism and Bioethics. Dr. Mueller is a fellow of the American College of Physicians and a member of the Board of Governors of the American Osler Society.

Dr. T. Jock Murray is Professor Emeritus in Neurology and Medical Humanities at Dalhousie and was its first professor of medical humanities. He is coauthor of *The Quotable Osler*; *Medicine in Quotations*, and *Sir Charles Tupper*. He authored *Multiple Sclerosis: A History of the Disease*, which won the ForeFront Silver Medal as the best book on medical history of 2005.

Allan Peterkin is Associate Professor of Psychiatry and Family Medicine at the University of Toronto. He is the author of *Staying Human During Residency Training* and edited *STILL HERE: A Post-Cocktail Aids Anthology*. Dr. Peterkin heads the Program in Humanities at Mount Sinai Hospital and is a founding editor of the literary journal *ARS MEDICA*.

Maureen Rappaport is Assistant Professor of Medicine at McGill University and St. Mary's Hospital Family Medicine Centre in Montreal. Aside from practicing and teaching family medicine, she writes about her clinical experiences in poetry and prose and leads writing groups for medical students and staff physicians.

M. Sara Rosenthal, PhD, is Director of the Program for Bioethics at the University of Kentucky, and Associate Professor of Bioethics. Her research interests focus on endocrine ethics, reproductive ethics, and clinical ethics education. Dr. Rosenthal serves on the Endocrine Society's Ethics Advisory Board, and has authored over 30 consumer health books.

Lawrence J. Schneiderman, MD, is Professor Emeritus at the University of California, San Diego, and Visiting Scholar in the Program in Medicine and Human Values at the California Pacific Medical Center, San Francisco. He has many publications, most recently, *Embracing Our Mortality* as well as short stories, plays, and a novel, *Sea Nymphs by the Hour*.

Audrey Shafer, MD, is Professor of Anesthesia at Stanford University School of Medicine and a staff anesthesiologist at the Veterans Affairs Palo Alto Health Care System. Her writings include *The Mailbox* and *Sleep Talker: Poems by a Doctor/Mother*. She directs the Arts, Humanities and Medicine Program, Stanford Center for Biomedical Ethics.

Ronald D. Stewart, MD, DSc, is Director of Medical Humanities in the Faculty of Medicine at Dalhousie. His initiatives in medical history and narrative medicine helped Dalhousie retain its rightful place as a leader in the humanities among medical faculties in Canada. He is an Officer of the Order of Canada and a member of The Order of Nova Scotia.

Jerry Vannatta, MD, is Professor of Humanities in Medicine at The University of Oklahoma. He teaches literature and medicine at the undergraduate campus in Norman, and in the Honors College at Oklahoma City University. He has published a DVD—*Medicine and Humanistic Understanding: The Significance of Narrative in the Everyday Practices of Medicine*.

Seth Vannatta, is a PhD candidate and Delyte and Dorothy Morris Doctoral Fellow in philosophy at Southern Illinois University Carbondale.

Arnold Weinstein is Professor of Comparative Literature at Brown University. His most recent books include *A Scream Goes Through the House*; *Recovering Your Story: Proust, Joyce, Woolf, Faulkner, Morrison*; and *Northern Arts: The*

Breakthrough of Scandinavian Literature and Art from Ibsen to Bergman. He has done six courses for The Teaching Company.

Dr. Omid Zargari received his MD from the National University of Iran in Tehran and then returned to the north of Iran to work as a dermatologist in a leprosy clinic. He has published several papers in different fields of dermatology. Dr. Zargari has a special interest in information technology and in 2001 he started a dermatology Web site: www.iranderma.com.

A Bedside Library

The best modern sources for the texts presented in this volume, as recommended by our contributors, and a suggested bedside library of your own (ordered as they appear in the text):

Dryden, John, trans. 2001. Plutarch's Lives Vol. I and II. Ed. Arthur Hugh Clough. New York: The Modern Library.

Browne, Thomas, The Major Works: Religio Medici, Hydrotophia, The Garden of Cyprus, A Letter to a Friend, and Christian Morals. C.A. Patrides (Ed.), New York, Penguin Classics, 1977.

Norton Shakespeare: Based on the Oxford Edition. Eds. Greenblatt S, Cohen W, Howard JE, Maus KE. New York: W.W. Norton & Company, 1997.

Complete Sonnets and Poems of William Shakespeare, Airmont Publishing Co. Inc., 1966.

Montaigne, Michel de, The Complete Works Essays, Travel Journal, Letters, trans. Donald M. Frame, intro. Stuart Hampshire. New York: A.A. Knopf, 2003.

Marcus Aurelius. Meditations, trans. Gregory Hays. New York: The Modern Library, 2002.

Epictetus, W.A. Oldfather (Translator) Epictetus: Discourses, Books 3–4. The Enchiridion. Loeb Classical Library No. 218. Cambridge, MA: Harvard University Press, 1928.

Don Quixote: Edith Grossman, the edition published by HarperCollins Publishers, 2003.

Ralph Waldo Emerson. Essays and Lectures, Library of America, 1983.

The Complete Writings of Oliver Wendell Holmes; The Autocrat of the Breakfast Table—Every Man His Own Boswell by Oliver Wendell Holmes. Paperback, 356 pages, published 2008.

Bible, King James New Revised Standard edition.

The Complete Poems and Songs of Robert Burns, Geddes & Grosset; illustrated edition (February 2002). ISBN-13: 978-1855349827.

The Complete Poems of John Keats, Modern Library. April 26, 1994. ISBN-10: 0679601082.

Eliot, George Middlemarch. W. J. Harvey, ed. London: Penguin, 1965 (reprinted 1988).

Dickens, Charles. A Tale of Two Cities. New York: Signet Classics, Penguin Group, Inc. (150th Anv Edition), 2007.

Sir Arthur Conan Doyle. The Complete Sherlock Holmes. Barnes and Noble Books, New York, 2003.

Sarah Orne Jewett. A Country Doctor and Selected Stories and Sketches. BiblioBazaar, 2007.

The Complete Stories of Robert Louis Stevenson: Strange Case of Dr. Jekyll and Mr. Hyde and Nineteen Other Tales. Modern Library pbk. edition, October 8, 2002.

The Decameron: Penguin Classics. G. McWilliam, editor. 2003.

The complete works of François Rabelais trans. by Donald Frame. University of California Press, 1991.

Robert Burton. The Anatomy of Melancholy. Kessinger Publishing, Whitefish, MT.

Autobiography and Other Writings. Oxford World's Classics by Benjamin Franklin and Ormond Seavey, 2009.

Barker W. The Adages of Erasmus. University of Toronto Press. 2001. [Contributor's note: This is a one volume edition of Erasmus's selected proverbs recommended as a single volume which fits on a night stand and is easy to hold and read in bed.]

Bos, G. Maimonides on Asthma: Volume 1 of the Complete Medical Works of Moses Maimonides. 2002. Brigham Young University Press.

Pascal, Blaise. Penseés and Other Writings, ed. Anthony Levi, trans. Honor Levi. New York: Oxford University Press, 1995.

The Essential Pascal, edited by Robert Gleason, New York and Toronto: The New American Library, 1966.

Block, Haskell M. ed. Voltaire: Candide and Other Writings, The Modern Library, New York, 1956.

Redman, Ben Ray, ed. The Portable Voltaire, The Viking Press, New York, 1949.

Ibsen, Henrik. An Enemy of the People. Translated by R. Farquharson Sharp. Fairfield, IA: 1st World Library, 2004.

John Wood's translation of Molière's selected plays (1959): The Misanthrope and Other Plays. Viking Penguin, New York.

Shaw, George Bernard. 2008. The Doctor's Dilemma. Huntington, VA: Standard Publications.

Daniel Defoe, A Journal of the Plague Year, ed. Paula R. Backscheider (New York: W. W. Norton, A Norton Critical Edition, 1992).

Avicenna, by Lenn E. Goodman, Cornell University Press, 2005.

Canon of Medicine, by Avicenna. Hardcover, 650 pages, Kazi Publications, 1999. ISBN-13: 978-1871031676.

Many of these works may be found at Project Gutenberg http://www.gutenberg.org

Medical Works of Maimonides

1. *Extracts from Galen, Art of Cure*. Also cited as (probably) *Abridgements of the Work of Galen* (2) or *Compendium of the Treatises of Galen* (3). This work only survived in part, has never been edited, and is available only in an incomplete English translation (2).

*2. *Commentary on the Aphorisms of Hippocrates*. Also cited as *Commentary to the Treatises of Hippocrates* (3) and *Commentary on Hippocrates' Aphorisms* (2).

*3. *Medical Aphorisms*. Also cited as *Aphorisms of Moses* (3) or *Medical Aphorisms of Moses* (1).

4. *Treatise on Hemorrhoids*. Also cited as *On Hemorrhoids* (3).

5. *Treatise on Sexual Intercourse*. Also cited as (probably) *On Cohabitation* (3) or *On Coitus* (2).

6. *Treatise on Asthma* (1190). Also cited as *Book on Asthma* (3) or *On Asthma* (2).

*7. *Treatise on Poisons and their Antidotes*. Also cited as *Poisons and their Antidotes* (3) or (probably) *On Poisons and Protections against Lethal Drugs* (2).

8. *Guide to Good Health* (1198). Also cited as *On the Regimen of Health* (2).

9. *Discourse on the Explanation of Fits or Coincidences* (1200). This is only cited by one source (1).

10. *Glossary of Drug Names*. Also cited as *The Names of Drugs* (3).

11. Medical Responsa. This is listed as a formal Medical Work by only one source (3).

*These works were only available in medieval Hebrew editions (based on the original Arabic) or modern Hebrew editions until Bos' translation of *Medical Aphorisms* from Arabic into English (2).

REFERENCES TO THE ABOVE BIBLIOGRAPHY ON THE WORKS OF MAIMONIDES

1. Gesundheit, B and Hadad, Eli. Maimonides (1138–1204): Rabbi, Physician and Philosopher. 2005 *Israel Medical Association Journal*; Vol. 7:547–552.

2. Bos, G. Preface: The Medical Works of Moses Maimonides: Toward Critical Editions and Translations. In: G. Bos, *Maimonides Medical Aphorisms: Treatises 1–5*. 2004, Brigham Young University Press, Provo. Pp. xvii–xviii.

3. Fishbein, M. Maimonides the Physician, In: Rosner, F. and Suessman Muntner. (Eds.) *The Medical Writings of Moses Maimonides, Volume III: Treatise on Hemorrhoids, Medical Responsa*. J.B. Lippincott Company, Philadelphia, 1969. p. xviii.

References and Permissions

Every effort has been made to take the quotes used in these essays from the public domain, since the works examined were all published more than 75 years ago, but if any errors have been made we will be happy to correct them. We gratefully acknowledge the following sources for public domain texts.

For the cover illustration: 1808, GUILLEMOT Alexandre-Charles, *Erasistratus Discovers the Cause of Antiochus' Disease*—permission was obtained from the Ecole nationale supérieure des Beaux-arts, rue Bonaparte, Paris, France, for its use.

Permission was obtained from Brigham Young University for the excerpts from Maimonides:

Bos, G. Translator's Introduction. In: *G. Bos, Maimonides Medical Aphorisms: Treatises 1–5*. 2004, Brigham Young University Press, Provo. Pp. xix–xxxii.

Bos, G. Maimonides on Asthma: Volume 1 of the Complete Medical Works Of Moses Maimonides. 2002. Brigham Young University Press, pp. 1–2; 5–18; 24–39; 51.

Bos, G. *Maimonides Medical Aphorisms: Treatises 1–5*. 2004, Brigham Young University Press, Provo.

Permission was obtained through the copyright clearance center for:

Gesundheit, B, Or, R, Gamliel, C, Rosner, F, and Steinberg, A. Treatment of Depression by Maimonides (1138–1204): Rabbi, Physician, and Philosopher. 2008. *American Journal of Psychiatry*. Vol. 165:425–428.

All remaining excerpted material from the works presented here have been taken from pre-1913 public domain books and from Project Gutenberg. (The excerpts from Epictetus' *The Enchiridion* are from a 1750 text, and those from Montaigne's *Meditations*, from an 1877 text, for example.) As much as possible, an attempt was made to match excerpted material with works that Osler would have had available to him, or had collected in his library.

References cited by authors are available to readers and to teachers of medical humanities courses using this book as text by accessing the following Web site at the American College of Physicians:

http://www.acponline.org/acp_press/osler_library/

The illustrations included in this book are from the public domain as well and their sources may be found at the above URL.

.

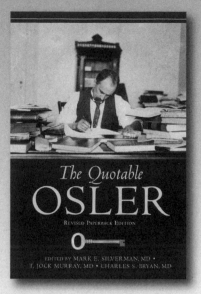